THE KNOWLEDGE BOOK

T0325363

THE KNOWLEDGE BOOK

KEY CONCEPTS IN PHILOSOPHY, SCIENCE AND CULTURE

Steve Fuller

MCGILL-QUEEN'S UNIVERSITY PRESS
MONTREAL & KINGSTON • ITHACA

© Steve Fuller 2007

ISBN 978-0-7735-3346-2 (bound)
ISBN 978-0-7735-3347-9 (paper)

Legal deposit second quarter 2007
Bibliothèque nationale du Québec

Published in 2007 simultaneously in the United Kingdom by Acumen Publishing Limited
and in North America by McGill-Queen's University Press

Library and Archives Canada Cataloguing in Publication

Fuller, Steve, 1959-
  The knowledge book : key concepts in philosophy, science and
culture / Steve Fuller.

Includes bibliographical references and index.
ISBN 978-0-7735-3346-2 (bound)
ISBN 978-0-7735-3347-9 (pbk.)

  1. Social epistemology. 2. Knowledge, Sociology of. I. Title.

BD175.F845 2007   001   C2007-902165-4

Designed and typeset by Kate Williams, Swansea.
Printed and bound by Cromwell Press, Trowbridge.

CONTENTS

INTRODUCTION

The Knowledge Book is an interdisciplinary reference work for students and researchers concerned with the nature of knowledge. It is probably the first work of its kind to be organized on the assumption that whatever else knowledge might be, it is intrinsically *social*. This explains the selection and treatment of the forty-two alphabetically arranged entries. Generally speaking, the entries gather around the intersection of philosophy and sociology, what used to be called SOCIOLOGY OF KNOWLEDGE but is nowadays increasingly called SOCIAL EPISTEMOLOGY. Even the entries that hail from the heartland of philosophy – such as RATIONALITY and TRUTH, RELIABILITY AND THE ENDS OF KNOWLEDGE – are given a sociological treatment. Several of the entries reflect knowledge-based issues of contemporary concern, such as FEMINISM, MULTICULTURALISM and KNOWLEDGE SOCIETY. Pride of place is given to topics relevant to SCIENCE AND TECHNOLOGY STUDIES, an emerging field that over the past quarter-century has posed the most interesting normative and empirical questions about the nature of knowledge. And while it is fair to say that *The Knowledge Book* takes science to be the paradigmatic case of knowledge, FOLK EPISTEMOLOGY, MASS MEDIA, RELIGION and RHETORIC are among several entries that come to terms with organized forms of enquiry that relate to science in interesting ways but are not usually themselves regarded as scientific.

The entries consist of self-contained essays of between 1000 and 3000 words. As illustrated in the previous paragraph, each entry includes capitalized references to other entries, ideally enabling readers to start anywhere in the book and move as their interests take them. One principle in selecting entries for inclusion has been the ease with which they could be cross-referenced with other entries. The same principle applies to the selection of bibliographic references that make up the further reading appended at the end of each entry. The reading list is not meant to be exhaustive. Rather, a work is included only if it could be recommended as a source for further thinking about more than one entry. The overall impression this should make on the reader is that there is a relatively well-defined set of issues relating to the nature of knowledge that are illuminated from a thoroughly sociological – or at least social scientific – standpoint. To be sure, there is always a measure of arbitrariness to the actual selection of entries, but a counterbalance is provided in the index, which effectively cross-classifies the entries by collecting together people, ideas and phenomena that appear several times in the book.

Readers familiar with my previous writing will recognize certain intellectual biases at play in this book for which I do not apologise but simply acknowledge.

In particular, I take what is generally called the "postmodern condition" as a problem that needs to be squarely faced but can be ultimately overcome by those who support a broadly Enlightenment approach to science as universal emancipatory knowledge. I believe that one should neither reject nor surrender to postmodernism – the typical responses these days – but use it as a basis for forging a more viable universalism that includes all of humanity but does not rely on a transcendent reality for its legitimization. In short, for me the quest for universal knowledge is simply the quest for universal government under a different guise. It does not refer to some parallel quest that might be realized even if our politics and economics remain unchanged or change in some arbitrary fashion. Here my own version of social epistemology diverges most clearly from ANALYTIC SOCIAL EPISTEMOLOGY, the branch of analytic philosophy that in the past two decades has rediscovered the social dimensions of knowledge, yet without ever straying too far from analytic philosophy's core predilections (e.g. for simple formal models, regardless of their relevance to what is modelled). Consequently, analytic philosophers never quite connect with the contemporary phenomena of knowledge production for which they would offer normative guidance. However, readers are provided scope in these pages to judge such matters for themselves.

For readers new to the intellectual terrain covered in this book, I recommend they start by reading the entry on SOCIAL EPISTEMOLOGY, which provides the most general treatment of the topic. Next it might be wise to examine the main contrasting disciplinary approaches: PHILOSOPHY VERSUS SOCIOLOGY, ANALYTIC SOCIAL EPISTEMOLOGY, SOCIOLOGY OF KNOWLEDGE. After that, the reader should be free to navigate through the book. The one general word of advice I would offer, especially to philosophical readers, is that the historical markers offered in the text need to be taken seriously. It makes a big difference whether a general statement about knowledge is made in, say, the seventeenth, eighteenth, nineteenth or twentieth century. (It goes without saying that such statements are almost always made in Europeanized cultures.) What counts as knowledge, who possesses it, the extent of its authority and the phenomena for which it is held accountable have varied significantly over time and space. Indeed, it remains an open question whether the very concept of knowledge has cross-cultural (and cross-temporal) validity. Readers intrigued by this question should begin with the entry on FOLK EPISTEMOLOGY, followed perhaps by the one on TRANSLATION.

The idea for this book was first proposed to me by Hidetoshi Kihara, one of the original Japanese social epistemologists, who persuaded the publisher Shin'yosha to include it in their "wordmap" series of concept dictionaries. My thanks goes to him and his co-translator, Tetsuji Iseda, for making the book possible in the first place. However, the book would not have appeared in English were it not for the diligent efforts and good will of Tristan Palmer at Acumen. Finally, this book is dedicated to Dolores Byrnes, a force of nature (and culture) who has stood by me during the difficult times that has marked its completion.

Steve Fuller

ANALYTIC SOCIAL EPISTEMOLOGY

Analytic social epistemology refers to the version of SOCIAL EPISTEMOLOGY pursued in the Anglophone analytic philosophical tradition. Indeed, the very phrase "social epistemology" reflects both the particular philosophical tradition and its mother tongue. The phrase was coined by the epistemologist Fred Schmitt in a special issue of the old logical positivist (see KUHN, POPPER AND LOGICAL POSITIVISM) journal *Synthese* in 1987, the same year Steve Fuller founded the journal *Social Epistemology*. That analytic philosophy – as opposed to one of the continental European schools – originated "social epistemology" as a phrase simply reflects that accounts of knowledge in the other traditions already presuppose a social dimension, which would make social epistemology superfluous. For example, from the nineteenth century onward, epistemologies descended from French positivism and German idealism have consistently stressed the systematic and collective character of knowledge. In contrast, analytic philosophy has remained wedded to the Cartesian individual – now occasionally presented as Darwinian – as the paradigm case of the knower. In that respect, "social epistemology" is designed to redress the individualist bias of analytic philosophical accounts of knowledge.

"Social epistemology" is equally an artefact of the English language. In English, "knowledge" is simply a nominalization of the verb "to know", which covers in an undifferentiated fashion the semantic space that in the other major Indo-European languages – ranging from Greek and Latin to French and German – would be divided more clearly between two distinct sets of words: one set stressing the internal process of knowing – that is, "consciousness" or "cognition" – and another set stressing the external products of knowing – that is, "discipline" or "science". Examples of this semantic division include, on the one hand, *nous, cognitio, connaissance* and *Erkenntnis* and, on the other, *episteme, scientia, savoir* and *Wissenschaft*. The former set of terms refers to activity concentrated in an individual's mental space, while the latter set refers to activity distributed among a community of collaborators. To each would correspond a distinct branch of philosophy and empirical specialty: on the one hand, philosophy of mind and cognitive psychology; on the other hand, philosophy of science and sociology of knowledge.

In *Social Epistemology* (1988), Fuller drew attention to the conceptual confusion concealed in the overextended use of "know" and "knowledge" by appealing to the *fallacies of composition and division*. Both fallacies refer to the tendency to regard a whole as exactly equal to the sum of its parts. It is therefore fallacious for epistemologists to identify social knowledge with the sum of what individuals know. "Composition" and "division" are, respectively, the names of the bottom-up and top-down versions of this fallacious tendency. On the one hand, analytic social epistemologists tend to aggregate the beliefs of a society's members to arrive at the state of social knowledge; on the other, they tend to take a socially sanctioned statement of knowledge as representative of what everyone in that society believes. Both inferences are fallacious because they fail to account for the effects of social interaction on what individuals accept (often passively) as counting for knowledge in their society. Otherwise, how is it possible that our lives are dominated by a scientific worldview, whose leading theories (e.g. Darwin's, Einstein's, Heisenberg's) are neither understood nor perhaps even believed by the vast majority of people? In the Marxist tradition, following Antonio Gramsci, this aspect of social epistemology ignored by analytic philosophy is called *hegemony*.

Working with an undifferentiated conception of knowledge, analytic philosophy has been concerned, unsurprisingly, with trying to adjudicate what that tradition itself calls *internal* and *external* approaches to epistemology. The internal approach says that knowledge requires consciousness of the causes (more precisely, reasons) of one's epistemic states, whereas the external approach says that the causes need not be available to consciousness but must be the products of reliable mechanisms that may be the object of scientific investigation. (See TRUTH, RELIABILITY AND THE ENDS OF KNOWLEDGE.) Since the 1970s, analytic philosophers have generally drifted from internalist to externalist approaches, as illustrated by the accounts of knowledge provided by, respectively, Roderick Chisholm and Alvin Goldman. Regarded from outside the Anglophone world, it must be striking that internalism and externalism are seen as irreducible alternatives and not complementary components of a comprehensive theory of knowledge.

Analytic social epistemology also tends to see the individual and the collective as alternative sources of epistemic authority. The social dimension of knowledge is presented as something superadded on the individual dimension, often overriding the individual's standpoint, for example, deference to authoritative testimony in everyday life, trust in collaborators on the research frontier, or simply some weighted aggregation of individual perspectives from which a consensus (see CONSENSUS OR DISSENT) or representative point of view may be inferred. Presupposed here is an interpretation of the "social production" of knowledge in conformist terms. Interestingly, analytic social epistemology tends to interpret conformism much more positively than some earlier philosophical theories of knowledge. In this respect, if Descartes is the inspiration for analytic individual epistemology, Plato is the inspiration for analytic social epistemology. Its "social" character is reducible to a chain of epistemic command between individuals. Consequently, analytic social epistemology specifically lacks two ideas that hark back to Kant's original coinage of "Enlightenment" and continue to be associated with Fuller's version of social epistemology: on the one hand, that individuals who think for themselves may be the products of a specific educational system or socialization process (see UNIVERSITY); on the other hand, that the epistemic community may be constituted so as to make CRITICISM, rather than conformism, the regulative ideal (see FREE ENQUIRY).

Analytic social epistemology's thorough rejection of the Enlightenment ideal is epitomized in its philosophical "Newspeak". For example, Goldman, perhaps the leading analytic social epistemologist, follows the practice of the great Scottish anti-Enlightenment theologian – and "common-sense" philosopher (see COMMON SENSE VERSUS COLLECTIVE MEMORY) – Thomas Reid in recasting intellectual autonomy as "epistemic egoism", an expression that implies a rejection of trust in others and perhaps an overestimation of one's own judgement. In contrast, he calls a social epistemology based on deferring to trustworthy testimony "epistemic altruism", which exhibits a generosity of spirit and a sense of humility in the face of one's epistemic superiors. Missing from this set of alternatives is the constitutive role of argumentation, or RHETORIC more generally, whereby reasoners – expert and lay – develop their respective positions in dialogue with each other. This dialogue need not lead to a meeting of minds, but it should empower people to take responsibility for whatever conclusions they reach, even ones that involve yielding to someone else's judgement. Rather than simply blaming the unreliability of an expert if her advice fails, one would be sufficiently aware of the expected outcomes to assume responsibility for changing course if the outcomes fail to materialize. In that case, the social epistemologist would make the great shift from Plato to Karl Popper – from designing institutions that fix belief and status to those that test and revise them. Instead of looking for certainty in others, one would learn – by making one's mistakes in public – to live with one's own fallibility.

Not surprisingly, analytic social epistemology gravitates towards politically conservative social formations. Indeed, the field has an uncanny tendency to turn such knowledge-bearing properties as competence and EXPERTISE (a.k.a. intelligence, were it not politically incorrect) into covert principles of social structure. The implied social order is sometimes akin to the mafia (i.e. the costs of not trusting the experts are likely to be higher than trusting them), other times to a royal dynasty (i.e. there are no legitimate grounds for a major change in perspective unless the current epistemic regime fails on its own terms). Together they point to a political perspective that is relatively primitive, or at least pre-constitutional.

Indicative of this pre-constitutional politics of knowledge is the recent elevation of *testimony* to a major epistemological principle. Testimony, the delegation of epistemic authority from oneself to another, was widely invoked – especially to justify religious orthodoxy – before the Enlightenment. Often it was presented, as it sometimes is today, as a complement to induction: where we lack personal experience, we must turn to the experience of others. Indeed, Goldman appears to accept Reid's theologically inspired design argument for the well-foundedness of our natural credulity: We would not believe others so readily, were their beliefs not true so often. For Reid, such epistemic reliability testified to God's benevolence, since only a sadistic deity would combine equally high degrees of credulity and fallibility in His creatures. (However, see **FOLK EPISTEMOLOGY** for a dissenting view about the reliability of folk beliefs.)

There are also more contemporary, or at least secular, defences of a testimony-driven social epistemology. Some are based on cognitive limitations: we have more beliefs than we can justify, and hence we must rely on the expertise of others to justify those beliefs. John Hardwig gave first major analytic-philosophical exposure to this idea only in 1985. His argument was based on the interdependence of enquirers on "big science" physics projects, as symbolized by the multiple authors found on their associated publications. Interestingly, Hardwig assumes without argument the normative acceptability of such scientific projects, a sign of how the naturalistic turn in analytic social epistemology has disarmed the critical impulse. (See **EXPLAINING THE NORMATIVE STRUCTURE OF SCIENCE**.) Philip Kitcher has generalized Hardwig's perspective by treating science as a self-organizing system subject to a division of cognitive labour, whose boundary disputes are internally resolved among the relevant experts and then externally applied to the rest of society, subject to the sort of ethical checks one finds on human-subject research panels.

Moreover, even analytic social epistemologists who seek common cause with **FEMINISM** or **MULTICULTURALISM** have been seduced by testimonialism. Thus, they interpret the slogan "knowledge is power" in terms of the transfer of power to the *true* knowers: in this case, women and ethnic minorities, who possess knowledge of their own bodies and ways of life that scientists and politicians lack but desire. Without denying that from a strictly empirical standpoint certain individuals possess generally relevant forms of knowledge simply by virtue of their membership in the relevant groups, the question remains of how to institutionalize such knowledge so that it genuinely benefits everyone and does not set up new barriers to access, whereby one mode of local domination is simply replaced by another, or in the more exact terms of economists, "rent-seeking". As John Stuart Mill fully realized, without the appropriate constitutional checks, a dogmatic group – be it elite or mass – can all too easily impose its will on everyone, even if only over a limited domain of their lives. (See **EPISTEMIC JUSTICE**.)

These lacunae point to a deep problem with analytic social epistemology. The field is alienated from not only the social sciences but also the other branches of normative philosophy (ethics, politics, law) that might provide guidance on designing a constitution for knowledge production. Such alienation is often presented as a kind of intellectual virtuosity, as if the goal were to reinvent SOCIAL SCIENCE by starting with as little knowledge of it as possible. This idealization might be seen, *pace* John Rawls, as analytic philosophy's original position. In any case, it reveals the extent to which analytic philosophers worry that their disciplinary identity may be compromised by sustained engagement with the special sciences, as the substance of their concerns is increasingly drawn from them.

Consider Robert Brandom's celebrated *Making it Explicit* (1994), a gargantuan opus that attempts to construct a social basis for NORMATIVITY from the most primitive semantic conventions recognized by analytic philosophy. Indeed, he wants to construct specifically Hegelian foundations based on the idea that freedom is rationalized through the codification of practice. But why undertake yet another project in the century-old tradition of inconclusive projects such as A. N. Whitehead and Bertrand Russell's *Principia Mathematica*, Wittgenstein's *Tractatus Logico-Philosophicus*, Rudolf Carnap's *Der logische Aufbau der Welt*, Nelson Goodman's *The Structure of Appearance*, Wilfrid Sellars's various false starts and even W. V. Quine's *Word and Object*? Perhaps Brandom's opus competes with projects in social ontology undertaken by social theorists such as Roy Bhaskar and Anthony Giddens, which provide a conceptual grounding for (at least some) of extant social research (see PHILOSOPHY VERSUS SOCIOLOGY). It may thus be read in the spirit of Peter Winch's *The Idea of a Social Science* (1959), in which empirical social research offers only exemplars but not "evidence" in the strict sense of something that adds to the validity of conclusions that could not have been reached by conceptual analysis alone.

FURTHER READING

R. Bhaskar, *Scientific Realism and Human Emancipation* (1987).
S. Fuller, *Social Epistemology* (1988).
S. Fuller & J. Collier, *Philosophy, Rhetoric and the End of Knowledge* (2004).
A. Goldman, *Epistemology and Cognition* (1986).
A. Goldman, *Knowledge in a Social World* (1999).
J. Hardwig, "Epistemic Dependence" (1985).
P. Kitcher, *The Advancement of Science* (1993).
M. Kusch & P. Lipton (eds), *Studies in History and Philosophy of Science* **33**, special issue on testimony (2002).
H. Longino, *Science and Social Values* (1990).
W. V. Quine, *Word and Object* (1960).
F. Schmitt (ed.), *Socializing Epistemology* (1994).
S. P. Turner, *Brains/Practices/Relativism* (2002).
P. Winch, *The Idea of a Social Science* (1959).

COMMON SENSE VERSUS COLLECTIVE MEMORY

Common sense and collective memory provide opposing paradigmatic images for the repository of social knowledge. They are based on rather different conceptions of knowledge acquisition. This difference, in turn, grounds the distinction between, respectively, Anglo-American and Franco-German philosophies of mind in the twentieth century. On the surface, the difference turns on the distinction between the individual and the collective as the locus of mind. But there is also a deeper distinction in metaphysical orientation. The common-sense approach envisages knowing as an attempt to solve the problem of *the one and the many*, namely, how to construct an economical yet faithful representation (the one) of reality (the many). In contrast, the collective memory approach takes knowing to be an attempt to solve the problem of *the whole and the part*, namely, how to provide direction, or "intelligent design" (the whole), to the collection of events that constitute history (the parts). ANALYTIC SOCIAL EPISTEMOLOGY, especially its conception of FOLK EPISTEMOLOGY, is wedded to the common-sense conception, whereas Fuller's version tends towards collective memory, especially its institutionalization as INFORMATION SCIENCE.

Common sense is typically described as a synthetic faculty that renders the inputs of the five senses into a coherent experience. The synthesis occurs by relating these inputs to the mind's default settings, which presume inductive continuity of experience over time and space. This continuity is grounded in a belief in the inherent reliability of our own and other people's senses, as well as the relative transparency of the external world to the senses. Common sense presupposes that the objects of knowledge are fully independent of the processes of knowledge acquisition. Thus, our minds are either in pre-established harmony with reality, such that we are born with ideas that are shaped like reality, or they are formed through a more contingent process – such as natural selection – in which our minds always turn out to be somewhat mismatched with reality and hence are in need of correction. These alternatives mirror the rationalist–empiricist dispute in modern epistemology, and show how a creationist conception of common sense (e.g. Thomas Reid) could yield to an evolutionary one (e.g. Charles Darwin).

In contrast, collective memory denies a clear distinction between the objects of knowledge and how we acquire them. In effect, the objects of knowledge are produced as residues of the knowledge-acquisition process, which in turn serves as a prompt for the residues to be organized into some meaningful experience. On the contrary, it reveals that one's mind has been carried along inertially by the residues of past events. Tradition is thus not venerated for its survival value, but rather distrusted as the herd mentality for its undeliberate – and, in that sense, unintelligent – character. The Italian founder of sociology, Vilfredo Pareto, developed this idea most systematically. For the theorist of collective memory, induction does not provide external validation of one's mental processes. However, equally distrusted is the view that history is inexorably drawing the mind to its natural fate. That view, demonized by Karl Popper as historicism, removes the element of choice required for genuine deliberation. (See KUHN, POPPER AND LOGICAL POSITIV- ISM.) Here sociological followers of Émile Durkheim, notably Maurice Halbwachs, have tried to split the difference by associating residues with multiply interpretable artefacts left to commemorate past events.

Despite their differences, both common sense and collective memory have a problem accounting for thinking as something more than the mere summation of experience. However, they deal with the problem in rather opposed ways. Common sense presumes that mind and world begin as separate entities, and thinking is the process of connecting them together. In contrast, collective memory presumes that mind and world begin as one, and thinking is the process of differentiating the former from the latter. We have here, then, what G. W. F. Hegel would have recognized as two careers of the mind: on the one hand, a mind in search of approval from the world; on the other, a mind in search of dominion over the world. This distinction is relevant not merely to epistemology but to value theory more generally. To put the contrast sharply, circa 1900, G. E. Moore argued, via the concept of common sense, that objects are valued because they are valuable, whereas Sigmund Freud argued, via the concept of collective memory, that objects are valuable because they are valued. (Moore's word for value was "good", Freud's "desire".) For Moore, our attitudes ideally reflect the inherent qualities of the objects we encounter; for Freud, they ideally reflect the contexts of our previous encounters with them or their surrogates. For most of the twentieth century, the contrast was marked as "linguistic analysis" versus "psychoanalysis".

Collective memory is central to the epistemological foundations of sociology (see PHILOSOPHY VERSUS SOCIOLOGY). Before Durkheim and Max Weber, it had been common in the history of philosophy and politics to argue that inequalities among those who live together at *the same time* are necessary to hold society together. In short, hierarchy was the universal social glue. However, Durkheim and Weber shifted the focus to the unequal significance assigned to people inhabiting *different times*: *time-discounting*, as welfare economists say. Sometimes people *discount the past*, as when they make it seem that what they are doing now is what they always have wanted to do. This strategy of *adaptive preference formation* is perhaps most familiar from the Ministry of Truth in George Orwell's *1984*, but it is also implied in Durkheim's attempt at a unified theory of solidarity that could incorporate both primitive and modern societies. (See TRUTH, RELIABILITY AND THE ENDS OF KNOWLEDGE.) However, sometimes people *discount the future*, which means that they use past behaviour as the baseline against which to plot their subsequent actions, without considering the long-term consequences of such blind obedience to precedent, regardless of negative feedback. In the psychological literature, future-discounting is normally seen as an unconscious process, as in the case of habits and addictions. However, Weber observed that this process takes a more self-conscious form in the legal and economic practices with which he associated that signature feature of modernity, rationalization.

At a societal level, then, RATIONALITY involves the disciplining of collective memory. Combining the insights of Durkheim and Weber, we can say that social order is maintained in the modern world by past-discounting compensating for the excesses of future-discounting. For example, the main reason that prophecies of ecological doom never seem to be vindicated is not that they turn out to be false, but rather that different people live with the relevant consequences. This allows time for the new generation to want (or at least tolerate) what is most likely to happen, which facilitates shifts in how these predictions are measured and interpreted, which is then retrospectively projected back on to the past. The state is strongly implicated in this process, especially in the production and maintenance of public records and a national education system, something that personally interested Durkheim and other founders of SOCIAL SCIENCE.

Finally, if one takes even slightly seriously Plato's view that knowledge is a form of reminiscence, perhaps even of past lives, then the natural sciences pose a special set of problems for collective memory, since their sense of PROGRESS appears to be intimately connected with *amnesia*. (See KNOWLEDGE MANAGEMENT.) In the 1960s, the founder of quantitative history of science, Derek de Solla Price, observed that scientific advancement is correlated with a shortened half-life for citations to previous work. A related point is that the harder the science, the more likely its historians will not be regarded as front-line contributors to the field. It is almost as if a sociological precondition for progress is that the short-term and long-term collective memories of a discipline must be radically severed from each other. Here social epistemologists could learn from the two main competing explanations for amnesia: Pierre Janet's theory of *dissociation*, according to which the past is simply detached from the present so that it is ignored as no longer part of oneself, and Freud's theory of *repression*, which involves the demonization of the past as false and hence a continuing threat to oneself. A relevant phenomenon for investigation is what Popperians call *Kuhn loss*, the problems from the old paradigm no longer retained by the new paradigm. (See HISTORIOGRAPHY.)

FURTHER READING

G. Ainslie, *Picoeconomics* (1992).

R. Aron, *Main Currents in Sociological Thought* (1965).

M. De Mey, *The Cognitive Paradigm* (1982).

J. Elster, *Sour Grapes* (1984).

J. Elster, *Alchemies of the Mind* (1999).

L. Fleck, *The Genesis and Development of a Scientific Fact* (1979).

S. Fuller, *Philosophy of Science and Its Discontents* (1993).

M. Kusch & P. Lipton (eds), *Studies in History and Philosophy of Science* **33**, special issue on testimony (2002).

E. Noelle-Neumann, *The Spiral of Silence* (1982).

P. Pettit, *The Common Mind* (1993).

K. Popper, *The Poverty of Historicism* (1957).

D. de S. Price, *Big Science, Little Science, ... and Beyond* (1986).

C. Price, *Time, Discounting and Value* (1993).

J. M. Robertson, *A History of Free-Thought in the Nineteenth Century* (1929).

S. P. Turner, *Brains/Practices/Relativism* (2002).

CONSENSUS VERSUS DISSENT

Consensus versus dissent arises as an issue in science because of science's aspiration to universal assent, a goal that is a secularized version of the universalist aspirations (see UNIVERSALISM VERSUS RELATIVISM) of the great proselytizing RELIGIONs, Christianity and Islam, according to which the truth is not fully realized until it is accepted by everyone. This made science central to the emancipatory project that democratic activists, especially socialists, derived from the eighteenth-century Enlightenment. (See SCIENCE AS A SOCIAL MOVEMENT, SOCIAL SCIENCE.)

Here it is worth observing that, with the possible exception of the Sophists, the Greeks had not generally presumed that an objective and rational account of reality would be accessible to all human beings, let alone derive its epistemic merit from such accessibility. (See RHETORIC.) Indeed, Plato was quite explicit that hard class divisions are ultimately justified in terms of clear differences in epistemic access. When Aristotle declared that the pure pursuit of knowledge required leisure, he was not recommending (as Karl Marx's son-in-law Paul Lafargue did) mass laziness; he was laying down a class marker that only the already leisured were in a position to know. ANALYTIC SOCIAL EPISTEMOLOGY continues this tradition by requiring consensus only at the second-order level of epistemic analysis, that is, there should be universal agreement over who holds the relevant EXPERTISE in a given situation where a decision needs to be taken. This second-order consensus is what Antonio Gramsci, in deference to the ancient Greek tyrants, called *hegemony*.

Contemporary philosophers often reduce the sociological dimension of knowledge to consensus formation, typically without distinguishing the first-order (emancipatory) and the second-order (hegemonic) type of consensus. (The contrast is familiar in politics as the difference between participatory and representative democracy.) Most notably in Jürgen Habermas, this conflation is achieved by a transcendental argument of the following sort: Communication and other fundamental forms of social interaction would be impossible without presupposing common standards of validation. Such an argument conveniently absolves philosophers from taking seriously two empirical possibilities that would force them to take the role of divergence, and especially dissent, more seriously as a feature of knowledge production: on the one hand, apparent agreement may mask deep conceptual differences, due to incommensurable assumptions that may surface only much later (see TRANSLATION); on the other, latent disagreements may be strategically suppressed for purposes of overcoming a common foe.

These countervailing considerations, which underwrite Fuller's social epistemology, are evident in the history of science. On the one hand, the charter of the first modern scientific body, the Royal Society of London, virtually invited the emergence of incommensurability by requiring members to have their metaphysical differences resolved by empirical and mathematical means. Of course, the metaphysical differences never really disappeared because they ultimately represented alternative directions in which any agreed knowledge claims could be taken. Thus, the seeds of conflict remained but germinated only once scientists were forced to seek the same degree of consensus from the context of discovery as from the context of justification. As Thomas Kuhn (see **KUHN, POPPER AND LOGICAL POSITIVISM**) observed, this happens only when a paradigm accumulates enough anomalies that a crisis is precipitated. At that point, the incommensurability of metaphysical assumptions is formally recognized, as scientists become explicitly concerned to move in the same direction. On the other hand, the suppression of latent disagreements may enable scientists to present an intellectually misleading but no less united front against an apparently powerful common foe. For example, biologists and philosophers supportive of **EVOLUTION** may suppress quite substantial differences (over, say, the theory's applicability to human beings or the primacy of natural selection as a mechanism) to oppose religiously inspired devotees of creationism and intelligent design. In such cases, one may reasonably ask whether the self-censorship that travels under the guise of consensus ultimately serves to pervert the flow of **FREE ENQUIRY**.

The general picture of knowledge dynamics implied by these countervailing considerations is that scientists are drawn together by common outside pressures, which help to set a shared normative framework, while they are prised apart by the freedom to pursue divergent paths within that common framework. This is somewhat different from the picture that emerged among historians and social scientists over the twentieth century, which is sometimes epitomized as "consensus versus conflict" or "cooperation versus competition". In both the philosophical and historical pictures, issues of first- and second-order consensus are blurred, but whereas philosophers and scientists have been preoccupied with the convergence of opinion, historians and social scientists have mainly focused on simply the problem of keeping the peace in complex societies where divergence of opinion is taken as given. In that case, consensus and conflict appear as poles along a continuum, or sliding scale, defined by the relative scarcity of usually material, but sometimes symbolic, resources. (See **SOCIAL CAPITAL VERSUS PUBLIC GOOD**.) However, this model has been typically proposed in an empirical spirit, such that the relationship between consensus–conflict and scarcity–abundance would be expected to vary across different sociohistorical settings.

The role of dissent as an outright virtue, something more than the absence of consensus in organized enquiry, has been underappreciated by philosophers (except Popperians), sociologists and even historians concerned with knowledge. Dissent only partially overlaps with *doubt*, whose virtues have been loudly advertised by sceptics who believe that, in many seemingly fundamental matters, the best course of action is to reserve judgement. In contrast, dissent is intimately related to CRITICISM, in that the dissenter presupposes a context of shared beliefs and values from which one then expresses a difference of opinion. The dissenter deeply cares about the issues over which a consensus has formed, whereas the sceptic is specifically dedicated to dissolving any such concern.

This point was perhaps most keenly felt by Joseph Priestley, the eighteenth-century Unitarian theologian who may be the greatest dissenter in the history of philosophy. Priestley is best known as the discoverer of oxygen, inventor of the utilitarian maxim "the greatest good for the greatest number" and confidant of the American founding fathers. But at the end of his life (1803), he authored a comparative evaluation of Jesus and Socrates as exemplars, where Jesus appears as a dissenter trying to deepen the spirituality of his fellow Jews, whereas Socrates appears as a doubter who started from the assumptions of his sophistic opponents only for the sake of argument, while hiding his own (or Plato's) distinct position. Although both Jesus and Socrates were eventually executed, Jesus appears morally superior because he explicitly identified with those whom he had challenged: he neither merely found fault nor advocated a completely alien point of view. He proposed a more fully realized version of what he took his audience already to believe.

The roots of dissent in the West are twofold, one pagan and one sacred. The pagan root is the obligation under Athenian democracy for citizens to express their opinions in the forum. Refrain from speech was seen as an act of cowardice. (See FREE ENQUIRY.) The sacred root is the proscription of idolatry in the great monotheistic religions, where believers were called regularly to renew their faith by distinguishing the nature and object of their belief *vis-à-vis* rivals and imitators. To be sure, this obligation seeded various waves of *heresies* (whose Greek root is "decision"). Originally, one was called to dissent from the worship of animals and artefacts. This explains the lingering colloquial connection between dissent and iconoclasm, which harks back to the smashing of idols. But after the Protestant Reformation, "idolatry" increasingly stood for institutions that were pale or corrupt representations of the spirit they were meant to embody. In the seventeenth and eighteenth centuries, the sense of justice associated with natural law came to be interpreted in light of this expanded understanding of anti-idolatry, thereby licensing political revolutions in England, America and France, as well as providing legitimacy to the idea that the populace is entitled on a regular basis (via elections) to decide whether their representatives truly represent its best interests. It is not by accident that Montesquieu's magnum opus in entitled *The Spirit of the Laws* (1748).

The great dissenter in modern science was Ernst Mach, after whom the logical positivists' (see **KUHN, POPPER AND LOGICAL POSITIVISM**) Vienna Circle was named. He believed that his own field of physics had become (at the end of the nineteenth century) a secular church that required disestablishment, preferably via mass education in science, comparable to the Reformation project of publishing the Bible in the vulgar languages. Mach himself pursued the project at the academic level in *The Science of Mechanics* (1883), a critical history of physics that presented the consolidation of Newtonian mechanics as a high church of science that had suppressed dissenting opinion – notably on such fundamental issues as space, time, matter and cause – for the next two centuries. Einstein and Heisenberg were inspired to revolutionize physics by reading Mach, who also informed the philosophical nonconformism of Popper and Paul Feyerabend.

FURTHER READING

H. Bergson, *The Two Sources of Morality and Religion* (1935).
R. Bhaskar, *Scientific Realism and Human Emancipation* (1987).
G. Evans, *A Brief History of Heresy* (2003).
S. Fuller, *Social Epistemology* (1988).
S. Fuller, *Thomas Kuhn* (2000).
J. Habermas, *Theory of Communicative Action* (1983–7).
J. Hecht, *Doubt* (2003).
A. Irwin, *Citizen Science* (1995).
W. Keith, *Democracy as Discussion* (2007).
E. Noelle-Neumann, *The Spiral of Silence* (1982).
J. Ravetz, *Scientific Knowledge and its Social Problems* (1971).
R. Sassower, *Popper's Legacy* (2006).
W. Shadish & S. Fuller (eds), *The Social Psychology of Science* (1994).
S. P. Turner, *The Social Theory of Practices* (1994).

CRITICISM

Criticism involves the formation of a judgement towards something that the critic believes could have been done or made otherwise (for better or worse). Thus, criticism presupposes not only a strong divide between subject (the critic) and object (the criticized) but also that the subject has an interest in the object even though she was not directly involved in constructing it. In this respect, criticism is always a constructive enterprise that occurs against a value consensus (see CONSENSUS VERSUS DISSENT). Thus, in ancient Athens, the *kritik* was the judge whose verdict converted a private dispute into a public matter, a *res publica*, from which everyone may learn and the polity grow stronger. This role is akin to that of the interested non-participant in knowledge production. (See NORMATIVITY.)

A key social condition for criticism – one difficult to establish and maintain – is the mutual recognition of critic and criticized. Criticism is impossible when the criticized is not, in some sense, accountable to the critic. (See RATIONALITY.) Historically, as Habermas has stressed, this condition has been tied to the fate of the public sphere, especially its sense of mutual peer accountability. (See FREE ENQUIRY.) It is easy to forget in these postmodern times (see POSTMODERNISM) that being ignored is not a subtle form of criticism, but its very antithesis. The Athenian *kritik* always judged an equal in public, and hence in a state of mutual accountability. This is in contrast to the *sceptic* who denied a level playing field sufficient for any such judgement. (After all, judgement is always at the mercy of more primitive passions and processes.) It also differs from the *cynic* who was capable of levelling all differences to the point of allowing human beings and dogs (the Greek word from which "cynic" derives) equal treatment.

After Kant's *Critique of Judgement*, the authority of critics has rested on the possibility of a subjective universal, which from the late-nineteenth century onward has been associated with the domain of *intellectuals*. (See EXPERTISE.) This subjective universality implies that somehow the whole can be represented from the standpoint of one of its parts. It follows that critics are themselves open to criticism from other subjects, whose judgements are not captured by what a critic says. The opposite of the critical standpoint is one that delivers "objective particular" judgements. Such judgements deny that the observer has an independent standpoint from the observed. When SCIENCE AND TECHNOLOGY STUDIES researchers obey Bruno Latour's injunction to "follow the actors", they are aiming to deliver objective particular judgements. In that case, if they are critical at all, it is only of other researchers not of the actors they are following. Unsurprisingly, Latour is generally dismissive of the critical attitude.

Schools of criticism are distinguished by the standards they use as a basis to judge a given object. These standards may be expressed in terms of either canonical works (what Matthew Arnold called *touchstones*) or exemplary patterns of reasoning (what Northrop Frye called *archetypes*). They correspond to Kuhn's two principal senses of *paradigm:* as exemplar and disciplinary matrix, respectively, except that Kuhn restricts the reach of the critical community to merely those who constitute it as colleagues. In this respect, Kuhn relativizes the critic's traditional subjective universality to a scientific specialty's peer review processes.

The so-called "two cultures" problem of the arts versus the sciences first emerged in the seventeenth century as a dispute over the appropriate standard of criticism: touchstone or archetype. The "ancients" argued for using entire works as the touchstones in terms of which any new work would be judged. This hermeneutical approach became central to the arts. It was typically accompanied by a view that recent works either elaborate the details of earlier works or otherwise fall short of the standards set by those original works. In contrast, the "moderns" argued that entire works are valuable only as archetypes, which may be better presented and developed in later works. Here is the basis for the attitude of the sciences, which regard works as testable hypotheses, or rough drafts, that are expected to be superseded over time.

Critics characteristically judge objects by the economy of effort exerted to the amount of value produced: Did the creator do the most with what she was working with or could more have been done? Critical judgements are contested by claiming that the work (or act) carries more meaning than the critic realizes, perhaps because the critic presupposes a standard alien to the work (or act). In other words, one tries to shift the burden of criticism from its hypothetical to its hermeneutical function, that is, the work does not conform to a pre-existent archetype but constitutes a touchstone in its own right.

Are there limits to criticism? This question was formally aired in the eighteenth century between Voltaire and Leibniz on the problem of *theodicy*, or divine justice. (See **RELIGION**.) Leibniz's God was beyond criticism. He held that God created the best of all possible worlds according to a principle of sufficient reason for everything that happens. God then compels human beings to discover this hidden order through science and thereby complete the divine plan by rendering the plan self-conscious. In contrast, Voltaire criticized God for wasting nature through catastrophes and senseless destruction, which suggested to him a role for human beings in correcting and improving this imperfect world through science. Most world-historic defences of science in the nineteenth century combined elements of these two views, with German idealism veering towards Leibniz and Anglo-French positivism towards Voltaire.

A major Enlightenment legacy was the academic institutionalization of criticism, as exemplified in the centrality of Kant in philosophy and the "higher criticism" in theology. Criticism was held to be the only universally reliable method of enquiry because it clearly accepted the epistemically fallen state of humanity, the secular equivalent of original sin. The very fact that we need to seek knowledge implicitly acknowledges our finitude and fallibility, such that the cost of acquiring any knowledge at all is that it will be biased by the conditions surrounding its acquisition. This line of thought had extended from the Young Hegelians (including Marx) to the French and Austrian positivists, including Ernest Renan and Ernst Mach. The main legatees of this tradition in the twentieth century were the Frankfurt School's "critical theory" and Popper's "critical rationalism". It is worth noting that this tradition has stood for the unity of enquiry against increasing academic specialization, as defended by neo-Kantianism, analytic philosophy and nowadays the followers of Kuhn.

Starting in the eighteenth century, the critical attitude has been associated with *sympathy*: a relationship between the subject and the object of criticism that is akin to what Popper called *the logic of the situation* and the field of science and technology studies calls *methodological relativism*. In both cases, the critic reconstructs how it was possible for someone to believe or act as they did, given their background beliefs and interests. However, the critic's capacity to function, in Adam Smith's words, as an "impartial spectator" does not imply that the critic actually endorses the criticized person's beliefs and interests. Rather, this capacity implies that there are other beliefs and interests common to the critic and criticized, in terms of which the criticized person may be understood and evaluated. However, it is not necessary to jump to the Kantian conclusion that these common beliefs and interests are transcendental (i.e. universally valid necessary conditions for the very possibility of criticism). Rather, the common beliefs and interests may constitute a *res publica*: a virtual public sphere that unites the critic and the criticized in a common fate in the empirical world. The relevant *res publica* may shift according to whom the critic is criticizing. This, once again, is the interested non-participant stance of the social epistemologist. (See UNIVERSALISM VERSUS RELATIVISM.)

Nevertheless, the defence of criticism on purely transcendental grounds escalated over the nineteenth century. This amounted to a limitation of the scope of permissible criticism. A key moment involved the introduction of *empathy* by Wilhelm Dilthey as the distinctive method of the human sciences. Empathy requires that the critic accept the fundamental soundness of the criticized person's beliefs and interests. Criticism is thus restricted to relatively peripheral matters: the sorts of things that would have enabled the criticized person to achieve their goals more effectively. If a critic cannot achieve that basic level of empathy, then she should not engage in criticism. In the twentieth century, both hermeneutical and analytic schools of philosophy have converged on this point, thereby erasing any sharp distinction between the perspectives of the critic and the criticized: in short, all of "them" are presumed to be versions of "us". The metaphorical distance traditionally required for criticism thus disappears. In this spirit, Hans-Georg Gadamer wrote of the fusing of cognitive horizons, while Donald Davidson denied the distinguishability of conceptual schemes. Helped along by the later Wittgenstein, and canonized by Richard Rorty, they have revived St Augustine's epistemic imperative, *crede ut intellegas*. In more secular terms, we understand people in other times and places only because we are prepared to believe most of what they say. It was over this principle that sociologists – especially those under the sway of Marx and Freud – most strenuously disagreed with philosophers in the twentieth century. (See PHILOSOPHY VERSUS SOCIOLOGY.)

Fuller's social epistemology stands with the sociologists in preferring the broad conception of criticism associated with sympathy to the narrow conception associated with empathy. Here Karl Mannheim's version of the SOCIOLOGY OF KNOWLEDGE provides an instructive precedent. He sharply distinguished between two types of criticism: *refutation* and *demystification*. The former addresses an explicit line of reasoning, the latter its presuppositions. Presuppositions are propositions that are only contingently interrelated but over time have come to appear necessarily connected together. Presuppositions congeal into ideologies, and when they take the form of a binary opposition (e.g. universal–particular, master–slave, male–female, white–black), their demystification is called, after Martin Heidegger and Jacques Derrida, *deconstruction*. Presuppositions require demystification – rather than refutation – because their constituent propositions have come to be mentally associated with each other without standing in some clear logical relationship. Not surprisingly, striking mental images tend to anchor ideologies. They are the stuff of declarative RHETORIC. Thus, the Dickensian factory worker of nineteenth-century England enabled Marx to launch his critique of capitalism. Reflecting on Charles Dickens's popular image, he thus could ask his readers: why must capitalism's high productivity be linked with worker exploitation? The suggestion that the two need *not* be so linked was a seminal moment in capitalism's demystification, as well as an argument for socialism.

Mannheim had been influenced not only by Marx but also by the great art historian Heinrich Wölflin, who distinguished between an internal and external history of art, the latter canvassing the possibilities out of which the former is only one of many possible realizations. For both Wölflin and Mannheim, the demystifying approach of external history is the profounder form of criticism, as it reveals the decisions that had to be taken for a particular artefact to appear as just the right one to both creator and observers.

However, this privileging of external history was subsequently clouded once Wöllflin's distinction was transferred to science. Both the logical positivists and Kuhn recognized a sharp difference between questions inside and outside a conceptual framework or paradigm. Yet here blanket appeals to the pragmatic realm conflated sheer contingency, free choice and irrationality as characterizations of the external factors that frame a paradigm. This led to a policy of *de gustibus non est disputandum*, which effectively lowered the epistemic status of demystification to an aesthetic complaint. Thus, today philosophers denigrate demystifiers as critics who practise guilt by association (with objectionable political motives) rather than engage in the hard work of refuting arguments on the terms of those they criticize. However, perhaps the truly hard work comes from holding people responsible for all the consequences of their decisions and not simply the logical ones to which their explicit reasoning draws attention. Not only are the consequences difficult to track, but also they may be at odds with what agents were trying to do or show. In this respect, the denigration of demystification reinstates a presumptively benign, and hence largely uncritical, view of the world. (See EXPLAINING THE NORMATIVE STRUCTURE OF SCIENCE.)

FURTHER READING

T. Adorno (ed.), *The Positivist Dispute in German Sociology* (1976).
A. Ahmad, *In Theory: Classes, Nations, Literatures* (1992).
D. Frisby, *The Alienated Mind* (1992).
S. Fuller, *Thomas Kuhn* (2000).
S. Fuller, *The Intellectual* (2005).
A. Gouldner, *The Future of Intellectuals and the Rise of the New Class* (1979).
J. Habermas, *The Structural Transformation of the Public Sphere* (1989).
I. Hacking, *The Social Construction of What?* (1998).
I. C. Jarvie, *The Republic of Science* (2001).
I. Lakatos & A. Musgrave (eds), *Criticism and the Growth of Knowledge* (1970).
B. Latour, *Pandora's Hope* (1999).
R. E. Macksey & E. Donato (eds), *The Structuralist Controversy* (1970).
K. Mannheim, *Ideology and Utopia* (1936).
J. Milbank, *Theology and Social Theory* (1990).
K. Popper, *Objective Knowledge* (1972).
R. Rorty, *Philosophy and the Mirror of Nature* (1979).
C. Taylor, "Interpretation and the Sciences of Man" (1971).

DISCIPLINARITY VERSUS INTERDISCIPLINARITY

Interdisciplinarity is more than simply a call for open borders between disciplines, so that cross-disciplinary borrowings are tolerated and even appreciated for the value they add to solving problems in one's home discipline. Rather, the persistent need for interdisciplinary work highlights the inherently conventional character of disciplines. Metaphysically speaking, disciplines are nothing more than holding patterns in the dynamic of enquiry. (See SCIENCE AS A SOCIAL MOVEMENT.) Of course, disciplinary conventions can be sociohistorically explained and epistemologically justified, but so could alternatives that perhaps already exist in neighbouring countries or had existed in earlier times. Rather than dispensing with disciplines altogether, disciplinarity should be treated as a necessary evil of knowledge production: the more necessary it appears, the more evil it becomes. One important way disciplinarity can appear *necessary* in this objectionable sense is by an overdeterminist (or Whiggish) historical perspective that cannot imagine alternatives to the current regime of disciplines. (See HISTORIOGRAPHY.)

Disciplinary success is largely a function of institutionalization. Any discipline can succeed if its members are provided with adequate resources to solve their own problems, which are in turn more generally recognized as problems worth solving. However, this commonplace continues to be shrouded in epistemological mystery because the ebb and flow of disciplines appears to happen without any central planning, let alone philosophical legislation. As a result, with a little help from secular theologies such as scientific realism, a trivial sociological insight is transubstantiated into a version of the "invisible hand" fashionable in the eighteenth century and vigorously pursued by the merchants of self-organization today, a very broad church that includes postmodernists (see POSTMODERNISM), evolutionary epistemologists and complexity theorists.

Thomas Kuhn's (see KUHN, POPPER AND LOGICAL POSITIVISM) influential account of paradigm formation has left the impression that scientists are the people who manage to wrest control of the means of knowledge production from the politicians, religious fanatics, and other folks who make it impossible to pursue the True without also pursuing the Good and the Just at the same time. This autonomization of enquiry – symbolized by the founding of the Royal Society and similar scientific societies in the seventeenth century – epitomizes all the perceived benefits of disciplinarity. These include: (i) secure borders for enquiry that keep larger societal demands at a distance; (ii) common standards for incorporating new members and topics, as well as for evaluating their efforts; (iii) discretion over the terms in which the concerns from the larger society are translated into new problems.

This account of disciplinarity strikingly presupposes the low prior probability that disciplines exist at all. It is considered a minor miracle that institutions of enquiry have been maintained in the face of various internal and external conflicts. Indicative of this perspective is the tendency to think that disciplined science had a rather specific origin – such as the founding of the Royal Society – and that its development cannot be, nor could have been, more perspicuous than it has been. Even contemporary philosophy of science, which has almost completely purged its old positivist fixation on the goal of unified science nevertheless takes for granted that it was better to dump Aristotle for Newton, Newton for Einstein and so on, and at roughly the times and for the reasons they were dumped. If contemporary philosophers of science engage in CRITICISM at all, it is with other philosophers or scientists who insist on a conception of scientific RATIONALITY that transcends normal scientific practice. Across the passing fashions in philosophy of science, from positivist unificationism to postmodernist disunificationism, the one constant has been that science normally is as it ought to be. This even applies to SCIENCE AND TECHNOLOGY STUDIES, which helps to explain its studiously descriptive stance towards the phenomena it studies.

Understandably, in the midst of the dynastic and religious wars that plagued early modern Europe, the survival of self-selecting and self-governing scientific societies that operated across warring factions was a considerable *political* feat. It was easily interpreted as promising the basis of a peaceful world-order, or what Stephen Toulmin has called a "cosmopolis". Not surprisingly, perhaps, this image again came to offer hope towards the end of the Second World War, when Herbert Butterfield and Alexandre Koyre each coined the phrase "Scientific Revolution" for this development. However, the history of disciplinarity before the canonization of the Scientific Revolution had covered most of the same people, events and institutions but discussed their significance rather differently.

First, disciplines were portrayed as more loosely bounded. From reading, say, Kuhn or Michael Polanyi, it is easy to get the impression that a discipline is akin to a monastic order in the stringency of its entry criteria, training procedures, evaluative standards and so on. However, until the late-nineteenth century, with the introduction of nationwide textbooks for discipline-based instruction in universities (see UNIVERSITY), an academic discipline was really little more than a collection of certification boards announcing that a piece of research met the standards upheld by the boards. Included here are what is common to doctoral examinations and peer-review journals. The exact nature of the training, the source of funding and the overarching programme of enquiry to which the research contributed were largely left open to discretion. Of course, some people aspired to stricter criteria – and the twentieth century has been the story of their steady ascent – but these have been always difficult to enforce for any great length of time or expanse of space. (See **EXPERTISE**.)

In intellectual histories written before Kuhn (e.g. Merz, Cassirer), disciplines were often portrayed as starting from worldviews designed to explain everything. They flourished as social movements in several countries, where they campaigned against each other to acquire professorships, funding, influence and so on. "Crucial experiments" and *Methodenstreiten* were symbolic events in the ongoing struggle. Over time, these clashes were institutionally resolved, especially through the creation of academic departments entitled to self-reproduction. (The nebular hypothesis proposed by Kant and Laplace for the origins of the universe could model how a molten intellectual movement cools down into a stable department structure.) In a sufficiently wealthy academic environment, even the losers could console themselves with a department they could call their own. Moreover, the resolutions were themselves subject to significant cross-national variation, such that the losers in one country may turn out victors in another. The apparent universalization of particular disciplines – the fact that, say, physics or economics may be taught the same everywhere – simply tracked the geopolitical interests of the nations whose universities housed the discipline.

Before 1945, "disciplines" were little more than the legitimizing ideology of the makeshift solutions that define the department structure of particular universities. Taken together across institutions and across nations, the history of disciplinarity constituted a set of test cases on how to resolve deep differences in cognitive horizons. Indeed, *interdisciplinarity* turns out to be the main *internal* motivator of sustained epistemic change: today's disciplines were born interdisciplinary, as social movements that aspired to address all manner of phenomena and registers of life, not simply the domain of reality over which they came to exercise custodianship. Here *positivism* holds a special place as a meta-theory of interdisciplinarity.

Common to the various self-described positivist projects has been an interest in constructing a medium of epistemic exchange across disciplinary boundaries. The ill-fated attempts by the logical positivists to unify science are not unreasonably seen as aiming to convert an interdisciplinary trade language into the official language of the disciplinary trading partners. In their original Viennese phase, the logical positivists tried to design a lingua franca from scratch, partly inspired by efforts in the 1920s to make Esperanto the official language of the League of Nations. Once in exile, at least one positivist, Philipp Frank, examined the strengths and weaknesses of two living examples of interdisciplinary social movements that showed no signs of retreating behind disciplinary boundaries and containing themselves to specialist puzzles: Thomism and dialectical materialism. Frank credited both movements, despite their obvious cognitive deficiencies and proneness to dogmatism, with upholding the ideal of enquiry that roams freely across domains of reality in the service of individual enlightenment and collective empowerment. However, Frank's movements in the US were monitored by the FBI, who feared that a totalitarian mindset lurked behind his critical appreciation of Thomism and Marxism. This lurid bit of Cold War history underscores the fact that interdisciplinary enquiry requires a secure site for its conduct. While interdisciplinarity may not respect disciplinary boundaries, it needs boundaries of its own, so that enquirers are not cut short when they attempt to challenge or bridge differences in existing bodies of knowledge.

For Frank, that site was the UNIVERSITY, especially its mission of liberal education, which continually forces academics – no matter how specialized their research – to return to the question of what future citizens will need to know to exercise their liberties most effectively. The value of research, one might say, is test-driven in the classroom. From that standpoint, one favoured by Fuller's version of social epistemology, the meta-theories of enquiry produced by both the German idealists and the logical positivists appear as alternative methodologies of curricular design. Yet, carrying through with the bold visions of these two movements presupposed that academics have the freedom – indeed, the obligation – to challenge the provincial assumptions of their disciplinary EXPERTISE. That sort of freedom was traditionally underwritten by *tenure*. (See FREE ENQUIRY.)

But tenure has become less central to the types of interdisciplinarity that have flourished since the onset of the Cold War. As universities expanded to meet national defence needs, a variety of "area studies" and "systems-theoretic" approaches were proposed as interdisciplinary fields. Some of these fields survive as SOCIAL SCIENCE disciplines, others as unrealized ideals. In either case, both have been removed from the context of liberal education. More typical has been the spread of a pattern of interdisciplinarity found in the natural sciences for most of the twentieth century and nowadays associated with "Mode 2" knowledge production. (See KNOWLEDGE SOCIETY.) It has less to do with liberal education than with filling in research gaps between disciplines or, in extreme cases, remapping certain domains of reality in a so-called "transdisciplinary" fashion. Because such interdisciplinary work has historically flourished off-campus in corporate laboratories and science parks, its educational implications are often not immediately apparent. All depends on how, if at all, the interdisciplinary projects make their way back into the curriculum: do they become bases for new disciplines and degree programmes? How is this interdisciplinary research institutionalized so that it becomes a genuine public good, that is, teachable, and not simply a piece of intellectual property? (See KNOWLEDGE MANAGEMENT, SOCIAL CAPITAL VERSUS PUBLIC GOOD.)

FURTHER READING

C. Bazerman, *Shaping Written Knowledge* (1987).

E. Cassirer, *The Problem of Knowledge* (1950).

W. Clark, *Academic Charisma and the Origins of the Research University* (2006).

P. Frank, *Modern Science and its Philosophy* (1949).

S. Fuchs, *The Professional Quest for Truth* (1992).

S. Fuller, *Thomas Kuhn* (2000b).

S. Fuller & J. Collier, *Philosophy, Rhetoric and the End of Knowledge* (2004)

P. Galison & D. Stump (eds), *The Disunity of Science* (1996).

T. S. Kuhn, *The Structure of Scientific Revolutions* (1970).

J. T. Merz, *A History of European Thought in the Nineteenth Century*, (1964).

P. Mirowski, *Machine Dreams* (2002).

M. Polanyi, *Personal Knowledge* (1957).

G. Reisch, *How the Cold War Transformed the Philosophy of Science* (2005).

S. Toulmin, *Human Understanding* (1972).

S. Toulmin, *Return to Reason* (2003).

I. Wallerstein, *Open the Social Sciences* (1996).

EPISTEMIC JUSTICE

The problem of epistemic justice concerns the optimal distribution of knowledge and power in society. The two main strategies for addressing the problem reflect two ways of understanding the slogan "knowledge is power". One supposes that more knowledge helps *concentrate* power, the other that it helps *distribute* power. Analytic social epistemologists (see **ANALYTIC SOCIAL EPISTEMOLOGY**) adopt the former perspective, while Fuller's version adopts the latter. To be sure, knowledge involves *both* the expansion and contraction of possibilities for action. Knowledge expands the knower's own possibilities for action by contracting the possible actions of others. These "others" may range from fellow knowers to non-knowing natural and artificial entities, in so far as they are capable of impeding the knower's will. Moreover, the "others" may even be one's own future states, in which case "knowledge is power" refers to an agent's sphere of autonomy.

Such a broad understanding of "knowledge is power" encompasses the interests of all who have embraced it, including Plato, Bacon, Comte and Foucault. But differences arise over its normative spin: should the stress be placed on knowledge *opening* or *closing* the possibilities for action? If the former, then the range of people recognized as knowers is likely to be restricted; if the latter, then the range is likely to be extended. After all, my knowledge provides an advantage over you only if you do not already possess it. In that respect, knowledge is a *positional good* (see **SOCIAL CAPITAL VERSUS PUBLIC GOOD**). From this standpoint, it may be misleading to treat the universally shared experience associated with **COMMON SENSE VERSUS COLLECTIVE MEMORY** as knowledge in the strict sense, since it typically exists in a tacit, unconscious or otherwise latent form that cannot be easily appropriated to inform action. (A simple example: someone with veridical perception does not *decide* to believe that the cat is on the mat.) Not surprisingly, the wide range of broadly ecological philosophers who stress this latent dimension (including Heidegger and the later Wittgenstein) tend not to regard knowing as separate from being, and hence do not worry about issues of epistemic justice.

Nevertheless, a profound ambivalence towards the "knowledge is power" equation haunts the history of Western philosophy, which has generally had an asymmetric focus on *producing knowledge* but *distributing power*. Consequently, epistemology has tended to concentrate on practices with the highest levels of epistemic productivity ("science"), regardless of their access to society at large, while ethics has focused on schemes for equitable distribution, without considering the costs of (re)producing the institutions needed for implementing those schemes. In the twentieth century, and especially in analytic philosophy, this ambivalence was institutionalized as epistemology (including philosophy of science) and ethics (including social and political philosophy) evolved into separate specialties. The result is what Paul Roth has called the "essential tension" of social epistemology. It is represented by, on the one hand, a Machiavellian side that aims to maximize the production of knowledge-and-power, even if the means of production are concentrated in the hands of an elite, and, on the other, a democratic side that aims to maximize the distribution of knowledge-and-power, even if this serves to undermine the autonomy and integrity of current scientific practices.

Epistemic justice may be achieved in one of two ways: either inhibit the power effects of new knowledge by distributing it as widely as possible, hence the **UNI- VERSITY**'s centrality to the production of teachable research; or define a piece of knowledge in terms of the functions it serves, thereby encouraging people to design more accessible and efficient means for serving those functions. The guiding intuition here is that if knowledge is truly universal, then it should not be restricted to a single kind of embodiment, medium or language. (See **MASS MEDIA**.) Since all theories of knowledge distinguish between the container and content of knowledge – or the representation and the represented – it should always be possible to transfer the same knowledge into different containers or representations, thereby increasing its accessibility.

This mode of thinking is familiar in the natural sciences from synthetic chemistry and so-called reverse engineering. Just such a view as presupposed by the logical positivist (see **KUHN, POPPER AND LOGICAL POSITIVISM**) quest for a universal language of science for testing all knowledge claims. The positivists treated the specialized technical discourses of science as relatively opaque epistemic vehicles in need of **TRANSLATION**. However, the historic failure of the positivist project arguably suggests that science is ultimately no more than a refined technology or even a fetish, whereby one needs to possess a unique set of skills or things in order to be declared in possession of the knowledge. (See **EXPERTISE**.) Unfortunately, **SCIENCE AND TECHNOLOGY STUDIES** tends to overlook this problem of epistemic justice. If anything it treats the problem as a virtue of "technoscience".

The quest for epistemic justice constitutes one of the strongest arguments for state support of science. This quest is modelled on the general market-failure argument for the existence of the welfare state. In other words, if all enquiries were purely self-interested – even when this self is a corporate agent (such as a professional body or a company's research and development division) – then it is not clear that knowledge of genuinely universal purchase would be produced. Instead, one would have a collection of techniques and technologies, many quite useful for a broad range of purposes when placed in the right hands, but without an overarching theme or unity. The result would be mere social capital. One specific state-based science policy principle aimed at redressing this form of epistemic injustice appeals to *epistemic fungibility*, which instructs the policy-maker to decide between only two types of science policy regimes. On the one hand, projects may be funded at a level that incurs the lowest opportunity costs (i.e. the fewest number of alternatives prohibited); on the other hand, decisions taken to fund projects with high opportunity costs must accommodate the disadvantaged researchers. Thus, one would either fund many little science projects or a few big science projects that include space for rival epistemic interests.

Thus, an epistemically just regime would be in the perpetual project of preventing *any* form of knowledge from becoming a vehicle of power. To be sure, specific forms of knowledge always privilege certain sectors of society. But then the state needs to regularly redistribute the advantage that these forms of knowledge have accumulated over time: what Fuller has called (with the teaching function of universities in mind) *epistemic trust-busting*. Affirmative action, or positive discrimination towards disadvantaged groups, is not simply a temporary strategy for getting the balance between knowledge and power right once and for all; rather, it is a long-term KNOWLEDGE POLICY for disintegrating the power effects of knowledge. This reflects the civic republican ideal associated with the Enlightenment, whereby the only power worth acquiring from knowledge is the power not to be dominated by others. (See FREE ENQUIRY.)

Can epistemic justice be institutionalized on a larger scale than simply through the teaching function of universities? Answers to this question bear on the normative foundations of national research ethics boards and international courts of scientific justice. The two principal models of judicial review are relevant for this purpose: on the one hand, a proactive *inquisitorial* system that promotes an independent standard of scientific propriety in terms of which many scientists may be found generally wanting; on the other hand, a more reactive *accusatorial* system that presumes scientists innocent of impropriety unless a formal charge is brought against them.

The natural context for an inquisitorial system is a field whose scientific integrity is regularly under threat because its research is entangled with political or financial interests. Often these entanglements are unavoidable, especially in the case of biomedical research. Here the inquisitors are part cost accountant, part thought police. They ensure that the funders of scientific research are getting their money's worth by threatening to cut off the funding for scientific transgressors. Equally the inquisitors uphold scientific standards by threatening the transgressors with "excommunication", which would make it impossible for them to practise or publish as scientists. Such a system is clearly more credible in centralized funding regimes that would leave the proved wrongdoer with no alternative source of support.

In contrast, the accusatorial system assumes that scientists adequately regulate their own affairs through normal peer-review procedures. Here scientific integrity is understood as a collective responsibility that is upheld by catching any errors before they cause substantial harm. The accusatorial system is then designed for those relatively rare cases when error slips through the peer-review net and some harm results. This harm may involve concrete damage to health and the environment, or the corruption of later research that assumes the validity of fraudulent work. The legitimacy of an accusation ultimately depends on the accuser establishing that some harm has been committed, which she alleges to be the fault of the accused. Sanctions relating to a restitution of the harm committed by the wrongdoer then need to be credibly imposed.

Both the inquisitorial and accusatorial systems have much to recommend them as models for institutionalizing epistemic justice, say, as a national research ethics board or an international court of scientific justice. Nevertheless, their complementary virtues do not sit easily together. Should scientists be presumed guilty until proved innocent or vice versa? The two systems presuppose rather different benchmarks of scientific propriety. For example, an inquisitorial system might set a standard that is above what most scientists are presumed to achieve, which would justify local spot checks on laboratory practice. In contrast, an accusatorial system might take a more *laissez-faire* approach, allowing the scientists themselves to set their own standards and perhaps even identify the wrongdoers for prosecution. The former would be tantamount to a police force, whereas the latter would approach self-regulation.

The question of judicial regimes for science is further complicated by the amount of responsibility that consumers of scientific research should bear in their dealings with scientists. Not only do scientists commit errors in the theories they endorse, but the public also commits errors in the scientists they endorse. Moreover, both are entitled to make their own mistakes and learn from them, in ways that enable them to do more of the same in the future. This is what Fuller calls "the right to be wrong", the first article in any decent Bill of Epistemic Rights. The liberal professions of law and medicine have traditionally enforced this right by licensing practitioners whose competence is presumed until a charge of malpractice is formally lodged. This structure presupposes that a clear line can be drawn between the practitioner's expertise and the client's interests, on the basis of which one can judge whether the former has served the latter. In effect, the client exercises her right to be wrong by volunteering to be treated by the professional, which functions as a test of the professional's expertise. To be sure, the line between expertise and interests is increasingly blurred. But arguably the line is even *more*, not less, blurred in the case of strictly scientific expertise.

The public image of scientists as detached and cautious experts who know their own limits is not endemic to the scientific enterprise itself but *merely* to its public image. On the contrary, as Popper saw very clearly, scientists *qua* scientists advance the course of enquiry by overstating their knowledge claims (a.k.a. going beyond the data) in settings where they will be subject to stiff cross-examination and possibly falsified. In other words, the right to be wrong is possessed individually but realized only institutionally, as scientists try to reveal error in each other's work. From this perspective, many of the ethical concerns surrounding scientific dishonesty may be misconceived, since scientists do not really need to believe what they put forward in the spirit of hypothesis. Moreover, the drive towards overstatement may well be motivated by ideological considerations, as illustrated by the alternative scenarios regularly put forward by environmental scientists. However, this need not be a problem, so long as rigorous checks are in place so that errors in the competing overstatements are caught. But how rigorous is rigorous? It is here that the public needs to take some responsibility for the conduct of science to ensure not only that all the relevant voices are heard but also that they are appropriately tested.

In response to this problem, a court of scientific justice might be empowered to determine whether the distribution of opinions in the media on a science-based topic is fair to the various scientific researchers and interest groups, as well as members of the public who are not obvious stakeholders. (This would be the court's inquisitorial side.) "Fairness" here would consist of an appropriate level of mutual examination among a wide enough range of competing views for their reasoned assessment. If the distribution is deemed unfair, then the court is empowered to redress the balance by releasing funds for the support of research and publicity into the underrepresented viewpoints. (This would be the court's accusatorial side.) To the maximum extent possible, these funds would be drawn from an independent source, so as *not* to involve a redistribution of the support already enjoyed by other viewpoints. This would help insulate the court from conflicts of interest and trade-offs that the public should make for itself. It would also underscore a basic insight of mass communications, namely, that a *relative* increase in the visibility of an alternative viewpoint is often sufficient to shift public opinion. The great advantage of the proposed court is that the import of its rulings would be, at once, to check and encourage scientific enquiry, thereby enabling the right to be wrong to be fully discharged.

FURTHER READING

J. Butler, *Excitable Speech* (1997).
S. Fleischacker, *A Short History of Distributive Justice* (2004).

S. Fuller, *The Governance of Science* (2000).
S. Fuller, *Knowledge Management Foundations* (2002).
F. Hirsch, *Social Limits to Growth* (1976).
A. Irwin, *Citizen Science* (1995)
M. Polanyi, *Personal Knowledge* (1957).
K. Popper, *Conjectures and Refutations* (1963).
J. Ravetz, *Scientific Knowledge and Its Social Problems* (1971).
J. Rawls, *A Theory of Justice* (1971).
P. Roth, "The Bureaucratic Turn" (1991).
J. Rouse, *Knowledge and Power* (1987).
S. P. Turner, *Liberal Democracy 3.0* (2003).

EVOLUTION

The Neo-Darwinian synthesis of natural history and experimental genetics forged in the 1930s and 1940s is what today passes as modern evolutionary theory, the first paradigm to encompass all the biological sciences. Charles Darwin had proposed the theory of evolution by natural selection in the mid-nineteenth century, largely by empirically extending Thomas Malthus's anti-welfarist tract *An Essay on the Principle of Population* from human beings to the rest of the animal kingdom (see SOCIAL SCIENCE). Thus, the only sense of PROGRESS countenanced in the theory was material survival, and even then understood in terms of number of offspring *vis-à-vis* the carrying capacity of an uncontrollably changing physical environment.

While Darwin's theory of evolution is normally seen as having dealt a death blow to theology's involvement in scientific matters, it is better seen as marking a radical shift in theological orientation. Whereas earlier creationists such as William Paley had expected the divine plan to be inscribed in the design of particular organisms (much as a watch bore the touch of the watchmaker), Darwin, following the example of Malthus (himself an ordained minister), displaced the problem of meaning to an indefinite future, as might be expected of an exceptionally radical Calvinist who wanted to reinforce the idea that divine and human knowledge differ in kind, not degree.

In any case, it is fair to say that Darwin demonstrated a way of doing science that, *pace* Newton, aimed to do justice to the phenomena of nature without pretending to enter the mind of God. Of course, the burden was then shifted to the Darwinist to explain why we should continue to pursue science, understood as a systematic understanding of reality, given these diminished expectations, not least the lack of reason for believing that reality is "mind-like". Unsurprisingly, Darwin was criticized roundly by the leading scientific methodologists of his day, William Whewell and John Stuart Mill (who disagreed on so much else), on precisely this point: for apparently denying what philosophers after Leibniz and Kant had called "the intelligibility of nature".

Setting aside societies whose RELIGIONs derive from the Old Testament's account of a supernatural creative intelligence (i.e. Judaism, Christianity and Islam), evolution has been a prominent feature in most worldviews. "Evolution" here means the belief that the world consists of a sequence of phenomenal forms that result from the recycling of a common material substratum. In the twentieth century this substratum came to be called "genes" (and has been further refined), but perhaps the most venerable precursor to genes is "karma" (Hinduism and Buddhism) and "ch'i" (Confucianism and Taosim). In the West, this viewpoint is most clearly associated with atomist metaphysics and Epicurean ethics. Common to all these conceptions are the following:

- one's own actions are somehow constrained by past lives, be it as a potential or a necessary determinant;
- actions can be taken in one's own lifetime (often related to lifestyle) to mitigate, but not completely eliminate, the worst aspects of one's legacy;
- there is no inter-generational or inter-species sense of progress, unless the goal is defined as peaceful physical extinction;
- the life force is common to all life forms, regardless of surface differences in appearance and emotional attachment.

Cultures espousing an evolutionary perspective in the above sense have typically regarded the overall process as blind to human concerns and even cognitive grasp. That human beings might take control of evolution and steer it to its own purposes was normally treated as an illusion, based on an unwarranted generalization from our proved cross-cultural capacity for domesticating nature to serve basic survival needs. Thus, India and China mounted vast technologically advanced civilizations that lasted several centuries without ever having systematically pursued forms of enquiry that could have resulted in the Newtonian worldview, let alone entertained ideas of intellectual **PROGRESS**. Atomism and Epicureanism themselves became pro-scientific worldviews in the West (as opposed to consolations for the world's ultimate unintelligibility) only with the advent of the scientific revolution that culminated in Newton.

The view that human beings might direct the course of evolution came to prominence in the early-nineteenth century as Jean-Baptiste Lamarck effectively gave Enlightenment progressive historiography a biological substratum, the most direct fruit of which was Comte's positivism, but which diffused throughout the **SOCIAL SCIENCES**, where Lamarckianism has existed as a free-floating heresy. According to Lamarck's peculiar Christian brand of **NATURALISM**, humanity was simply nature in a state of maturity, or self-consciousness, in relation to which all subordinate species represented intermediate stages aimed at this common goal. What palaeontologists had already recognized in Lamarck's day as the mass extinction of past species, Lamarck treated as earlier versions of the same generic life force present in nature (immortalized a century later by Henri Bergson as *élan vital*). The most fertile idea associated with Lamarck's evolutionism was that the memory trace of traits acquired in one's lifetime could somehow enter the germplasm to be inherited by offspring: that is, the existence of a genetic collective memory (see **COMMON SENSE VERSUS COLLECTIVE MEMORY**).

In the past two centuries, this idea has sometimes been taken literally, especially when applied to lower organisms (e.g. Trofim Lysenko's disastrous Soviet agricultural policy) but even in terms of the transmission of very general cross-culturally recurrent ideas (e.g. Jungian archetypes). However, Lamarck-inspired research has generally adopted the population-thinking perspective associated with modern genetics. This is already present in the US founder of developmental psychology, James Mark Baldwin, who in the early twentieth century moved to Paris where he seeded what, after Jean Piaget, has been known as "genetic structuralism". Baldwin argued that a reproductive advantage would be enjoyed by later generations of individuals who already possess traits like the ones that advantaged individuals who acquired, or otherwise manifested, them in their own lifetime. Richard Dawkins extended this idea to bring all of culture into the Darwinian framework under the rubric of "extended phenotype", namely, the positive feedback loop whereby those who benefit from having certain traits will reconstruct the selection environment with the effect of promoting others who share those traits. Thus, macro-level progress is simulated by what, at the micro-level, remain blind evolutionary processes. A controversial dirigiste version of this perspective would cultivate mutations as harbingers of higher evolution: the so-called "hopeful monsters" valorized by Donna Haraway. It was proposed by Julian Huxley, UNESCO's first scientific director, who coined the phrase "evolutionary synthesis" for neo-Darwinian theory but was increasingly dismayed by Darwinism's residual racialist fixation on our origins rather than our destinies.

In contrast, Herbert Spencer's "survival of the fittest" marked a reversion to the ancient Epicureans, although that did not stop his self-styled "social Darwinism" from becoming the most influential evolutionary social theory of the past 150 years. Spencer held a cyclical view of evolution that alternated between ordered and disordered phases and that was expressed across all levels of reality, albeit governed by a vague naturalistic sense of cosmic progress. Friedrich Nietzsche refashioned Spencer in light of Darwin in his method of *genealogy*, which in the hands of Foucault came to colonize the research practices of the humanistic end of the social sciences in the final quarter of the twentieth century.

Nietzsche's *On the Genealogy of Morals* (1887) updated worries of legitimate lineage that had dominated the reproduction of social life prior to modern state constitutions. Replacing traditional legal concerns that political succession might be based on fraudulent documents, Nietzsche argued that contemporary morality might rest on forgotten etymologies, whereby obligations turn out to be strategies for the weak to inflict a sense of guilt on the strong, simply for being stronger. At that time, an evolutionary school of medical science known as "racial hygiene" introduced the term "counter-selection" to capture morality's role in instilling an unnatural dedication to welfare of the weak.

In addition, Nietzsche cleverly recast the slogan of Ernst Haeckel, Darwin's staunchest German defender, who famously declared, "Ontogeny recapitulates phylogeny", by which he meant the biological development of the individual organism (i.e. the gestation period) repeats the stages undergone in the evolution of all organisms. In Nietzsche's hands, it became one of the earliest statements of SOCIAL CONSTRUCTIVISM: "Ontology recapitulates philology". In other words, reality is the ongoing outcome of language use, a thesis familiar from such latter-day Nietzscheans as Heidegger and Derrida. However, much more than a pun unites Darwinian and Nietzschean genealogies.

Darwin had depicted – and Haeckel popularized – evolution as a tree of life founded on a principle of common ancestry of morphologically similar species, ultimately deriving from a unitary origin of life. The imagery remains powerful today as both a principle of biological taxonomy and an account of migration patterns within species or closely related species (e.g. the idea that all human beings emerged out of Africa). Both uses are indebted to Darwin's own inspiration, the comparative linguist August Schleicher, who drew the first tree of life (or cladogram) to show the interrelatedness of Indo-European languages, which together implicated an ultimate common ancestor, a pure Aryan language probably spoken in Western India. Many of Schleicher's fellow philologists were inclined to think of this inferred source as the medium in which the biblical deity originally communicated with Adam. However, Darwin and Nietzsche were prepared to take at least one aspect of the tree of life metaphor literally, namely, that language – and life – began *arbitrarily* at a particular place and time.

The contingency of origins is crucial for the genealogical method. To see this point, consider that history may be considered from two general perspectives: from the past looking forwards into the future, and from the present looking back at the past. The former standpoint focuses on turning points when the future is open to multiple alternate futures, with the decisions taken at those times generating what economists call "path-dependent" outcomes. In contrast to such *underdeterminism*, the latter standpoint tends to presume *overdeterminism*, whereby when and where the origin actually occur is irrelevant because eventually the outcome will turn out the same. Overdeterminism produces teleology, underdeterminism genealogy. In the latter, the perceived sense of necessity in current ways of knowing and being merely reflects the reinforcement of an original moment of decision.

In a period that strongly wanted to believe in inexorable progress, Nietzsche's re-specification of evolution as genealogy appeared scandalous in a manner best illustrated by Henrik Ibsen's "bourgeois dramas", whereby some apparently ordinary situation turns out to betray the traces of a sordid past that persists, albeit in some hidden form that veers between sanctification and mystification. The moral dilemma that repeatedly arises in Ibsen's plays is whether knowledge of that past should be allowed to influence contemporary judgements. Can some idealized, perhaps secularized, Christian sense of good overcome the genetic load of the human condition? Invariably the answer seemed to be no.

However, Darwin, Nietzsche and Ibsen all lived before the incorporation of Mendelian genetics into modern evolutionary theory, which occurred in earnest only in the 1930s. Thus, they operated with a semi-coherent sense of hereditary transmission, in which an older Lamarckian view of the inheritance of acquired traits was grafted on a much less teleological view of offspring simply manifesting a blended version of their parents' family traits. Yet, despite its semi-coherence, it was precisely this view that fuelled the imagination of Freud, who saw his psychoanalytic practice as a micro-application of Nietzsche's genealogical method. Freud replaced the rogue ancestor, whose identity is revealed in the course of the bourgeois drama, with the rogue incident in the patient's past – say, the source of the Oedipus or Electra complex – that anchored his or her subsequent conduct.

In terms of earlier theories of genealogy and inheritance, Mendelian genetics constitutes a turn towards essentialism that undermines the need for extensive historical investigation. In Mendel's wake, the traits expressed in an individual's life (i.e. its phenotype) reflect a limited range of possibilities circumscribed by its genetic programme (i.e. its genotype). In other words, an individual's inheritance can be ascertained simply through an intensive examination of that individual. A case in point is the increasing use of genetic profiling, whereby susceptibility to, say, crime or disease is determined by genetic sequences that an individual shares with others who bear no obvious family relation. In this context, Gilles Deleuze's views about the virtualization of identity (i.e. a shared actuality rooted in different potentials) have considerable purchase.

FURTHER READING
D. T. Campbell, *Methodology and Epistemology for the Social Sciences* (1988).
C. Degler, *In Search of Human Nature* (1991).
G. Deleuze, *Difference and Repetition* (1994).
P. Dickens, *Social Darwinism* (2000).
M. Foucault, *The Order of Things* (1970).
S. Fuller, *The New Sociological Imagination* (2006).
D. Haraway, *Primate Visions* (1989).
D. Haraway, *Simians, Cyborgs, Women* (1991).
M. Mandelbaum, *History, Man and Reason* (1971).
R. Richards, *Darwin and the Emergence of Evolutionary Theories of Mind and Behavior* (1987).
U. Segerstråle, *Defenders of the Truth* (2000).
H. Simon, *The Sciences of the Artificial* (1977).
D. Sperber, *Explaining Culture* (1996).

EXPERTISE

Expertise represents an innovative development in the history of relativism (see RELATIVISM VERSUS CONSTRUCTIVISM), whereby epistemic authority is claimed over a *conceptually* rather than *physically* defined domain. The *locus classicus* for this point is Émile Durkheim's *The Division of Labour in Society* (1895), which defined the transition from mechanical to organic solidarity in terms of precisely this shift. The culture of expertise is usually associated with a discipline (see DISCIPLINARITY VERSUS INTERDISCIPLINARITY) whose members practise in a dispersed, as opposed to a well-bounded, space. (See KUHN, POPPER AND LOGICAL POSITIVISM for the emergence of expertise as paradigm.) "Expert", a contraction of the participle "experienced", first appeared as a noun in the French Third Republic, the final quarter of the nineteenth century. The first experts were called as witnesses in trials to detect handwriting forgeries. When evaluating putative forgeries, experts were *not* expected to exhibit their reasoning publicly. They were not casuists who weighed the relative probability that various general principles applied to the case. Rather, an expert's previous experience in successfully identifying forgeries licensed the trustworthiness of his judgement, subject to the objections of a fellow expert called to testify in a case. The mystique of expertise is created by the impression that an expert's colleagues are sufficiently scrupulous that, were it necessary, they would be able and inclined to redress any misuse or abuse of their expertise. That they do not means that the expert must be doing something right.

This climate of collegiality harboured a mystique that led Émile Zola, France's leading novelist and self-declared *intellectual*, to dub experts the "new clerics", as distinguished from the "lay" public. Zola was conjuring up a spectre raised by Auguste Comte's more zealous "positivist" followers, who would have science replace religion as society's ultimate source of authority. Unlike the expert, the intellectual takes the entire world as fair game for her judgements, while opening herself to scrutiny from all quarters. Indeed, intellectuals often (gladly) spend more time defending and attacking positions than developing and applying them.

There are four senses in which expertise is socially constructed (see SOCIAL CONSTRUCTIVISM):

- The skills associated with an expertise are the product of specialized training. Expertise cannot be picked up casually or as the by-product of some other form of learning.
- Both experts and the lay public recognize that expertise is relevant only on certain occasions. No expertise carries universal applicability.

- The disposition of expertise is dependent on the collegial patterns of the relevant experts. Protracted internecine disputes over fundamentals typically erode expertise.
- The cognitive significance of an expertise is affected by the availability of expert training and judgement, relative to the need for the expertise. Too many experts or too little need typically devalue the expertise in question. Thus, expertise is a positional good. (See SOCIAL CAPITAL VERSUS PUBLIC GOOD.)

A plethora of conflicting knowledge claims, and the differences in background knowledge that they presuppose, arguably means that it is no longer rational to evaluate each claim on its own merits. Under the circumstances, rule by expertise (or cognitive authoritarianism) becomes *prima facie* attractive (see KNOWLEDGE SOCIETY). Unfortunately, expert advice tends to be sought in matters where the framing of the problem is itself part of the problem. For example, the first step towards solving the problem of world poverty involves determining the sort of problem poverty is: put vividly, who (or what) is to blame?

A traditional difference between the liberal professions and academic disciplines is that the former deal with these messier problems whose social relevance is not matched by neat scientific solutions, but rather require discretionary judgements that are best informed by the experience of having already made such judgements in real world settings. In the end, deference to expertise is a licence for the expert to model your problem against the background of her experience. However, this can easily lead to an epistemic bait-and-switch, whereby the client is persuaded to accept a refocusing of the problem that better addresses the expert's abilities than the client's needs. (See TRUTH, RELIABILITY AND THE ENDS OF KNOWLEDGE).

Expertise involves a transaction between a client and vendor, broadly construed to include, among others, doctor–patient and politician–constituent relations. Two complementary senses of *wisdom* are implied: on the one hand, wisdom in selecting the right vendor for the job, which is a matter of *acumen*; on the other hand, wisdom in the vendor's self-representation as appropriate for the job, which is a matter of *propriety*. Both senses involve trial-and-error, whereby client and vendor adapt to each other's competences, desires and expectations. Clients typically desire things that extend beyond vendor competence, in response to which vendors try to persuade clients to accept their competence as a better rendering of their desires. In this potentially fluid situation, experts need to be held to explicit standards of accountability, be it defined as informed consent (medicine) or consent of the governed (politics).

The flipside of this need for consent is that clients must take responsibility for the vendors they select to speak and act on their behalf. The recent emphasis on trust and testimony in both ANALYTIC SOCIAL EPISTEMOLOGY and SCIENCE AND TECHNOLOGY STUDIES obscures this sense of responsibility as expert incompetence is explained in terms of a breakdown in trust. This form of words, which suggests expert betrayal, lets clients off the hook too easily, as if the acknowledgement of a division of labour in society implies the wholesale devolution of authority to those who perform specialized tasks on one's behalf. The *reductio ad absurdum* of this blame-shifting is the endless "chains of delegation" (Bruno Latour) and "cycles of credibility" (Pierre Bourdieu) based on alleged track records that feed future hopes and expectations. (See EXPLAINING THE NORMATIVE STRUCTURE OF SCIENCE.) If a chain breaks or a cycle spins out of control, blame tends to be distributed equally across the affected parties as co-producers of the outcome. This blurring of the jurisdiction of expertise only serves to render accountability and hence improvability virtually impossible, for *both* the client and the vendor of expertise. In particular, the vendor cannot tell whether the problem lies mainly with the content of her expertise or the context of its application. Moreover, if expertise is socially constructed in the four senses noted above, the value assigned to accountability and improvability may turn out to be quite low. After all, if an expert is presumed to be one of many people who possess control over a highly circumscribed domain of knowledge, then the content of that knowledge, including the thought processes involved, may be much less at issue than the function it serves. In principle, then, the expert human being could be replaced by a computerized *expert system* that is programmed to give set answers to set questions. That the computer does not think like a human being is irrelevant under the circumstances.

Here we enter the world of KNOWLEDGE MANAGEMENT, in which knowledge is valuable solely as a means and not an end in itself. The model for this view of knowledge is, of course, industrial labour, which has been gradually replaced by automated technology that can manufacture more efficiently the same or similar products. Because expertise is, by definition, domain-specific, it is susceptible to knowledge management if experts lack a strong sense of collective identity focused on developing their knowledge as a set of skills beyond its current applications. In the Middle Ages, the collective identity of knowledge producers was cultivated by *guilds*, which were legally entrusted to reproduce a high-quality craft beyond the need to secure the livelihoods of their members. Academic disciplines and liberal professions retain much of the guild mentality, including its traditionally hierarchical social arrangements, epitomized in apprenticeship. However, as expertise has come to be associated more with abstract principles than work conditions, the guild mentality becomes harder to enforce. Chemistry was perhaps the first science to suffer this fate, although it arguably now affects all the sciences.

Not surprisingly, the past half-century has witnessed repeated failures to establish a Hippocratic Oath for science, whereby scientists would prohibit the use of their expertise to do harm. Beyond the usual difficulties of defining "harm", scientific activists have faced the far more basic problem of establishing an agency with the moral authority to license such an oath and administer sanctions for its violation. All trained and practising scientists no longer share a common worldview, if they ever did. A telling precedent was the mid-twentieth-century campaign by British physicist John Desmond Bernal to align scientists with the industrial proletariat. Although by then scientific training had become a vehicle of upward social mobility for people from working-class backgrounds, nevertheless the increasingly thorough interpenetration of science and society meant that scientists lacked a common relationship to the means of production, a necessary condition for the emergence for that updated version of the guild mentality that Marxists call "class consciousness".

Generally speaking, the guild mentality that historically informed the autonomy of expertise has come to be seen as singularly unattractive. Guilds acquired the conservative disposition of insurance bodies, censoring deviant practices that did not meet with the governing board's approval. In the 1870s, Bismarck made German academics more manageable by turning FREE ENQUIRY into the guild right of academic freedom. Thus, the state had no need to intervene to stop the spread of politically subversive positions, since the academics themselves already had a collective interest to do so. The mutual criticism of the peer-review process simultaneously launders out more radical positions and ensures that what remains is of sufficiently high quality to be appropriated for orthodox political purposes. Moreover, the hierarchical character of guilds, still dignified as Robert Merton's "principle of cumulative advantage", is widely seen as corrupt when practised in science. This negative sentiment has less to do with fraud perpetrated by elite scientists than the simple fact that the elites are out of touch with the interests of rank-and-file scientists. This point became painfully obvious in the early 1990s when the American Physical Society (APS) could not wholeheartedly endorse the construction of the Superconducting Super Collider, despite heavy lobbying by Nobel Prize winners, because most of its members would not benefit from it. Nevertheless, besides curbing their own elites, professional scientific bodies can do little more for their members than urge as many employers as possible to hire them.

FURTHER READING

R. Aron, *Main Currents in Sociological Thought* (1965).
D. Bell, *The Coming of Post-Industrial Society* (1973).

J. D. Bernal, *The Social Function of Science* (1939).

P. Bourdieu, "The Specificity of the Scientific Field and the Social Conditions of the Progress of Reason" (1975).

H. M. Collins, *Artificial Experts* (1990).

H. M. Collins & M. Kusch, *The Shape of Actions* (1999).

G. Delanty, *Challenging Knowledge* (2001).

J. Franklin, *The Science of Conjecture* (2001).

S. Fuller, *Knowledge Management Foundations* (2002).

S. Fuller, *The Intellectual* (2005).

A. Gouldner, *The Future of Intellectuals and the Rise of the New Class* (1979).

W. Keith, *Democracy as Discussion* (2007).

E. Krause, *The Death of the Guilds* (1996).

M. Kusch & P. Lipton (eds), *Studies in History and Philosophy of Science* **33**, special issue on testimony (2002).

B. Latour & S. Woolgar, *Laboratory Life* (1986).

W. Lippmann, *Public Opinion* (1922).

R. K. Merton, *The Sociology of Science* (1977).

R. Sassower, *Knowledge without Expertise* (1993).

A. Schutz, "The Well-Informed Citizen" (1964).

H. Simon, *The Sciences of the Artificial* (1977).

S. P. Turner, *The Social Theory of Practices* (1994).

S. P. Turner, *Brains/Practices/Relativism* (2002).

S. P. Turner, *Liberal Democracy 3.0* (2003).

EXPLAINING THE COGNITIVE CONTENT OF SCIENCE

The knowledge-like character of science is often called its cognitive content, or, more simply, content. The word "content" is based on the metaphor of container and contained, with lingering medieval connotations of body and spirit, matter and form, statement and proposition. The underlying intuition is that the universal character of scientific knowledge is tied to its capacity for being conveyed in multiple containers. (See EPISTEMIC JUSTICE.) Thus, the content of a scientific theory is what is common to its linguistic formulations and technological applications.

But suppose we take seriously the strong social epistemological thesis that science's cognitive content is coextensive with its social context. In other words, it is just as misleading to claim that science is done only by professional scientists in laboratories as it is to claim that finances are transacted exclusively by professional bankers: just as all of society can be regarded from a financial standpoint, so too from a scientific standpoint. To capture this totalizing sense of science – its socio-cognitive identity, so to speak – the various solutions to the mind–body problem offers a model for understanding the possible interrelations of cognitive and social factors, which together can provide alternative explanations for scientific knowledge.

In terms of this model, most philosophers and sociologists remain dualists of some sort. They assume that cognitive and social factors are separable entities, somewhat like experimentally manipulable variables. Thus, philosophers imagine knowledge and reason as independent of any social embodiment, whereas sociologists tend to see knowledge and reason as dependent on rather specific social factors. (See EXPLAINING THE NORMATIVE STRUCTURE OF SCIENCE.) The first social epistemologist to break away from this dualist mindset was Popper. He clearly envisaged scientific RATIONALITY not as a detachable abstract logic, but as an embodied community of "conjecturers and refuters" who in concert enact his celebrated falsifiability principle.

The fact that "the social" and "the cognitive" figure in largely separate discourses helps to maintain the illusion of a social–cognitive dualism, as in the case of mind–talk and body–talk. Yet, few confessed dualists remain these days in the philosophy of mind. Instead one finds *functionalists*, *reductionists* and *eliminativists*, all of whom believe that mind is, in some sense, a property of certain arrangements of matter. Likewise social epistemologists hold the correlative view that knowledge and reason are ways to embody certain kinds of social relations. Consider these possibilities, which follow from pursuing the mind–body analogy (see also SCIENCE AS A SOCIAL MOVEMENT):

- *Functionalism*: Various social structures – although probably not all – can instantiate a given cognitive relation. For example, we are psychologically ill disposed to falsifying our own theories. It follows that Popper's falsification principle would probably not be instantiated in isolated individuals. Equally unlikely is that the CRITICISM stipulated by the principle will be effective if individuals do not receive prompt unequivocal feedback from people whose judgement they respect. Thus, cognitive relations – in this case, relating to the falsifiability principle – are sensitive to the spatiotemporal dimensions of the social enterprise in which they are embedded.
- *Reductionism*: The categories of social and cognitive accounts of science diverge simply because they have not been developed in conjunction with each other. Just as psychological states can be more closely monitored and refined if we attend to their physiological correlates, so too the cognitive character of science may lose its seeming disembodiment if we attend to the social circumstances in which cognitive claims are made.
- *Eliminativism*: Cognitive categories are the vehicles by which scientific claims and practices are officially justified. However, in fact those claims and practices can be best explained and predicted solely based on social categories. For example, one explains the widespread acceptance of a scientific theory not by a common perception of an underlying reality, but by examining the social mechanisms of belief acceptance. These mechanisms may vary significantly across cases, perhaps ultimately leading to a denial that some common cognitive content exists on which all sides agreed.

These three strategies for interrelating social and cognitive factors bear interesting relationships with each other. Consider functionalism and eliminativism. At first glance, several different social contexts may generate the same cognitive content. In other words, the content would supervene on the multiple contexts. But on closer inspection, this appearance of multiple realization may turn out be the *post facto* narrative achievement, a discovery that would have the effect of eliminating the illusion of common content.

Consider the alleged phenomena of multiple or simultaneous discoveries, to which Kuhn (see KUHN, POPPER AND LOGICAL POSITIVISM) drew attention in his early work. If several scientific teams reach roughly the same result at roughly the same time – especially if they hail from different national traditions and research agendas – then it would seem that they have perceived a common reality that transcends their social divisions. Yet, even if we assume (implausibly, in the case of modern science) that these teams are completely ignorant of each other's activities, simultaneous discoveries can be explained in sociologically more palatable ways.

Principally, these discoveries may be creatures of HISTORIOGRAPHICAL artifice, for example, a twenty-year spread for rather varied expressions of the energy conservation principle, the touchstone for Kuhn's insight into the historical unreliability of science textbooks. Instead of presuming that the simultaneous discovery is the same *thing* appearing on different occasions, we can follow Kuhn and deconstruct this alleged "thing" into a set of *unique* events that are collapsed in the textbook account. Some social epistemologists have gone further, adopting the social constructivist (see SOCIAL CONSTRUCTIVISM) strategy of sociologically reducing the idea of a common reality underlying these events to an epiphenomenon that, once observed, is reinforced by the scientific community. Metaphysically speaking, instead of a thing or an event, the alleged discovery would be a *mode of appearance* common to several distinct processes. This would be tantamount to eliminating the luminous character of the discovery.

For example, imagine three scientific teams, each with its own distinctive patterns of organization, interaction and decision-making. Each set of patterns is itself explainable in terms of more general features of the society in which a team is embedded. All three teams might arrive at what would appear to an observer as the same discovery, but simply because that discovery is the natural outcome of their respective team processes. To make this point, one need not presuppose a radically idiographic approach to history and sociology. Rather, one can invoke general sociohistorical principles to explain why each team discovered what it did, as in the following mock explanatory scheme, where an *explanandum* is the phenomenon in need of explanation and *explanans* the explanation:

- *Explanandum*: Three independent teams – *A, B* and *C* – discover something that appears as *X* at roughly the same time.
- *Explanans*: In each case, *X* emerged as the expected outcome of the team's standard operating procedure. The proponent of *X* beat his rivals in winning the favour of team *A*'s director. The charismatic director of team *B* became personally committed to *X*. The hypothesis-testing machine regularly used by team *C* deemed *X* the most probable rendering of the data.

In short, there is nothing more to why all three teams arrived at the finding than an explanation of why each team arrived at the finding. Convergence here turns out to be a rough coincidence that seems deep only as long as one abstracts from the underlying causal (sociohistorical) processes. Of course, once this coincidence is observed, efforts may be taken to standardize the discovery across the teams so that it becomes common property of the discipline, constitutive of its NORMATIVITY, and hence a source by which subsequent claims and practices are justified. This process of social construction involves journal citations, textbook accounts and official histories.

The virtue of the eliminativist sociological approach to the cognitive content of science becomes clear on turning to the metaphysical version of the social–cognitive divide: namely, *culture versus nature*. Thus, instead of, say, the social construction of three superficially similar moments of discovery in independent locations as pointing to a common cognitive content, we have the social construction of three superficially similar phenotypic displays across the animal kingdom pointing to an underlying genotypic identity. This tendency to see cross-species convergence in traits is aided by overwhelming genetic overlap (i.e. more than 95 per cent among species). In this context, the appeal to natural factors – notably in fields related to sociobiology and evolutionary (see EVOLUTION) psychology – often conveys a sense of finality, or overdetermination, that forecloses considerations of alternative causes or even alternative effects through further interventions. Overall this serves to limit the sphere of public deliberation and restrict the policy imagination. (See SOCIAL SCIENCE and KNOWLEDGE POLICY.) This version of NATURALISM can easily turn faith in science to superstition, or "methodolatry" in Feyerabend's terms.

FURTHER READING

R. Bhaskar, *Scientific Realism and Human Emancipation* (1987).
D. T. Campbell, *Methodology and Epistemology for the Social Sciences* (1988).
P. Feyerabend, *Against Method* (1975).
P. Forman, "Weimar Culture, Causality, and Quantum Theory" (1971).
S. Fuller, *Philosophy of Science and Its Discontents* (1993).
R. Giere (ed.), *Cognitive Models of Science* (1992).
A. Goldman, *Epistemology and Cognition* (1986).
P. Kitcher, *The Advancement of Science* (1993).
T. S. Kuhn, *The Essential Tension* (1977).
R. K. Merton, *The Sociology of Science* (1977).
J. Rouse, *Knowledge and Power* (1987).
W. Shadish & S. Fuller (eds), *The Social Psychology of Science* (1994).
D. Sperber, *Explaining Culture: A Naturalistic Approach* (1996).
S. P. Turner, *The Social Theory of Practices* (1994).
S. P. Turner, *Brains/Practices/Relativism* (2002).

EXPLAINING THE NORMATIVE STRUCTURE OF SCIENCE

The biggest mistake that both philosophers and social scientists make when trying to explain a stable knowledge-producing activity such as science is to assume that the task requires that one explain science-as-successful or knowledge-as-true. Unlike explanations of, say, the capitalist economy, few explanations of science imply CRITICISM of science as it normally is. Rather, a broadly functionalist explanatory logic is invoked to infer that science works as well as could be expected. (See TRUTH, RELIABILITY AND THE ENDS OF KNOWLEDGE.) As these explanations have come to incorporate more of the actual history of science, the tendency – especially among epistemologists and philosophers of science – is to pursue invisible-hand strategies whereby even prima facie suboptimal day-to-day features of science, such as its ruthlessness, its drudgery and elitism, are said to be necessary for its overarching good features. Included here are the most recent generation of naturalistic (see NATURALISM) epistemology (e.g. David Hull, Philip Kitcher), as well as sociologists and economists who point to knowledge as a uniquely legitimizing or productive element in the modern world. (See KNOWLEDGE SOCIETY.)

Before turning to this functionalist explanatory logic – whose natural home is Talcott Parsons's social systems theory – three critical responses are worth noting. The first simply reinforces the boundary between how science is and ought to be, arguing that most science performs suboptimally most of the time. This response presumes a normative philosophy of science that is independent from the practice of science itself. It is associated with the logical positivists and the Popperians, especially Imre Lakatos, who argued that part of the philosophical task involves rationally reconstructing the history of science to show how it should have proceeded (see KUHN, POPPER AND LOGICAL POSITIVISM). The second response, associated with the strong programme in the sociology of scientific knowledge, is to short-circuit sociological functionalism by arguing that both good and bad outcomes in science must be explained symmetrically, that is, in terms of the same empirical principles. In what follows, these two responses are called, respectively "social realist" and "social verificationist" (see SOCIAL CONSTRUCTIVISM). Finally, a "panglossian" strategy tries to combine elements of the first two, asking – much as Marx did of capitalism – how can a system with so many in-built suboptimal features manage to survive and flourish as well as it has? Who and what are served by such a system? This is a largely empirical enquiry into the de facto ends of knowledge production, which may be rather different from the officially declared ends. From this point of view, functionalist explanations of science are literally instances of ideology.

It would be a mistake to suppose that philosophical and sociological versions of functionalist explanations of science are the same; rather, they are complementary (see **PHILOSOPHY VERSUS SOCIOLOGY**). Thus, analytic social epistemologists (see **ANALYTIC SOCIAL EPISTEMOLOGY**) tend to introduce sociological elements only on a "need-to-know" basis, namely, when the ideal epistemological conditions have failed to be met in concrete cases that happen to concern the social epistemologist. Thus, in the guise of W. V. Quine's "underdetermination thesis" it is argued that specifically social factors are needed to bring closure to an episode of theory choice that would otherwise allow for several plausible alternatives. Here appeals to the social function "phlogistemically", recalling that eighteenth-century substance, phlogiston, which was invoked to explain combustion once all the other known factors have been removed or accounted for. Sociologists practise a reciprocal form of "phlogistemics", which invokes "knowledge" or "information" as uniquely adding value to contemporary society. In this case, epistemic factors are introduced as a "god of the gaps" to explain aspects of today's society that elude the usual sociological variables.

In both philosophical and sociological contexts, words such as "trust", "tacit knowledge", "**EXPERTISE**" and "practice" function phlogistemically to explain how the socio-epistemic units are held together. Over the past hundred years, words such as "tradition", "custom", "habit" and "culture" have also been on this list, although all but the last seem to have lost their original positive valuation. The last eight terms in quotes pick out phlogistemic factors, in that they share the following characteristics:

- The factor is not reducible to a formal procedure or set of behavioural indicators, yet those who possess the factor can make appropriate socio-epistemic judgements in real-life settings.
- The same act may be counted as manifesting or not manifesting the factor, depending on the social status of the agent (e.g. a novice's error may count as an innovation if committed by an expert practitioner).
- There is little direct evidence for the factor's presence. Rather, it is presupposed in the lack of disruption in the community's day-to-day activities.
- Conversely, the factor operates as a default explanation for the community's survival when other aspects of the community are under explicit contestation (e.g. scientists may argue about theories but leave the tacit knowledge of laboratory practice intact).
- The denial of the factor, to either the entire community or one of its members, is taken to be at least as much a moral judgement as a social or epistemic one, thereby inviting the charge that the denier is not merely critical, but uncharitable to the point of misunderstanding how the community works.

Taken together, these five phlogistemic features establish a presumption in favour of treating the society under investigation as operating in a normatively acceptable fashion. However, doubts may be cast on this presumption from two standpoints: social realist and social verificationist.

On the one hand, a social realist may wonder: just because pronounced patterns of deviance, conflict and change are not apparent on a day-to-day basis, why conclude so quickly that the society is normatively acceptable? Perhaps the society lacks normatively acceptable ways of *expressing* deviance, conflict, and change; it is not that there is none to express. Moreover, because so many important changes in a society occur in ways that are either imperceptible or unpredictable to its members, even given adequate freedom of expression, the social epistemologist may be warranted in treating any set of seemingly stable socio-epistemic phenomena as hiding certain unexpressed and unrealized conditions that would alter the character of these phenomena, were they revealed. The search for these conditions would be propaedeutic to identifying the "emancipatory interest" of the members of that society.

On the other hand, a social verificationist may wonder: if a society can only specify the people who are qualified to pass appropriate socio-epistemic judgements but not the standard by which they pass such judgements (given their tacit nature), is there anything more to passing appropriate judgements than merely being one of those people? If so, "qualified people" and "appropriate judgements" would be interdefined terms that are mutually reinforced in practice. If a society appears capable of living with the consequences of such elite discretionary judgements, that would testify only to a minimal sense of social functionality: the stability of the society's power structure. In the case of science, this situation becomes especially problematic as it implies a curious asymmetry between those to whom the knowledge is directly accessible (the few) and those to whom it is meant to apply (the many).

Notice that neither the social realist nor the social verificationist is actually making a claim contrary to that of the phlogistemologist. The former does not claim that what appears to be normatively acceptable behaviour is really repressive; nor does the latter claim that it is really arbitrary. Rather, both hold that evidence adduced for inferring the phlogistemic factors could just as easily be adduced for inferring features that would challenge the behaviour's normative acceptability. In other words, the social realist and social verificationist are pointing to the *normative underdetermination of social regularities* (or NUSR). This is different from what Kuhn first observed under the rubric of "incommensurability" and sociologists of science have subsequently demonstrated; namely, that the same epistemic norms can be instantiated in many different, perhaps even incompatible, ways. (See **TRANSLATION**.) For example, there is considerable historical evidence that something called "simplicity" has operated as a norm in scientific theorizing throughout the ages, yet the norm has been subject to so many different interpretations – depending on whether it is taken as a psychological or logical notion – that a scientist's appeal to simplicity is a relatively poor indicator of the sorts of theories she will prefer.

NUSR's sense of underdetermination is related to the insight of Pierre Duhem and Quine that for a given experimental outcome, scientists who adhere to the same canons of scientific method may nevertheless differ on the outcome's evidential bearing on a set of rival theories. However, in contrast, NUSR implies that even where there is enough evidence of social constraint to enable the reliable prediction of actions taken by epistemic agents, the question remains whether the constraints are indeed normatively appropriate in the sense of increasing the overall welfare of the society in which they are embedded. The appearance of social order is not necessarily its own reward, even when the society in question is explicitly devoted to scientific enquiry.

To illustrate NUSR, consider the famous account of the normative structure of science put forth by the sociologist Robert Merton, based on the testimony of philosophers and scientists but *not* any first-hand investigation of contemporary scientific practice. Where the sociologist can easily show that Merton's norms – universalism, communism, disinterestedness, organized scepticism – fail to explain or predict day-to-day research activities, the social epistemologist should ask two further questions:

- What patterns of social phenomena would lead so many philosophers and scientists to infer the existence of Merton's norms? Even if these patterns are not found in the average research site, they may be traced to folk histories, anecdotes or even emergent macro-sociological features of the scientific enterprise, knowledge of which is transmitted through professional education, publication and popularization.
- Can those patterns be described and explained in ways that do not presuppose their normative appropriateness? Persistent social phenomena already tend to be explained "functionally" as maintaining a desirable social order. To redress this bias, we need to specify less desirable orders that may be equally maintained by the same social regularities. For example, actions that enable the successful pursuit of a research programme may, at the same time, perpetuate gender and class discrimination within the prospective community of enquirers, and otherwise cause problems for third parties who are forced to absorb the applications of that research.

Consider each of Merton's norms in the spirit of our two questions. A popular sign of universalism is that scientists from around the world can agree on the leading professional journals. But since these journals are preponderantly in English and conform to Euro-American stylistic conventions, one may equally characterize this pattern as cultural imperialism (see UNIVERSALISM VERSUS RELATIVISM). As for communism, the willingness of scientists to share data and credit is legendary. But if scientists feel they have no choice but to share – say, for fear of retaliation by an aggrieved party who happens to review their next grant proposal – then communism starts to look more like insurance against risk or, less delicately, protection money. "Distinterestedness" is the name given to what enables scientific knowledge to transcend its ideological moorings. However, if both the Allies and the Nazis need the same physical principles to build an atomic bomb, then a knowledgeable physicist can work effectively for either side. Thus, evidence of disinterestedness can equally be of opportunism. Finally, the relentless scrutiny of widely cherished beliefs by the likes of Galileo and Darwin is the mark of organized scepticism in science. But were we not inclined to see ourselves as the long-term beneficiaries of the cultural dislocations caused by these revolutionary scientists, we would probably dismiss organized scepticism as collective irresponsibility. Once the social epistemologist admits these alternative appraisals of the same social phenomena, she must articulate the ends of science in terms of which either the positive or the negative appraisal is a normatively appropriate interpretation.

FURTHER READING

R. Bhaskar, *Scientific Realism and Human Emancipation* (1987).
P. Feyerabend, *Against Method* (1975).
S. Fuller, *Social Epistemology* (1988).
S. Fuller, *Science* (1997).
S. Fuller, *The Governance of Science* (2000).
S. Fuller & J. Collier, *Philosophy, Rhetoric and the End of Knowledge* (2004).
P. Kitcher, *The Advancement of Science* (1993).
P. Kitcher, *Science, Truth and Democracy* (2001).
I. Lakatos & A. Musgrave (eds), *Criticism and the Growth of Knowledge* (1970).
R. K. Merton, *The Sociology of Science* (1977).
P. Mirowski, *The Effortless Economy of Science?* (2004).
P. Mirowski & E.-M. Sent (eds), *Science Bought and Sold* (2002).
W. V. O. Quine, *Ontological Relativity and Other Essays* (1969).
J. Ravetz, *Scientific Knowledge and its Social Problems* (1971).
S. P. Turner, *The Social Theory of Practices* (1994).
S. P. Turner, *Liberal Democracy 3.0* (2003).

FEMINISM

Feminism is relevant to social epistemology because most of humanity is female, and gender has always been an important basis for demarcating spheres of knowledge and power. However, a defining ambiguity running through the heart of feminism is whether it is primarily about women as such or women as a privileged perspective from which to pursue the universal project of humanity. This ambiguity is captured in the dual meaning of "standpoint" in terms of both specific location (or situatedness) and source of an overarching vision. The word "standpoint" derived from the kind of epistemic privilege that the Marxist philosopher Georg Lukács had attributed to the proletariat. Specifically, as the bulk of the labour force, the proletariat are necessary for the operation of capitalism, yet their subordinate social position renders their stake in the perpetuation of capitalism minimal. This semi-detachment constituted a sociological simulation of objectivity. It was also exactly the position alleged for women, according to feminist theorists such as Sandra Harding and Donna Haraway. Women and workers shared several salient characteristics that gave them epistemic power, which (hopefully) could be translated into political power: their numerical majority, their relative invisibility from society's legitimizing narratives, and their material centrality to crucial moments in societal reproduction.

Nevertheless, by the time the concept of standpoint migrated from Marxism to feminism in the early 1980s, its universalist (see UNIVERSALISM VERSUS RELATIVISM) pretensions had already been seriously eroded within Marxism. This was part of a general metamorphosis of the concepts of *ideology* and *class* into *identity* and *culture*, which tracked the retreat of Marxism from a global political movement to an academic pursuit. In its heyday, Marxism had treated class distinctions as a sociological projection of human alienation. The division between working and managing as classed activities thus corresponded to a separation of the hand from the head in the individual. Similarly, in its heyday, the women's movement saw such characteristically gendered distinctions as the feminized "home" versus the masculinized "workplace" as signs of alienation that would be redressed once the sexes were political equals. However, in their academic guises, both Marxism and feminism have increasingly reinterpreted the presence of distinct classed or gendered standpoints as marks of positive cultural identity. Such standpoints are critical (see CRITICISM) only in that they demand recognition from the other, but without demanding recognition of a common project joining oneself to the other. (For related developments, see MULTICULTURALISM.)

The philosophical upshot of this transformation is that a previously universalist epistemology now became a particularist ontology. In this guise, women's knowledge came to be valued for its own sake, sometimes as constituting a radically alternative sensibility to the world: one that stresses intuition, care, the natural and community. Usually, as in Carol Gilligan, Evelyn Fox Keller and Valerie Walkerdine, this difference was explained in terms of the rather different ways boys and girls are raised and treated in the larger society. However, more essentialist explanations were also given for the relative stability of the gender divide over time and space, especially the lingering inequalities that remained between men and women even after affirmative action social policies. These explanations drew on primatology and more recently, evolutionary psychology and behavioural genetics (see **EVOLUTION**).

However, such attempts to shift the philosophical locus of feminism from epistemology to ontology have been at best a mixed blessing. On the one hand, the supposedly defining traits of women can be found, sometimes better developed, in men (and vice versa, of course). On the other, the retreat to ontology may lower the ambitions of gender-based politics. For example, one implication that the animal rights philosopher Peter Singer draws from his call for the left to abandon Marx for Darwin in *A Darwinian Left* (1999) is that gender differences – the "sexual division of labour" demonized by Marxists – may be grounded in reproductive processes that are unavoidable for the survival of most evolved forms of life. (See **SOCIAL SCIENCE**.) A salutary trend in response to this tendency has been so-called cyberfeminism, championed by Haraway, which is willing, at least at the level of theory, to free the female identity from a conventional sex-based biology. The idea here is to re-inscribe the feminine in both (non-human) animal and cyborg forms, of the sort traditionally both valorized and demonized in science fiction, which, in light of new developments in biotechnology and prosthetics, is laying the foundation for a post-human or trans-human future.

By the end of the 1980s, the ontological interpretation of a feminist standpoint was subject to radical internal critiques. These were epitomized by the notoriety surrounding Judith Butler's *Gender Trouble* (1990), which argued for the performative character of gender identity: if there is an essence to our gender identity, it is queer, with "male" and "female" being two possible social constructions of that queer identity. Aside from the challenge posed to conventional sexual mores, this thesis drew attention to the displacement of women inside feminism itself. Butler's conclusions were immediately seen as radical in a sense that had become familiar in the humanities; namely, a deconstruction of a binary opposition definitive of our culture – in this case, male–female. But the political import of this radicalism was more ambiguous. Butler seemed to presume that the status of women in society was sufficiently secure that it would be better now for them to treat femininity as a "floating signifier", in Jacques Lacan's sense, than as a source of solidarity.

Butler's anti-essentialist, even discretionary, appeal to the feminine highlighted just how class-divided the status of women in society had become. Her radical overtones notwithstanding, Butler spoke for women who had already achieved a virtual equality with men in their own lives, and hence were in a position to overthrow the last vestige of gender inequality, namely, the very gender marker itself. Such "queers" – the middle sex? – resemble the middle-class advocates of revolution in eighteenth-century America and France, for whom "liberty" meant the removal of the final hereditary barriers to their equality with the traditionally dominant aristocrats. Like the bourgeois revolutionaries *vis-à-vis* poor unpropertied commoners, it is not clear that the post-revolutionary order would benefit those who continue to suffer economic and cultural disadvantage simply by virtue of their status as women. Just as the achievement ethic stressed by the middle classes does not serve the interests of the poor who lack the opportunity to achieve, the performative approach to gender may deprive the bulk of subjugated women of their main rallying point for opposing their oppressors, namely, their appeal to sexual difference. Consequently, the literary critic Jonathan Dollimore has dubbed Butler's stance "wishful theory", a phrase that merits comparison with Marx and Engels's derogation of "utopian socialism".

Perhaps the most interesting social epistemological question to ask about feminism concerns the relationship between its growth as an intellectual movement within the academy – as exemplified by the rise of women's studies programmes – and the fate of the women's movement in the larger society: are they mutually reinforcing or has the former come to absorb the energies of the latter? The question is complicated by the fact that the UNIVERSITY – as a major site of affirmative action – is probably the institution that has most clearly reflected the social advancement of women. Does the rise of prominent female academics mark a genuine success in transforming the institution or simply the co-optation of particular individuals into the establishment? Those sceptical of feminism's success, including many self-professed leftists, point to what has happened to that slogan of 1960s campus radicalism, "The personal is political". This was originally a call to raise consciousness, so that people could turn their everyday lives into sites of political activity. Nowadays the slogan refers more passively to the "always already" politicized nature of everyday life, which simply requires academic analysis for its recognition to be complete.

To be sure, unless one holds to an essentialized approach to gender difference, it remains an open empirical question whether the influx of women into academia has already or will inevitably change the ends and means of knowledge production. It is entirely possible that an academic environment consisting primarily of women would conduct its business in much the same way as men have. Nevertheless, this would not detract from the value of affirmative action and the general aim of making the knowledge-production system representative of the society to which its products, procedures and principles are applied. This aim can be justified purely on grounds of **EPISTEMIC JUSTICE**, specifically the ideal that universal knowledge should be universally accessible.

FURTHER READING

J. Butler, *Gender Trouble* (1990).
J. Dollimore, "Bisexuality, Heterosexuality, and Wishful Theory" (1996).
D. Haraway, *Primate Visions* (1989).
D. Haraway, *Simians, Cyborgs, Women* (1991).
S. Harding, *The Science Question in Feminism* (1986).
S. Harding, *Whose Science? Whose Knowledge?* (1991).
H. Longino, *Science and Social Values* (1990).
P. Singer, *A Darwinian Left* (1999).

FOLK EPISTEMOLOGY

This branch of social epistemology studies conceptions of knowledge as products of cultural variation. (See **MULTICULTURALISM**.) The "folk knower" typically travels under such names as the "native speaker", "naive knower" or, more abstractly, the "first-person perspective". Originally, under the influence of imperial anthropology and positivist science, folk epistemology had the derogatory connotation of pre-scientific or even primitive accounts of knowledge. However, in contemporary analytic philosophy, the value placed on the expression "folk epistemology" varies considerably. For example, folk views of the mind, which typically define mental states in terms of a grammar of thought without making reference to brain states, are still given at least some credence by most philosophers of mind, and figure prominently in the sort of philosophical writing (e.g. by Jerry Fodor, Thomas Nagel) likely to appear in the *Times Literary Supplement* or the *London Review of Books*. (See **EXPLAINING THE COGNITIVE CONTENT OF SCIENCE**.)

Nevertheless, for the past quarter-century, Stephen Stich has queered the pitch by treating philosophical theories of knowledge as themselves instances of folk epistemology. Thus, as a folk epistemologist, Stich is less concerned with defending epistemological relativism than with undermining the assumption that there is a universal problem of knowledge to which relativism attempts to provide one general solution. (See **UNIVERSALISM VERSUS RELATIVISM**.) Indeed, the fixation on defeating the sceptic as the ultimate goal of a theory of knowledge may turn out to be an elite Western preoccupation. Among contemporary philosophers, Stich has most persistently drawn on social and cognitive psychological research to cast doubts on the universal status of the epistemological intuitions that motivate classical philosophical problems. Indeed, far from being untutored, he regards these intuitions as very much the product of a specifically Western philosophical education.

Stich first drew on the studies of the social psychologist Richard Nisbett, who in the 1970s had shown that people normally use heuristics that enable them to adapt to their environments even though they fall short of philosophical norms of **RATIONALITY**. Following the Oxford philosopher, L. Jonathan Cohen, **ANALYTIC SOCIAL EPISTEMOLOGISTS** had tended to interpret these heuristics as merely an imperfect manifestation – perhaps reflecting an incomplete understanding – of the underlying rational processes. In contrast, Stich doubted the existence of any such underlying rational processes. Later, armed with Nisbett's cross-cultural studies of the US and the Far East, Stich observed that Asians are more sceptical than Americans of beliefs caused by reliable processes of which they are unaware, yet they are less disturbed by what epistemologists call the "Gettier problem", whereby someone holds a justified true belief with a false background assumption. This result suggested that Westerners, especially those schooled in analytic philosophy, are more inclined to evaluate knowledge claims in terms that are detached from other aspects of the knower's experience. Thus, for Westerners, the knower's state of consciousness is less likely to be an overriding consideration in determining that someone knows something than for Asians.

Either a positive or a negative gloss may be placed on this cross-cultural difference. On the one hand, it may be taken to show that Western epistemology cultivates a connoisseurship with regard to knowledge claims that is comparable to the wine taster who can judge the qualities of different vintages independently of the meals with which they are served. On the other hand, the detachability of epistemic evaluation from the overall psychology of knowers may be taken to imply the alienation of Western judgements about knowledge claims from the knowers who generate them. Fuller's version of social epistemology tends towards the latter viewpoint, although he agrees with Nisbett that this alienation entails epistemic strengths as well as weaknesses. For Nisbett, the difference between Western and Eastern folk epistemologies is traceable to fundamental differences in their respective founding societies: ancient Greece and China. However, here Nisbett tends to stereotype the Greeks as innately curious in a way the Chinese were not. Thus, according to Nisbett, the Greeks were not inclined to take appearances at face value. This led them to reorganize their experience in terms of some deeper mode of classification that could be tested against subsequent experience. In contrast, Nisbett argues, the Chinese took appearances at face value, which is to say, they regarded all of equal value in contributing to a harmonious sense of reality. (See **RELIGION**.)

However, given the past 2500 years of East–West relations, it might be more illuminating to recast the Greeks' curiosity as an unrelenting interest to overcome whatever differences in perspective exist among themselves, an interest that in the ancient world was most directly addressed by **RHETORIC**. The aim would be for the interlocutor to see things as the speaker does, and hence grant him a measure of epistemic authority. This image of enquiry, whose language was borrowed from war and its spirit from games, was in sharp contrast with the more tolerant and contemplative attitudes of the Chinese. This explains a pattern commonly observed in cross-cultural history of science. The East was often first in adopting metaphysical perspectives commonly associated with modern science – such as action-at-a-distance in physics and evolution by natural selection – yet because these were perspectives accepted for their *prima facie* plausibility without having undergone much resistance or rigorous testing, they never developed beyond a relatively superficial or impressionistic level.

While generally averse to the kinds of cross-cultural considerations associated with folk epistemology, analytic philosophy was nevertheless exposed to the challenge posed by Stich and Nisbett by virtue of its default tendency to motivate classical philosophical problems by drawing on untutored intuitions that the philosopher regards as universal. This starting-point reveals the ease with which philosophers continue to turn the classroom into the site for original research. Thus, philosophers treat the untutored intuitions of their students as the raw material out of which rational thought is to be forged. The results of these pedagogical experiments can be seen in the arguments and counter-arguments published in analytic philosophy journals. In the case of epistemology, the intuitions usually concern the possible illusoriness of our knowledge: that our beliefs may not be as well-grounded as we thought. Once we are persuaded of this point, the problem of knowledge becomes a matter of defeating the personified planter of these doubts, the sceptic. (See CONSENSUS VERSUS DISSENT.)

A version of this image of philosophical enquiry can certainly be found in Socrates and, say, William of Ockham. However, in the ancient and medieval contexts, untutored intuitions were often treated like prejudices that the philosopher seeks to overcome through discipline. This attitude was popularized during the Enlightenment, where the distinction between tutor and tutee was levelled in what Kant called the "public sphere": critical discourse was thus about eliciting and challenging each other's intuitions. (See FREE ENQUIRY.) This sensibility came to characterize modern thought more generally, perhaps most clearly championed by Russell and Popper. Fuller's version of social epistemology is very sympathetic to this general re-specification of scepticism as CRITICISM. Here it is worth noting that one can accept the Stich–Nisbett thesis that the problem of scepticism is a contrivance of the Western philosophical tradition, while still recognizing the power of that contrivance to challenge what we take for granted. It only follows from the Stich–Nisbett view that those who refuse to engage with the problem of scepticism are not irrational but rather need to be persuaded of the problem's significance.

However, there have always been differences of opinion on the status of untutored intuitions: does rational thought *replace* or *develop* them? Does the philosophically tutored student acquire a new mind or does she simply become self-conscious of how her mind has always worked? As analytic philosophy struggled to remain autonomous from the findings and practices of the special sciences in the twentieth century, untutored intuitions have been ontologically boosted to the status of Platonic universals. This strategy is traceable to G. E. Moore's systematic attempt to distance the philosophical method from the naturalistic encroachments of Mill, Spencer, James and Dewey. Following Moore, alternative philosophical positions are theories that aim to best explain – that is, to justify – those presumptively perennial intuitions. Moore's strategy was associated in its day with a common-sense approach to philosophy traceable to the eighteenth-century Scottish theologian Thomas Reid, who regarded common sense as evidence of the preordained harmony between the human mind and the divine plan. Moore secularized Reid's insight by suggesting that common sense might be located in the semantics of ordinary language, which over the twentieth century came to be known as "conceptual analysis". (See COMMON SENSE VERSUS COLLECTIVE MEMORY.)

The turn to ordinary language was a natural one for Moore to take, since he had been trained as a classicist. The nineteenth-century German classicists routinely regarded the history of a language as the main empirical trace of a nation's mentality, or culture. Moreover, German philosophers from Hegel and Heidegger had been convinced that their language had inherited the mantle of Attic Greek as the natural language of philosophy, the medium of universal culture, or civilization. What is striking, in retrospect, is that comparable charges of linguistic chauvinism were not raised against Moore and his successors Gilbert Ryle and J. L. Austin, respectively, a Plato and an Aristotle scholar, both trained at Oxford. Rather, it took the Popperian anthropologist Ernest Gellner to reveal, in his 1959 book *Words and Things*, that the common sense of ordinary language philosophy meant English as spoken in the Oxbridge common room. Why had no one else detected the English language's centrality in grounding the universal objects of philosophical enquiry? The main part of the answer is probably to be found in British imperialism and (especially after 1960) the globalization of US culture. However, it is also noteworthy that this Anglophone chauvinism was attached to a systemic critique of the illusions of "surface grammar" that was typically associated with German linguistic chauvinism. Thus, British idealist philosophers, such as F. H. Bradley, Bernard Bosanquet, J. M. E. McTaggart and R. G. Collingwood – all of whom had seen some merit in Hegel's formulations – were deemed profoundly confused on matters of the self, time and logic by philosophers who followed in Moore's footsteps.

This anti-German sentiment was abetted by the émigré logical positivists (see KUHN, POPPER AND LOGICAL POSITIVISM), who had seen at first hand the deployment of German philosophical language for nefarious political ends. Thus, in his best-selling Anglophone popularization of logical positivism, *Language, Truth and Logic* (1936), A. J. Ayer relied on Rudolf Carnap's own native demystification of German metaphysicians such as Martin Heidegger, who made pseudo-profound assertions in syntactically correct German that were then used for Nazi propaganda. For the next half-century, an artificial barrier was erected between the English- and German-speaking worlds, which divided the ranks of broadly "constructivist" or "anti-realist" philosophies. Indeed, logical positivism shared more with German idealism than it cared to admit. Specifically, both denied the meaningfulness of a mind-independent reality. Rather, they identified reality with the material realization of human intelligence (a.k.a. self-consciousness), be it defined as a decision procedure in mathematics, an operationalization in experimental science or a legally constrained political institution. The common roots of positivism and idealism started to be recovered in the 1960s by Ayer's successor at Oxford, Michael Dummett, whose anti-realist philosophy was grounded on a rereading of the German and Austrian metaphysicians who influenced Ayer's mentor, Russell, a staunch opponent of ordinary language philosophy throughout his long career.

While Dummett did much to undo the Germanophobia of analytic philosophy, Moore's original problem of protecting philosophy's domain from the special sciences intensified as the twentieth century drew to a close. Analytic philosophers did themselves few favours by claiming that they were engaged in a descriptive rather than revisionist project, to recall P. F. Strawson's distinction. This invited the invidious question: do philosophers *really* describe our conceptual life better than, say, linguists, psychologists, sociologists or anthropologists? Richard Rorty took perverse pleasure in championing the negative point of view. Rorty had begun his career in the 1960s defending Paul Feyerabend's comparison of ordinary talk about mental states with eighteenth-century talk about the pseudo-substance phlogiston, whose seemingly paradoxical nature as the essence of combustion concealed a variety of distinct physical causes. The Chemical Revolution associated with Antoine Lavoisier resolved phlogiston's properties into several elements, notably oxygen and nitrogen. Similarly, Feyerabend and Rorty argued that philosophical puzzles surrounding the identification and explanation of beliefs will be ultimately resolved, or eliminated, as a variety of causally distinct phenomena explainable by the behavioural and neuroscientific disciplines.

Specifically responding to Rorty's demotion of philosophy to cultural criticism in *Philosophy and the Mirror of Nature* (1979), Cohen launched a rearguard defence of analytic philosophy that has continued to influence philosophers of mind and epistemologists relatively unconcerned with science (e.g. Alvin Goldman). Cohen's strategy was to identify Moore's search for Platonic Forms with Noam Chomsky's "generative grammar", a deep structure of thought that one may access through intuition but not application (e.g. one can recognize a grammatically correct sentence without normally speaking in grammatical sentences). Thus, in response to the cognitive psychologists Amos Tversky and Daniel Kahneman, who provided experimental evidence for the heuristic value of philosophically irrational forms of inference, Cohen argued that they dealt with matters too superficially, for example, failing to explain the contradiction that subjects perceived between their own responses and expected norm. Of course, the very experience of contradiction could just as easily testify to a social system that routinely fails to shape individuals in accordance to its norms, thereby creating opportunities both retrenching and changing the norms. (See **NORMATIVITY** and **EXPLAINING THE NORMATIVE STRUCTURE OF SCIENCE**.)

FURTHER READING

G. Ainslie, *Picoeconomics* (1992).

A. J. Ayer, *Language, Truth and Logic* (1936).

D. T. Campbell, *Methodology and Epistemology for the Social Sciences* (1988).

L. J. Cohen, *The Dialogue of Reason* (1986).

H. M. Collins & M. Kusch, *The Shape of Actions* (1999).

P. Feyerabend, *Against Method* (1975).

S. Fuller, *Philosophy of Science and Its Discontents* (1993).

S. Fuller, *Science* (1997).

R. Giere (ed.), *Cognitive Models of Science* (1992).

A. Goldman, *Epistemology and Cognition* (1986).

S. Nichols, S. Stich & J. Weinberg, "Meta-Skepticism" (2003).

R. Nisbett, *The Geography of Thought* (2003).

E. Noelle-Neumann, *The Spiral of Silence* (1982).

R. Rorty, *Philosophy and the Mirror of Nature* (1979).

W. Shadish & S. Fuller (eds), *The Social Psychology of Science* (1994).

S. Stich & R. Nisbett, "Expertise, Justification, and the Psychology of Inductive Inference" (1984).

FREE ENQUIRY

This concept includes the free expression of enquiry, also known as "free speech". It is central to the civic republican politics of knowledge associated with Fuller's version of **SOCIAL EPISTEMOLOGY**. In the equation "knowledge is power", knowledge enables one to be free of the power exerted by others, *not* to exert power over others. (See **EPISTEMIC JUSTICE**.) The relevant sense of "freedom" here implies the recognition of objectively alternative courses of action, that is, an "undeterminist" **HISTORIOGRAPHY**. In other words, one is free to speak only if the options of which one speaks are likely to lead to significantly different outcomes, even if they are ones that the speaker ends up regretting having chosen. In this sense, free enquiry embodies a "right to be wrong". This sensibility is the cornerstone of autonomy, which, especially after Kant, has often been the mark of personhood. Unfortunately, still following Kant, modern moral philosophy has tended to see the pursuit of autonomy as somehow divorced from considerations of the consequences of one's actions. For example, a vulgarized Kantian might say that ethics requires that one act on principle without regard to consequences. Yet, the anticipation of consequences is vital to the construction of a society in which autonomy is feasible.

Historically the paradigm case of autonomy, classical Athens, restricted citizenship to male hereditary landholders. This enabled citizens to speak their minds openly without threat to their lives, even if they turned out to be wrong. As Popper put it, their ideas could die in their stead; they could return to the forum the next day to argue another round. The eighteenth-century European Enlightenment was about recovering precisely this original sense of autonomy for the emerging urban middle classes who lacked a say in government on genetic grounds. The open question was how much beyond the original Athenian precedent should the project of Enlightenment be extended. Already by the end of the eighteenth century, arguments were beginning to be made for the enfranchisement of indentured servants and slaves, itinerant and wage labourers, and women. By the end of the twentieth century, reflecting the successes of the previous 200 years, similar arguments were beginning to be made for securing the autonomy of children, the disabled and animals.

In all these cases, arguments have had to be made for extending the state's control over individual lives – especially involving the redistribution of income and power but increasingly the redesign of social space, allowing for the relevant mobility and security. **SOCIAL SCIENCE** and socialism have been instrumental in this extension of the physical prerequisites for autonomy. However, as the line is crossed from adult human beings to non-adults and/or non-human beings, conceptual and material resources have been strained. The main locus for this strain arises over the appropriateness of rights and obligations, the traditional legal categories in which the sphere of autonomy has been defined. For example, how might animals be accorded legally enforceable rights and obligations, given that these categories were designed with adult male human beings in mind?

Modern discussions of free enquiry started in the sixteenth century as a by-product of the secularization brought on by the Protestant Reformation, which effectively converted Christendom from a Roman Catholic monopoly to a free market of independent churches, each catering to a constituency that had lacked a voice in the traditional dominant Catholic power structures. The spirit of these original discussions was one of *tolerance*, a term that implied that differences in belief could not be resolved yet different believers had to live peacefully in one space together. Thus, by virtue of declaring a stalemate on the search for ultimate truth, tolerance constitutes a "second best" epistemology. Not surprisingly, John Milton and John Locke, the great seventeenth-century English defenders of tolerance, did not extend the principle to Catholics, who still wanted to resolve all differences in belief in one church doctrine. This idea of tolerating only the tolerant became a cornerstone of modern liberalism, a philosophy that differs from civic republicanism in its preoccupation with minimizing violence, even if that requires the kind of self-censorship that often passes for "tolerance". However, such liberalism has come under increasing fire from two religious sources. On the one hand, US fundamentalist Christians have argued that, contrary to the Constitution's doctrine of tolerance (enshrined as the separation of church and state), a scientific NATURAL-ISM has become the *de facto* national RELIGION, which has restricted the expression of supernaturalist views about the origins of life and the universe, especially in tax-based public-school classrooms. On the other hand, Muslims worldwide have questioned the very principle of tolerating only the tolerant, which they see as a formula for value corrosion, since ethics gravitates to the path of least resistance for those who already enjoy autonomy. In the liberal "utopia", the plight of the poor and dispossessed is ignored, if not censured or persecuted, if only highly inconvenient political solutions are proposed to alleviate their plight.

John Stuart Mill's 1859 essay *On Liberty* is normally seen as the classic defence of free enquiry. For Mill, the value of such freedom is that it increases our chances of reaching the truth, which often lies with dissenters from the crowd. (See CONSENSUS VERSUS DISSENT and TRUTH, RELIABILITY AND THE ENDS OF KNOWLEDGE.) Mill was sometimes read in his day as covertly anti-democratic for expressing this rationale, which seemed to privilege an intellectual elite. In any case, it is a clear expression of the positive correlation between scientific and political interests that goes beyond classic religious defences of tolerance, which had been based on our lack of privileged access to God's mind. In contrast, Mill wanted to *oblige*, not merely allow, citizens to speak and enquire freely so as to benefit their common interest in knowing the truth. Thus, he called for universal education (albeit self-organized, as in the US) and detested class-based politics of the sort that enabled people to hide their true beliefs in the anonymity of a group.

Here Mill recalls classical Athens, where cowardice was worse than defeat in debate. In Athens, free speech was considered a civic duty for reasons of national defence: someone might know something that is relevant to the security of every-one in society. While Mill downplayed the nation-building capacity of free speech, he advocated the exportation of political and economic freedom worldwide in the name of truth. Indeed, during his brief term in the 1860s as a Liberal Party Member of Parliament, Mill clearly supported the imperialist banner under which such policies normally travelled, since the global enforcement of free trade appeared to be the most politically expedient way to promote truly free enquiry.

The hidden aggressiveness of the principle of free enquiry brings to light the role of CRITICISM as institutionally sublimated confrontation. In this respect, civic republicanism presupposes many of the conditions of classical social contract theory. On the one hand, liberty requires a certain level of natural wealth so that criticism does not turn into the chronic hostilities over scarce resources associated with a Hobbesian state of nature. People must find losing an argument sufficiently tolerable to remain within the bounds of the law until they are given the opportunity to restate their case. On the other hand, republican liberty presupposes that there are limits to this natural wealth, so that different courses of action are likely to bring about substantially different effects. Only then does the decision one takes – and hence the criticism of alternatives – matter. These limits compel the engagement in other people's interests and projects beyond their own immediate concerns, as opposed to, say, the benign indifference of Jean-Jacques Rousseau's "noble savage". It is between these extremes that a *res publica* can properly be constructed and maintained. The corresponding critical attitude is fostered in settings that oblige people to debate matters of equal import to all but without fear that the opinions they express will undermine their capacity to participate in similar debates in the future. Historically the most effective institutions for maintaining this attitude have been related to *duty-driven lifelong tenure*, which has been applied to citizenship itself (especially when tied to a guaranteed income or comprehensive social welfare), high court appointments and, most controversially perhaps, academic posts.

On Liberty is dedicated to Wilhelm von Humboldt, the famed Prussian education minister credited with the modern UNIVERSITY ideal as a vehicle for building national identity. However, Mill had in mind Humboldt's youthful work *The Limits of State Action* (1792), which argued that a fully educated ("enlightened") citizenry would be capable of legislating for its own collective interests and thereby cause the paternalistic state to "wither away" (an expression later immortalized by Marx and Engels) in favour of a purely administrative entity that implements and monitors the actions taken by the legislature. Popper acknowledged the Humboldt–Mill link as relevant to his own views of the ethic of the open society. Here one might envisage the Humboldtian distinction between legislative and administrative powers as akin to that between theory and method in Popperian philosophy of science.

Nevertheless, as the nineteenth century progressed, the departmental structure of universities came to be institutionalized and academics shifted their focus from citizen education to specialized research. Free enquiry thus became a kind of guild right that required self-policing, which became the meaning of "self-legislating". The German professoriate instituted peer-reviewed journals to screen research contributions prior to publication, since publication meant that a community of scholars took collective responsibility for the research. (See EXPERTISE.) Not surprisingly, then, special emphasis was placed on not offending the political authorities whose funding enabled the scholars to flourish in the first place. This meant that much social science research potentially critical of government policy had to be done outside academia, especially by Marxists, who were generally suspected as enemies of the state. By the time Max Weber was extolling the virtues of free enquiry in "Science as a Vocation" in 1918, he was partly referring to freedom from entering political controversy.

This intellectual dependency on the state for academic autonomy escalated in the twentieth century – now across the entire world – as the conduct of research became increasingly incompatible with the academic's traditional teaching and administrative functions. Consequently, for everything from laboratory equipment to teaching assistance, academics have required more external funding, first from the state but increasingly from private foundations and industry. In most cases, constraints are placed on what one may research or publish. To be sure, "peer review" is arguably a euphemism for academic self-censorship, the precedent for which was already set in the charter of the Royal Society of London, a body that secured its autonomy by refusing to promote political and religious controversies. The potential for institutional censorship grew markedly once academics were forced to secure grants and hence continually undergo scrutiny for their very eligibility to do research. In recent years, however, ideological considerations have been eclipsed by financial ones – that is, intellectual property protection – as the principal grounds cited for restricting free enquiry in academia.

Nevertheless, the attempt to restrict free enquiry for ideological reasons remains, largely on grounds Mill himself would have recognized. Mill wanted citizens to have the right to speak, but not act, freely. The model was the difference between what transpires inside and outside parliament: in principle, anything may be discussed but action requires specific institutions of decision-making and implementation. Philosophically, "speaking" versus "acting" amounted to forms of expression that are "general" versus "specific". On the one hand, Mill would permit general claims that capitalists exploit the workers, since such claims invite public debate and perhaps corrective legislation. On the other hand, Mill would prohibit naming-and-shaming campaigns against specific capitalists accused of exploiting specific workers, because that would put the capitalists' lives at risk from angry protesters. Clearly Mill had in mind restrictions on journalistic licence. He had not anticipated that social policies targeting specific individuals might be made on the basis of general scientific knowledge outside the simulated environment of the laboratory, as in, say, twentieth-century correlations of race and intelligence. In this respect, Mill treated the *ceteris paribus* ("other things being equal") clause in the formulation of a scientific law as an institutional safeguard that kept science at a safe distance from society. Indeed, in his day, the capacity to convert an experimental paradigm to a large-scale technology was limited to the science of chemistry. The rest of the sciences were relatively low-tech and non-invasive, although medicine had begun to introduce some allopathic practices. The only obvious threat that free enquiry posed was to the cosmology of the established Christian churches, but not to the well-being of individual Christians.

Today the lack of adequate institutions to hook up the generalizations of science and the specificities of policy has increased the tendency to censor research with controversial political import. Often this involves principled appeals to political correctness, namely, that certain things are too dangerous to know because they would upset social conventions. Arguments of this sort, familiar down through the ages and across cultures, fail in the long run because they presuppose that the well-being of science and society necessarily trade off against each other. Some more productive attitudes include the following:

- Scientific generalizations can be taken to establish default positions against which policy can be rationally made. Concerted state action has historically involved the reversal of such default positions. In this way, politics can convert an allegedly brute fact into a soluble problem. Thus, the welfare state was designed to set a standard of human existence that exceeded statistically normal indicators such as income level and life expectancy. The use of science to discourage such compensatory policy-making would take us back to Thomas Malthus's ideas of "natural mortality", thereby reducing us to mere animals.
- The gap between the generalities of the laboratory and the specificities of reality can be used as the basis of criticism. For example, are the differences

studied in the laboratory the most salient ones for understanding human populations, and can implications for human beings be drawn so easily from animal experiments? Answers to these questions may result in efforts to tighten the connection between what lies inside and outside the laboratory – as in Popperian "reversible social experiments", whereby human beings volunteer, as part of their civic duty to promote the truth, to participate in scientific experiments and make judgements about the policy import of those experiments in consensus (see **CONSENSUS VERSUS DISSENT**) conferences.

FURTHER READING

J. Butler, *Excitable Speech* (1997).
W. Clark, *Academic Charisma and the Origins of the Research University* (2006).
G. Delanty, *Challenging Knowledge* (2001).
P. Feyerabend, *Science in a Free Society* (1979).
S. Fuller, *The Governance of Science* (2000).
S. Fuller, *The Intellectual* (2005).
J. Habermas, *The Structural Transformation of the Public Sphere* (1989).
J. Hecht, *Doubt* (2003).
R. Hofstadter & A. Metzger, *The Development of Academic Freedom in the United States* (1955).
A. Irwin, *Citizen Science* (1995).
S. C. Jansen, *Censorship* (1991).
I. C. Jarvie, *The Republic of Science* (2001).
W. Keith, *Democracy as Discussion* (2007).
P. Kitcher, *Science, Truth and Democracy* (2001).
E. Noelle-Neumann, *The Spiral of Silence* (1982).
P. Pettit, *Republicanism* (1997).
K. Popper, *The Open Society and its Enemies* (1945).
J. Rawls, *A Theory of Justice* (1971).
J. M. Robertson, *A History of Free-Thought in the Nineteenth Century* (1929).
C. A. Willard, *Liberalism and the Problem of Knowledge* (1996).
R. Wuthnow, *Discourse Communities* (1989).

HISTORIOGRAPHY

Historical knowledge transpires along two dimensions: on the one hand, a historian may (or not) presuppose a common history to which everyone contributes; on the other, a historian may (or not) write from the standpoint of a historical winner. In the 1930s, Herbert Butterfield usefully distinguished between *Whig* and *Tory* historiography as the standpoints of, respectively, the winners and the losers of a common history. The common history behind Butterfield's coinage of Whig and Tory historiography involved the ascendancy of parliament over the king in seventeenth-century England. For the monarchist Tories, this was the story of decline from a natural order into fractiousness and chaos, whereas for Whiggish defenders of parliament, it marked the removal of obstacles to the spread of liberty, which has eventuated in peaceful enterprise and prosperity for all. In other words, while the Whigs and Tories recognized each other as characters in the same historical narrative, they interpreted the plot of that narrative in radically different terms: specifically, where the Whig saw freedom, the Tory saw decadence; where the Tory saw order, the Whig saw stagnation. To the Tories, the Whigs were the lucky beneficiaries of monarchical weakness, not riders on the wave of historical destiny, as the Whigs saw themselves. If the Whigs controlled the letter of history, the Tories laid claim to its spirit in exile.

The difference between Whig and Tory historiography is epitomized by their contrasting attitudes towards the past, which Fuller has called, respectively, *overdeterminist* and *underdeterminist* (see **EVOLUTION**.) In the former, the same outcome is assured regardless of the historical starting-point, while in the latter, the current trajectory is the product of historically specific, and potentially reversible, decisions. Expressed in the logic of counterfactual conditional statements, here are their attitudes towards the relationship between two temporally successive events, X and Y:

Overdeterminist: Even if X had not happened, Y still would have happened.
Underdeterminist: If X had not happened, Y would not have happened.

Whig historiography has religious precedents (see **RELIGION**) in the Christian salvation story and is the characteristic narrative of **PROGRESS** in the modern period, elements of which can be found in thinkers as otherwise different as Smith, Hegel, Marx and Mill. Despite its political origins, Whig historiography is more likely to be found today in accounts of science than politics, although some hopeful histories of democracy continue to be Whiggish. Kuhn (see **KUHN, POPPER**

AND LOGICAL POSITIVISM) notoriously argued that Whig histories are little more than edifying myths, but no less necessary to motivate both scientists and the public in the often specialized and inconsequential activities that constitute day-to-day science. The RHETORICAL value invested in Whig histories – especially as prods to perseverance in the face of adversity – draws attention to what Polanyi regarded as the "unconditional commitment", or even "religiosity", required of today's scientists, even when the ultimate end of enquiry always seems to recede from view (see TRUTH, RELIABILITY AND THE ENDS OF KNOWLEDGE).

Tory historiography is more often applied to accounts of the arts and politics than science. Yet, it too has religious precedents. For example, the seventeenth-century Tories echoed a widespread Renaissance sentiment that history has been one long steady decline from an original moment of pristine wisdom, in which human beings were in harmony with nature and in communion with God (as represented by the king). In biblical terms, this fall from grace was epitomized by the Tower of Babel, which Tories have invoked to symbolize the dispersion of languages, schools and viewpoints. The positivist preoccupation with unifying the sciences under a single standard of epistemic currency arguably modernizes this Tory sensibility. Tory historiographies have also drawn on the *dirty hands* principle, according to which there are no clean wins. Every victory is lucky and ultimately pyrrhic, incurring hidden costs that come to light only later. This principle typically reveals the tragic dimension of human fallibility, as qualities that initially led to success eventually arrest development and may become the source of failure. In that event, one may witness Tory wish fulfilment, *the return of the repressed*, whereby what had been previously expelled comes to reclaim its rightful legacy.

The Tory sensibility to history is by no means limited to defeated generals like Thucydides or exiled politicians like Viscount Bolingbroke, the original English Tory from whom Voltaire and Hegel acquired the idea of philosophical history (i.e. history as philosophy teaching by examples). As the idea of a common history was broadened in the eighteenth century from alternative branches of a family tree to encompass the entirety of humanity, the "losers" came to stand for much more than disinherited elites. They came to incorporate non-males, non-nobles, non-whites and even one's own non-rational self. Marx, Nietzsche and Freud thus transformed Tory historiography into a narrative of potential emancipation, if only (as in Freud) from one's ordinary self-understanding. If winning and losing is always a matter of contingency, then there is always hope that past losses may be reversed in the future. In the late-nineteenth century, there even appeared to be a scientific basis for these views in, say, the "eternal recurrence" of all atomic combinations in an infinite universe and the periodic return of what evolutionary biologists called "atavistic" species.

A peculiar feature of the history of the philosophy of science is that the people primarily regarded as philosophers today were on the losing side of the major scientific battles of their time, sometimes even being forced into philosophy because of their failure to find acceptance in the scientific community. The seventeenth century provides a striking confirmation of this point. Not only Galileo, Boyle and Newton, but also Descartes, Hobbes and Leibniz were all called "natural philosophers", yet today the first set are called "scientists" and the second set "philosophers". In effect, the philosophy of science is the natural home of Tory history of science. When history's unrealized potential, the stuff of Tory historiography, is the subject matter of philosophy, it becomes a standpoint from which to criticize contemporary scientific practice.

This was certainly the standpoint from which Kuhn, the logical positivists and the Popperians developed their respective normative (see **NORMATIVITY**) visions of science. Despite their often quite considerable differences, all bemoaned science's twentieth-century metamorphosis into *technoscience* (see **SCIENCE AND TECHNOLOGY STUDIES**). Where Kuhn differed from the positivists and the Popperians – especially Popper's students Imre Lakatos and Paul Feyerabend – was his acceptance of the phenomenon that Lakatos dubbed *Kuhn loss*. This refers to the tendency of scientific revolutions to result in not only improved problem-solving effectiveness but also the official removal of intractable problems from the new paradigm's agenda. For the Popperians, science's systematic forgetting, or perhaps even repression, of its past – the stuff of Kuhn's Whig histories – inhibited its potential as universal enquiry. (See **COMMON SENSE VERSUS COLLECTIVE MEMORY**). Not surprisingly, the aspects of the old paradigm that tend to be lost are the more subjective ones wrapped up with publicly contested issues that scientists would prefer to avoid, perhaps so as not to expose the limits of their own authority.

In these postmodern times (see **POSTMODERNISM**), it is easier to presuppose multiple historical lineages and trajectories. In this context, we may distinguish *Prig* and *Subaltern* historiography, to evoke terms coined by, respectively, the historian of science Stephen Brush and the Marxist philosopher Antonio Gramsci. The Prig is the professional historian who appreciates the multiplicity of history from a standpoint of equanimity. The superiority of her position – a mark of her **EXPERTISE** – is the Zen attitude she displays towards the different strands, regardless of the hostilities that had originally existed among the strands themselves. In contrast, the Subaltern experiences the multiplicity of history as radical "otherness", specifically her exclusion from and even subordination to the dominant strands. (See **FEMINISM, MULTICULTURALISM**.) The Whig sense of superiority differs from the Prig in its treatment of history as a source of personal legacy rather than impersonal transcendence. Similarly, the Tory sense of inferiority differs from the Subaltern in its treatment of history as a source of specific disenfranchisement rather than a more general expression of social marginality. Fuller's version of social epistemology is naturally aligned to Tory historiography, especially as a basis for CRITICISM, and least sympathetic to Prig historiography.

FURTHER READING

A. Ahmad, *In Theory: Classes, Nations, Literatures* (1992).

J. Elster, *The Logic of Society* (1980).

S. Fuller, *Science* (1997).

S. Fuller, *Thomas Kuhn* (2000).

S. Fuller, *Kuhn vs Popper* (2003).

S. Fuller & J. Collier, *Philosophy, Rhetoric and the End of Knowledge* (2004).

I. Hacking, *Scientific Revolutions* (1981).

J. Kadvany, *Imre Lakatos and the Guises of Reason* (2001).

T. S. Kuhn, *The Structure of Scientific Revolutions* ([1962] 1970).

T. S. Kuhn, *The Essential Tension* (1977).

M. Mandelbaum, *History, Man and Reason* (1971).

S. Toulmin, *Human Understanding* (1972).

S. Toulmin, *Return to Reason* (2003).

INFORMATION SCIENCE

The first discipline called "social epistemology" was information science, as envisaged by the University of Chicago librarian, Jesse Shera, in the 1960s. According to Shera, social epistemology applied social scientific knowledge to synthesize the theoretical and practical functions of librarianship. It married a universal classification system to what, after the cognitive scientist Donald Norman, is called a "smart environment" for browsing that would enable library users to cultivate their epistemic interests and make educated choices with minimum friction. Nowadays we might say that Shera's image of the information scientist was that of a "mindscape designer". Shera introduced social epistemology at a time when computers had begun to enhance librarians' capacities in the search and retrieval of information. However, Shera did not want the emerging field of information science to become captive to the new technology, which would only lead to the deprofessionalization and perhaps even the redundancy of librarians. Instead, he urged librarians to regard documents as sites for studying the multiply embedded social relationships among producers, consumers and objects of knowledge.

Shera was fighting an uphill battle that has been largely lost, as librarians have shifted their focus from the construction and maintenance of "holdings" (i.e. the documents contained in the library) to a user-friendly conception of access to such holdings. Accordingly, information science research has gravitated towards the design of indicators that do little more than summarize spontaneous patterns of citation and usage. Indeed, these indicators are now often used to justify cutting and aggregating library holdings. Shera's failure reflects the replacement of the classical ideal of the library as a single physical structure that contains all knowledge, in favour of a potentially infinite – albeit virtual – space of universal access. The former ideal required organization according to explicit normative principles, whereas the latter is presumed to be a self-organizing free market of ideas. Corresponding to this change in worldview has been a shift in the demographics of librarianship in its transition to information science during the Cold War. A formerly humanistic field with a tendency to fetishize texts came to be dominated by people trained in the physical sciences who regarded texts as means to other ends, akin to the standpoint of KNOWLEDGE MANAGEMENT.

To appreciate the ideal that Shera had sought to reinstate under the rubric of "social epistemology", it is worth recalling that before Wilhelm von Humboldt's rededication of the UNIVERSITY to both the production and distribution of knowledge, librarians had provided the main impetus for the organization of enquiry. Gabriel Naudé, librarian to the powerful seventeenth-century French Cardinals Richelieu and Mazarin, collected together news of the research of Galileo and other innovative enquirers and passed it along to Marin Mersenne, who spread the news to other scientists and coordinated their correspondence. This became the basis for the first medium specifically devoted to scientific communication, the journal. In the seventeenth and eighteenth centuries, several major philosophers developed their views on the nature of knowledge in the context of librarianship. For example, David Hume, librarian to the Edinburgh law courts, nurtured his sceptical outlook by observing the countervailing judicial applications of legislation in particular cases. Even more characteristic was Gottfried von Leibniz, librarian to the Duke of Hanover, whose omnivorous appetite for collecting books enabled Leibniz to envisage a conceptual unity to knowledge – symbolized in a universal logic – that could justify the existence of libraries. This ideal was recovered in the early-twentieth century by Paul Otlet, whose universal decimal classification system of documentation was consulted by Otto Neurath when the logical positivists were pursuing their own unificationist ambitions (see **KUHN, POPPER AND LOGICAL POSITIVISM**). Crucial to this line of thought was the idea that any book's contents could be reduced to a unique combination of finite elements. The idea of "genetic information" and the associated field of "bioinformatics" preserve this older view of information science.

However, with the modern ascendancy of the university, the mission of librarianship increasingly shifted towards making everything known available to all knowers. Classification systems came to be valued more for the efficiency with which they enable access to holdings than their organizational and mapping functions. This service ethic democratized librarianship, but over time the field became subservient to its dominant users. Thus, academic librarians were reduced to technical support, a fate not unlike that of nursing *vis-à-vis* an increasingly powerful medical profession. Even in local community settings, where librarians have most clearly retained their autonomy, there is a clear tension between envisaging the reading public as a constituency to be nurtured proactively and a clientele to be served reactively: do librarians open minds to new ideas or simply serve pre-existing needs?

The door to modern information science was opened once "the customer is always right" mentality came to prevail in librarianship. This new breed of information scientist generally regarded the growth of knowledge as proceeding on too many fronts at once to achieve the Enlightenment goal of a universal system of classification. As Jean-François Lyotard famously observed, information science was the original postmodern (see **POSTMODERNISM**) science. The more fruitful course was to map the allegedly self-organizing patterns of knowledge production and distribution. Perhaps the most influential advocate of this approach has been Eugene Garfield, a chemist who studied under Robert Merton, the sociologist who did the most to promote the idea that science is a self-regulating system.

Garfield's combination of chemistry and sociology turned out to have diabolical consequences. Once chemistry was shown to be reducible to atomic physics in the early-twentieth century, it came to be regarded as a closed science, that is, one whose growth was limited to pursuing implications and applications of known fundamental principles. This level of core agreement meant that its knowledge base could be treated as a stable domain of knowledge that could be mapped like a geographical region and exploited like a region's raw materials. Even in basic research, interest shifted from re-posing fundamental problems to refining known solutions. This mentality spread to all the sciences (including the humanities) with the onset of the Cold War, when the US National Science Foundation provided Garfield with seed money to develop what became the Science Citation Index (SCI). SCI was designed to help the US compete more effectively against the Soviet Union by enabling scientists to see what their colleagues had done, and hence not duplicate research needlessly. Over the years, however, this tool has been converted into a normative model for the conduct of science, whose principal theorist has been Derek de Solla Price, the founder of "scientometrics". (See **EXPLAINING THE NORMATIVE STRUCTURE OF SCIENCE.**) One might say that the SCI has been reflexively applied to bring out more clearly the latent market-like tendencies in scientific enquiry. In this spirit, one now speaks of being on the "cutting edge" of research, as if it were the latest business fashion.

What would it mean to return to Shera's original vision of information science as social epistemology today? First, one would look at **EXPERTISE** through a different lens. An expert is not someone with special mental powers acquired by elite training but a kind of authorized information scientist who can control the search procedures for a given field. In that respect, to be credentialed as an expert is like having received the deed to a piece of land. The key point is that the expert is not identical with the expertise, just as the deed-holder is not identical with the land: in both cases, only usage and passage is controlled. Against this backdrop, university librarians perform the vital role of organizing all of the library's holdings, an interest not shared by the disciplinary experts, who are simply concerned with protecting and cultivating their own domains. Indeed, the integrationist tendencies of librarians may go against expert judgement, as they prioritize relevance to education over research as the criterion for inclusion in the holdings. A good way to contrast the conceptions of information science presupposed by the disciplinary expert and the librarian-as-social-epistemologist is that the expert is concerned with *only the truth*, while the librarian focuses on *the whole truth*. Thus, in order to maintain the reliability of her expertise, the expert will err on the side of excluding controversial but possibly true works from the library holdings (i.e. what statisticians call "type I error"), whereas the librarian will err on the side of including relevant but possibly false works (i.e. "type II error").

In this context, the librarian-as-social-epistemologist can determine just what portion of a field's publications is actually cited, or even consulted, in the preparation of new research, and hence new publications. Limited studies into this matter already suggest that a vanishingly small percentage of publications is used, a fact reflected in the increase in the serials and books that are *both* added and dropped from library holdings on a regular basis. Of course, this regularly culled material may be simply an inferior version of what survives. However, more likely, this material is unorthodox along a variety of dimensions and hence not readily assimilated into the disciplinary mainstream. Indeed, the rejected material may project a rather different intellectual trajectory for the discipline. (See **HISTORIOGRAPHY**.) In any case, from the systemic standpoint afforded to the librarian, this gravitation towards an elite appears downright irrational as it amounts to a routine waste of collective effort. At worst, it results in the ritualized destruction of collective memory (see **COMMON SENSE VERSUS COLLECTIVE MEMORY**) (i.e. self-induced historical amnesia), leading not only to the reinvention of the wheel but, worse, the neglect of precedents that are already available to solve urgent problems.

In this respect, information science is well placed to become a counter-hegemonic practice devoted to undoing the damage done by the dominance of discipline-based expertise. (See **DISCIPLINARITY VERSUS INTERDISCIPLINARITY**.) The field would employ the usual search heuristics (a.k.a. text mining) to recover lost precedents to pre-empt the efforts of those funded on the promise of doing cutting-edge research. Donald Swanson presented the paradigmatic case of this strategy as "undiscovered public knowledge", whereby librarians such as him might combine two normally non-overlapping technical literatures to arrive at a testable solution to a significant biomedical problem. In an ideal world where enquirers' talents were optimally deployed, information scientists would remind disciplinary practitioners of what they have forgotten before the latter are licensed to embark on original research. A systematic reading of the existing literature would itself be considered a form of original research. In this way the difference between the humanities and the sciences would be finally bridged. But all of this depends on information scientists asserting that what is neglected is at least the equal of what is noticed.

FURTHER READING
M. De Mey, *The Cognitive Paradigm* (1982).
S. Fuller, *Knowledge Management Foundations* (2002).
J. F. Lyotard, *The Postmodern Condition* (1983).
F. Machlup, *The Production and Distribution of Knowledge* (1962–80).

F. Machlup & U. Mansfield (eds), *The Study of Information* (1983).
R. K. Merton, *The Sociology of Science* (1977).
D. Norman, *Things That Make Us Smart* (1993).
D. de S. Price, *Big Science, Little Science, ... and Beyond* (1986).
H. Simon, *The Sciences of the Artificial* (1977).
D. Swanson, "Undiscovered Public Knowledge" (1986).

KNOWLEDGE MANAGEMENT

The very idea that knowledge needs to be managed suggests that its growth should not be left in a wild state: at best it remains unused and at worst it wastes resources. Yet, this managerial mindset goes against the grain of the past 2500 years of Western thought, which has valorized the pursuit of knowledge for its own sake, regardless of its costs and benefits. What has changed in the interim? Has it been for the better?

The rise of knowledge management represents a backlash against scientific professionalism in the pursuit of knowledge, but without the interest in reviving the old amateur ethic that had existed when the pursuit of knowledge was expected of any leisured person. (See RHETORIC.) When academics hear the phrase "the most knowledge produced at the lowest cost", they presume it implies an interest in an absolute increase in society's knowledge stock. In contrast, the knowledge manager wants a return on investment. Not surprisingly, the most profitable firms do not devote too much of their budgets to research and development (R&D).

Knowledge managers are mainly interested in exploiting existing knowledge more efficiently so as to capture a larger share of the markets in which they compete. Their interest in producing and distributing *new* knowledge extends only to what will enable them to realize that goal. Indeed, knowledge managers are masters of what may be called "counter-entrepreneurship": they find innovative ways of inhibiting or disciplining innovation by manipulating scarcity in either the supply or the demand for knowledge (understood as a good or a service). Thus, knowledge managers either restrict the production and open up the distribution of knowledge, or vice versa. An example of the former strategy is "outsourcing", whereby a firm rents knowledge that others can produce more cheaply. An example of the latter is "specialization", whereby a firm carves out a niche for itself in the knowledge market that discourages the entry of potential rivals. Increasingly, this latter strategy is abetted by a liberalized conception of intellectual property law.

These features of the *realpolitik* of knowledge management begin to explain why an increase in scientific publications and patents does not necessarily enhance a nation's competitiveness in global markets. To be sure, there is some truth to the widespread view that scientists and industrialists do not communicate with each other very well, and so even the details of a patent application may not provide the kind of information a manufacturer needs for its purposes. (Perhaps this provides evidence of different cultures for translating knowledge into practice.) Nevertheless, a deeper problem is the difference in value that science and business, respectively, attach to knowledge as such. In particular, business regards the need for new knowledge as the moral equivalent of a necessary evil: the more necessary, the more evil. In other words, the anticipated benefit-to-cost ultimately determines whether it is advisable for a firm to engage in potentially difficult and expensive encounters with new specialists or specialities.

Economists often fail to recognize this point because of the rather patronizing attitude towards business that is enshrined in their "constrained maximization" model of rational action. In this model, the average corporate executive appears as a harried and impatient person who must strike a balance between doing what is best in the short and long terms, which may end up curtailing the work of the R&D division. However, so the economists believe, had the corporation a limitless supply of time and resources, it would increase its R&D investments and eventually reap the corresponding benefits, since new knowledge is presumed to be the royal road to an increased market share.

The rise of knowledge management reveals that the average corporate executive does not think like that at all. Indicative of that is the difference in the biological imagery to which the economist and the knowledge management specialist typically appeal. Economists regard new knowledge as spontaneously generated, much like a mutation that eventually becomes the basis for a new species. Despite their pessimism about the prospects for controlling the growth of knowledge, economists are generally optimistic that such uncontrolled growth will ultimately result in overall good. In contrast, knowledge managers regard the uncontrollable character of knowledge growth as itself a problem. Where economists imagine a proliferation of new variations and species, knowledge managers see only potential weeds that crowd out the effort needed to maximize profitability. Where economists see "factors of production" in the staff and equipment of the average knowledge-intensive firm, knowledge managers see "conspicuous consumption", the cost-effectiveness of which is presumed dubious until proved otherwise.

Difference in historical perspective plays an important role here. Economists' views of knowledge remain anchored in the industrial revolution of the late-eighteenth and early-nineteenth centuries, when capitalized innovation did indeed result in a general expansion of markets and increase in wealth. However, knowledge management is anchored in the information explosion of the late-twentieth and early-twenty-first centuries, in which corporations are struggling to cope with overflowing computer databases, care of which has been left to a highly skilled but mobile labour force.

While it should be clear that knowledge management threatens to overturn the value structure of the UNIVERSITY, perverse inertial tendencies within academia already serve the interests of knowledge management. On the production side, the entry costs for engaging in research continue to escalate. This fact grants an effective monopoly to those with access to just the right pedigree, funds and publication outlets. On the distribution side, this monopoly restricts the flow of knowledge products in two senses: intentionally through intellectual property rights, but also unintentionally through the specialized training that is increasingly needed even to make sense of those products, even if one has acquired access to them. The overall result is the conversion of academic knowledge to intellectual real estate (or EXPERTISE), an object of knowledge management.

Of course, at least as a matter of ideology, academics continue to assert that knowledge is produced by hard work that is never fully rewarded, the fruits of which are nevertheless distributed as widely as possible. For economists, this is what distinguishes knowledge as a public good. (See SOCIAL CAPITAL VERSUS PUBLIC GOOD.) But for the knowledge manager, that is merely to concede that universities are not very economical in ordinary market terms. It would be better for the reverse to occur. Effort towards innovation would then be discouraged except where a profit is likely to result, even in universities. This would license, on the one hand, the redundancy of research staff and, on the other, the acquisition of intellectual property rights. In both cases, *capturing* knowledge takes precedent over *cultivating* it.

Not surprisingly then, the university appears, in the words of former *Fortune* editor Thomas Stewart, a "dumb organization" that is "high on human capital" but "low on structural capital". In contrast, a fast-food chain such as McDonald's is a "smart organization" because it makes the most of its relatively ill-trained staff by maximizing the interconnectedness of their activities. Business as usual in academia proceeds almost exactly in reverse. Indeed, the university would seem to be a whole much less than the sum of its parts. Imagine a firm whose goals are dictated almost entirely by the various trades unions from which its labour force is drawn. Each union has the final say on the performance standards to which its members are held. Management ensures that the firm's employees do not interfere with each other's work, without aspiring to any greater level of cooperation and coordination of effort. If we replace "trade union" with "academic discipline" or "professional association", the firm starts to look like a university.

Of course, the past 20 years of public sector liberalization have forced universities to set goals that transcend the interests of their constituent disciplines. Unfortunately, instead of setting their own organizational aims, university administrators have let those aims be dictated by others who would see academic institutions as means to their own ends. The result still fails to impress knowledge managers, who now wonder whether each competing demand might not be more efficiently served by such post-academic institutions as electronically administered degree programmes (a.k.a. diploma mills) or privately funded science parks that rent space on university campuses. We would seem, then, to be heading for a world where the pursuit of knowledge is de-professionalized and perhaps even de-skilled, as the teaching and research functions of the university are subject to increasingly polarized demands. For some this institutional meltdown is returning us to the liberating conditions of the original industrial revolution. According to this line of thought, academic disciplines are like medieval guilds that restrict free trade: in this case, trade in knowledge. Yet, there is also reason to believe that both business and government are slowly rediscovering what academics have traditionally done better than anyone else, namely, to give a shape and direction to entire bodies of knowledge.

Knowledge managers make much of the frustration that the pioneering scientists felt within the disciplinary confines of their home universities. Yet, it was the subsequent establishment of academic departments and degree programmes that ultimately ensured that these fields, which may have been originally interdisciplinary (see DISCIPLINARITY VERSUS INTERDISCIPLINARITY) or even transdisciplinary, remained in the public domain as scientific knowledge, and not converted into trade secrets and other bits of intellectual real estate.

The combined commitment to efficiency, systematicity and publicity point to the institutional uniqueness of universities. These three virtues are most clearly realized in the design of the curriculum, which routinely forces academics – both for purposes of general education and specialized training – to organize innovative and traditional knowledge into a coherent whole that then can be disseminated in a logical fashion to many students of varying backgrounds over a short time (including a period in which performance is evaluated). This routinization, often derided as "scholasticism", provides an important institutional safeguard against the problem of what knowledge managers call "corporate amnesia", the negative by-product of quickly formed, flexibly organized associations of providers and clients. (See COMMON SENSE VERSUS COLLECTIVE MEMORY.) While the existence of these nimble networks has enabled the business community to adapt to a changing competitive environment, the only knowledge traces they leave are those embodied in their joint products. For, once its mission is accomplished, a network's human nodes simply disperse and connect with other nodes to form new networks in pursuit of new projects. (See KNOWLEDGE SOCIETY.)

The precedent for this diabolical situation is captured by the term "market failure", which is the economist's way of talking about goods that markets fail to generate because no one finds it in their interest to produce them. This is because the cost of producing the goods can never be completely recovered in profits. In welfare economics, market failure defines the frontier where state provision of public goods begins. Similarly, we may speak of the role of universities in redressing *network failure* by reproducing and extending knowledge that might otherwise be lost through network dispersion.

Knowledge managers have yet to realize the full significance of universities in this capacity because they tend to diagnose network failure much too locally, as mere instances of "knowledge hoarding". The idea here is that companies become dependent on the services of certain employees – often information technology personnel – who do not make their knowledge directly available. We are then asked to envisage these human nodes as blocking the flow of information in the network by refusing to share what they know with the other nodes. Thus, the knowledge hoarder appears as a moral failure who needs to be taught greater concern for her colleagues. Little is said about the emergence of knowledge hoarding as a defensive strategy for remaining employed or even employable in the knowledge economy's volatile labour market.

The targeting of the individual knowledge hoarder by knowledge managers aims to ensure that firms receive an adequate return on their investments, as measured by the clients, contacts or Web links that employees accumulate. It is very much the point of view of managers trying to keep their firms afloat. However, from SOCIAL EPISTEMOLOGY's more global perspective, the tendency of knowledge to escape from its formative networks is a positive market mechanism for counteracting the *corporate* hoarding of knowledge, which could result in that ultimate blockage of free exchange, a monopoly.

In this context, the university institutionalizes "knowledge escape" so as to redistribute the corporate advantage accumulated in a firm's staff, databases and intellectual property. Classically this task has involved synthesizing disparate cases from their original contexts of discovery and inferring larger explanatory principles, which are then subject to further study and ultimately dissemination through teaching and publication. Nowadays this strategy extends beyond the contemplation of nature's design to troubleshooting and reverse-engineering products that may lead to their improvement and ultimately even their replacement.

FURTHER READING

J. D. Bernal, *The Social Function of Science* (1939).

G. Delanty, *Challenging Knowledge* (2001).

P. Drucker, *Post-Capitalist Society* (1993).

S. Fuller, *Knowledge Management Foundations* (2002).

M. Gibbons *et al.*, *The New Production of Knowledge* (1994).

E. Krause, *The Death of the Guilds* (1996).

F. Machlup, *The Production and Distribution of Knowledge* (1962–80).

F. Machlup & U. Mansfield (eds), *The Study of Information* (1983).

H. Simon, *The Sciences of the Artificial* (1977).

KNOWLEDGE POLICY

K nowledge policy differs from conventional science policy by recognizing that policy is always being made, even when the status quo is maintained, or, as Popper (see **KUHN, POPPER AND LOGICAL POSITIVISM**) might say, induction rules. In the case of science, such *institutional inertia* can have significant consequences. It underlies the self-organizing, self-selecting and self-stratifying processes associated with the various levels at which peer review occurs in science. Originally, peer review was limited to the publication of completed research but in the twentieth century, once science was subsumed under the state, peer review spread to cover the funds required even to be eligible to do research. The result is an ever expanding and interlocking system of elites, for which Robert Merton coined the euphemism "the principle of cumulative advantage", whereby you cannot do research unless you have been part of a group that has done research. It is tantamount to a providential vision of history of science that would have been familiar to the early modern purveyors of what Max Weber called the "Protestant Ethic": the dominant strands of scientific research would not be so well resourced and efficacious if they were not doing something right – even if we cannot as yet specify their target realities. In this context, the maxim that scientific research does not experience diminishing marginal returns on investment acts as an article of faith with trivially true consequences, since *any* research funded for *enough* time will yield *some* benefit. At the same time, this maxim could be invoked to redistribute resources to a wider array of scientific projects. In the name of **EPISTEMIC JUSTICE**, Fuller's version of social epistemology supports the redistributionist interpretation of the maxim.

Conventional science policy tends to be problem-centred without evaluating the discipline-based knowledge relevant to addressing the problems. (See **DISCIPLINARITY VERSUS INTERDISCIPLINARITY**.) Indeed, the science policy analyst rarely figures in *discovering* or *constructing* problems; they are simply treated as given. In contrast, knowledge policy critically examines the maintenance of institutional inertia: why don't research priorities change more often and more radically? Why do problems arise in certain contexts and not others, especially why is there more competition for resources within a discipline than between disciplines? These questions are addressed on the basis of three presumptions that take seriously the normative (see **NORMATIVITY**) implications of the social constructivist (see **SOCIAL CONSTRUCTIVISM**) premises of **SCIENCE AND TECHNOLOGY STUDIES**:

- *The dialectical presumption*: The scientific study of science will probably serve to alter the conduct of science in the long run, in so far as science has reached its current state largely through an absence of such reflexive scrutiny.
- *The conventionality presumption*: Research methodologies and disciplinary differences continue to be maintained only because no concerted effort is made to change them, not because they are underwritten by the laws of reason or nature.
- *The democratic presumption*: The fact that science can be studied scientifically by people who are themselves not credentialed in the science under study suggests that science can be scrutinized and evaluated by an appropriately informed lay public.

Together these presumptions highlight the collectively embodied and contingently maintained character of our knowledge practices, which are always eligible for change.

To address institutional inertia, the social epistemologist can begin by identifying the diverse interest groups that derive enough benefits, each in its own way, from the status quo so that there is little incentive to change. In response, the social epistemologist might periodically restructure the environments in which researchers compete for resources. For example, they might be put in direct competition with one another where they previously were not. Or, they may be required to incorporate the interests of another discipline in order to receive funding. This strategy draws on the principle of *epistemic fungibility*, whereby a research project is designed so as to obtain reasonably adequate results in rough proportion to the available funding. The logic of statistical research fits such a principle, since studying a representative or random sample constitutes value for money *vis-à-vis* studying the entire population from which the sample would be drawn. Finally, researchers may be forced to account for their findings, not only to their own discipline's practitioners but also to the practitioners of other disciplines and the lay public.

In manipulating these variables of knowledge production, the social epistemologist can ensure that disciplinary boundaries do not solidify into "natural kinds" and that the scientific community does not acquire rigidly defined class interests that impede communication both between disciplines and within society. Effective knowledge policy is ultimately an exercise in RHETORIC. Specifically, the social epistemologist must overcome the classical stereotypes of the philosopher (as Platonist) and the rhetorician (as Sophist). The philosopher invokes norms as an excuse for distancing herself from the people, who fail to meet her lofty standards. The rhetorician abandons norms for gimmicks that can secure short-term success for her client. The social epistemologist's way out of this stalemate is to realize that the normative is constitutively rhetorical, that is, no prescription can have force, if the people for whom it is intended refuse to obey it. This raises the question of whether knowledge policy really requires a meeting of minds or simply a confluence of behaviours. Only a philosophical conceit, backed by a dubious mental ontology, makes agreement on meanings, values and beliefs a necessary condition for coordinated action. Instead, parties to a knowledge policy decision need to realize that they must serve the interests of others *in order* to serve their own. That is, their diverse perspectives are causally entangled in a common fate, a *res publica*. (See FREE INQUIRY and UNIVERSITY.) Unfortunately, much public-policy thinking reifies zero-sum gamesmanship, illicitly presuming that opposing interests require opposing courses of action that result in one side succeeding at the expense of the other. But the complexity of the world order makes it more likely that, in the long term, both sides to a dispute will either win or lose together.

FURTHER READING

J. D. Bernal, *The Social Function of Science* (1939).
P. Feyerabend, *Science in a Free Society* (1979).
S. Fuller, *Social Epistemology* (1988).
S. Fuller & J. Collier, *Philosophy, Rhetoric and the End of Knowledge* (2004).
M. Gibbons *et al.*, *The New Production of Knowledge* (1994).
P. Kitcher, *Science, Truth and Democracy* (2001).
F. Machlup, *The Production and Distribution of Knowledge* (1962–80).
F. Machlup & U. Mansfield (eds), *The Study of Information* (1983).
K. Mannheim, *Man and Society in an Age of Reconstruction* (1940).
R. K. Merton, *The Sociology of Science* (1977).
P. Mirowski & E.-M. Sent (eds), *Science Bought and Sold* (2002).
W. Schaefer (ed.), *Finalization in Science* (1984).

KNOWLEDGE SOCIETY

Talk of a "knowledge society" (Nico Stehr) and its corresponding study of "epistemic sociology" (Karin Knorr-Cetina) is diametrically opposed to the spirit of **SOCIAL EPISTEMOLOGY**. It is no secret that the upbeat character of most discussions of "modernity" and "modernization" have been due to the special status accorded to science and technology. The same applies to discussions of **POST-MODERNISM**, whose roots in the works of Daniel Bell and Jean-François Lyotard in the 1970s are identical to those of the knowledge society. From the standpoint of social epistemology, the postmodern valorization of science and technology (which usually means *information* technology, that is, the commodification and routinization of scientific knowledge) amounts to little more than confirming normative status on empirical tendencies whose ultimate significance has yet to be fully fathomed. (See **INFORMATION SCIENCE**.)

These tendencies include the increasing percentage of state and corporate budgets devoted to scientific research but more importantly the increasing appeal to scientific concepts and arguments to justify non-scientific beliefs and actions, and the increasing use of science and technology indicators as measures of social and economic superiority in the international arena. At the very least, they bear the imprint of an academic or otherwise intellectual mindset not so different from that of the average knowledge society analyst. Thus, when Bell, Lyotard and, in the post-Cold War era, Francis Fukuyama point to the "irreversibility" of the spread of science and technology, they are simply admitting that they do not know how to stop the spread of what they hope to be a generally beneficial trend, since their fellow "knowledge workers" are bound to benefit personally from the development. In a related but more critical spirit, the sociologist Alvin Gouldner argued that this obvious convergence between the interests of the analyst and the analysed, who together form an increasing percentage of the entire workforce, signalled a second-best solution to the crisis of advanced capitalism for which the collective ownership of the means of production would have been the first-best solution. Gouldner wishfully called this "flawed universal class" the "culture of critical discourse".

In sum, the knowledge society is what advanced capitalism looks like to intellectuals, once they have been assimilated into its mode of production: a classic case of what economists call the "internalization of a negative externality". Since Wilhelm von Humboldt's first bold attempts to co-opt the Enlightenment into the **UNIVERSITY** in 1810, intellectuals have gradually evolved from alienated critics outside the system to professional academics whose peer sanctioned **CRITICISM** provides the basis for the credentialing process that structures modern social relations. The subtlety of this transition has been assured by an overlay of two moments of feudalism: the first, that of the credentialing process itself, which in its expansion has increasingly become a symbol of social frustration; the second, that of the new intellectual property regime, which will follow in the wake of the academic credentials monopoly being destroyed by a new set of "critical outsiders", or *infopreneurs* (a contraction of "information entrepreneur").

Infopreneurs earn a living by combining written materials from disparate sources and then distributing them to users whom the original authors would not have otherwise reached. In effect, they creatively destroy textual integrity and authorial intent. The rise of infopreneurship reflects the new incapacities and capacities created by the knowledge society. On the one hand, the surfeit of available texts often makes it difficult to access exactly what one needs to know without expert guidance (see EXPERTISE); on the other hand, the ease with which texts can be either photocopied or cut-and-pasted in cyberspace has removed most of the material obstacles to customizing information to users' needs. One common and legally contested form of infopreneurship is the course pack that university instructors compile to provide students with selected chapters from recent books. Despite the tendency to see infopreneurs as parasites, it is worth recalling that before early-nineteenth-century German Romanticism, "authorship" was based more on the authority carried by the writing, as we think of editorship today, than the writer's own originality.

The story of the knowledge society is one of large-scale historical deception, mostly self-imposed by those who are paid to be in a position to know better. Sometimes one need only step back a generation to see the deception at work. The difference in emphasis between two of the original knowledge society gurus, Bell and Lyotard, proves very instructive.

Bell's image of "intellectual technologies" enabling an increasingly observant administrative state to curb the excesses of advanced capitalism was clearly grounded in Keynesian economics and the subsequent growth of the welfare–warfare state in the Cold War. Bell's "intelligent system" was a top-down processor, be it the central government or a computer model of the mind. Whatever else one may wish to say about Bell's vision of post-industrial society, it was designed in large part to rationalize or contain the effects of capitalism, so that it produced a sufficient level of prosperity without destabilizing the balance of power between and within nations.

However, the end of the Cold War has resulted in a new vision of the knowledge society. What Bell had regarded as signs of intelligent life in the social system were seen by Lyotard as misguided acts of will to disrupt what turns out to be knowledge's naturally fragmented and fluctuating state. The dominant image of this revised knowledge society is that of the market, or a "parallel distributed processing unit", to quote the corresponding model of brain. Computers are themselves envisaged as many personal terminals connected together in a network rather than all to one mainframe generator. Even computer languages are now valued less for their algorithmic powers than for the conceptual spaces left open by their incompleteness and undecidability. Unsurprisingly, John Maynard Keynes's main opponent, Friedrich Hayek, was among the very first to have interrelated the political, economic and psychological aspects of this new decentralized image of knowledge society. Moreover, two other godfathers of today's image of the knowledge society, the phenomenologist Alfred Schutz and the management theorist Peter Drucker, were trained economists and frequenters of the Hayek Circle in Vienna in the 1930s. (See **SOCIAL CONSTRUCTIVISM**.) Indeed, virtually all the intellectual components of the knowledge society were already in place by the eve of Nazism, although they were only brought to fruition with the demise of communism.

The most disturbing feature of the historical amnesia that marks today's enthusiasm for the knowledge society is the ease with which what is essentially a purified and sanitized version of free-market capitalism is presented as a revolutionary moment in the history of social relations, comparable, say, to the first wave of the industrial revolution. Consider that celebrated theorist of "informationalism", Manuel Castells, whose three-volume *The Information Age* has been compared to Marx's *Capital* and Max Weber's *Economy and Society*. In calling ours a "network society", Castells stresses the reduction of social norms to the recognition that several parties may realize their goals by temporarily acting in a concerted fashion, which in turn defines a specific network. Stripped of Castells's tables and jargon, this is little more than the definition of **NORMATIVITY** put forward by Hayek's Austrian school, which provides the intellectual foundation of contemporary neoliberalism. The Austrians had drawn a sharp distinction between *dispersed* and *divided* labour, the former varying across spacetime and the latter not. According to Austrian thinking, the idea that labour is optimally divided makes sense only if the design of a factory is projected on society at large (i.e. the route from Adam Smith to Émile Durkheim). In that case, skill corresponds to a relatively fixed sense of social status. However, in a purely capitalist order unfettered by feudal vestiges and hence open to a competitive labour market, skill becomes nothing more than scarce locally relevant knowledge, the value of which may change (and may even be converted to non-human capital) according to market conditions. Thus, your knowledge is most valuable if it complements that of others in your immediate situation, thereby enabling all of you to collaborate in activities that will benefit each of you differently.

The fate of labour in Castells's network society differs from this perspective only in the role assigned to computerization and the increasing ease with which one's interests and situational relevance may change. However, Castells adds another wrinkle to the neo-liberal story, since the Austrians did not anticipate the robustness of social movements that use the network infrastructure to promote longer-term interests that counter those of the dominant networkers at any given time. In that sense, Castells's neo-liberal future manages to find space for a salutary backlash: the sort of "have your cake and eat it too" scenario that may placate transnational policy-makers, while giving hope to virtual revolutionaries, such as the anarchist Antonio Negri.

Knowledge society discourse epitomizes the Orwellian regime of Newspeak, which threatens to erase the intuitions that originally made compelling the idea of the SOCIAL SCIENCES as a body of knowledge distinct from both the humanities and the natural sciences. In its wake has emerged "KNOWLEDGE MANAGEMENT", an oxymoron in earlier times but now a field that promises to teach universities – formerly the centres of societal knowledge production – how to collectivize their intelligence effectively as, say, a fast-food franchise routinely does. Like other totalitarian ideologies, from Nazism to Maoism, this one involves a radical reversal of values, typically a subordination of the elites to the vulgar through the complicity of disenfranchised members of the elite. Thus, academic researchers on short-term contracts, and hence with tenuous loyalties to universities, are in the forefront of ushering this new era by levelling the distinction between academic knowledge and other cognitively adaptive responses to the environment.

Perhaps the best display of knowledge society Newspeak is the Glossary to *The New Production of Knowledge* (1994), a multinational collaboration that is the single most influential academic work in European science policy circles since the end of the Cold War. The notoriety of this book comes largely from the distinction between "Mode 1" and "Mode 2" knowledge production as a roughly two-stage process that marks the transition from knowledge being driven by internal to external mechanisms. *Prima facie* the distinction captures the difference between enquiry governed by strictly academic interests and by more socially relevant interests. But in practice, the scope of Mode 1 is much narrower than the university – closer to a Kuhnian paradigm – and Mode 2 is much more diffuse than "relevance" normally connotes – closer to a market attractor. As a result, the university is reduced from an institution with the aim of unifying knowledge to a convenient physical space that enables the "communication" of various knowledge interests. Here "communication" resonates both of a Habermasian "ideal speech situation" for establishing CONSENSUS and a Hayekian "clearing house" for setting prices. Table 1 lists the major terms in "Modespeak", alongside their *prima facie* innocent meanings ("not this ...") and their more sinister practical ones ("but that ...").

Modespeak	Not this ...	But that ...
"Codified/tacit knowledge" (conversion principle)	Performance/competence (creativity)	Fixed/variable capital (knowledge management)
"Context of application"	Applied research	Client-centred research
"Globalization"	Universalization	Specialization
"Heterogeneity"	Anti-homogeneity	Anti-autonomy
"Hybrid agora/forum" (university redefined)	Knowledge unifier	Knowledge advertiser
"Informatization of society"	Knowledge mediates social relations	Knowledge alienated from individuals
"Knowledge industries"	University privileged	University de-privileged
"Massification of higher education"	Knowledge adds value	Knowledge devalued
"Pluralization of elites"	Knowledge workers respected	Knowledge workers modularized
"Reflexivity"	Critical of context	Adaptive to context
"Social capital"	Public good	Corporate property
"Social distribution of knowledge"	Integrated unit (institution)	Dispersed network (interaction)
"Socially robust knowledge"	Universally resilient knowledge (science)	Locally plastic knowledge (culture)
"Technology transfer"	Academia legitimates industry (nineteenth century)	Academia services industry (twenty-first century)
"Transdisciplinarity"	Interdisciplinarity	Antidisciplinarity

Table 1. "Modespeak": knowledge society Newspeak.

The overall impression conveyed by this table is that some recognizably capital-ist, and even pre-capitalist, forms of domination are masked by a pluralist RHETORIC that disperses power and responsibility. Indicative of the workings of Modespeak is the translation effected in the first row of Table 1: "codified/tacit knowledge". What academics routinely celebrate as our capacity "to know more than we can tell" appears as a nightmare to managers trying to maintain the corporate knowl-edge base in the face of mobile workers in a flexible economy. Not surprisingly, then, when academics advise managers that their competence is not reducible to their performance, managers conclude that they must find ways of replacing that competence with a more reliable source of performance that can be made a permanent feature of corporate memory, or what Marx called "fixed capital". In that case, employees are best regarded as transient sources of knowledge – or "variable capital" – that need to be captured while they are still on site. Towards this end, computerized expert systems have offered much promise to a business world that, for the most part, has historically succeeded by modelling the human mind only on a need-to-know basis.

The two most insidious features of knowledge society Newspeak are: (i) the devaluation of knowledge, such that all organizations are now said to be in the business of producing knowledge in the same sense; (ii) the assimilation of democratic processes to market processes. This feature is symbolized in the use of the words "agora" and "forum", the Greek and Latin words for the physical space in ancient cities where both business and politics were conducted. This image of a common space is then used to create a blurred image of the public character of knowledge, leading to the following confusions: free speech is confused with advertising (see FREE ENQUIRY), CRITICISM with "niche differentiation", the public interest with an array of "revealed preferences", voting with trading, power with sales, RATIONALITY with efficiency, and PROGRESS with profits.

FURTHER READING

D. Bell, *The Coming of Post-Industrial Society* (1973).
M. Castells, *The Information Age* (1996–8).
G. Delanty, *Challenging Knowledge* (2001).
P. Drucker, *Post-Capitalist Society* (1993).
S. Fuller, *The Governance of Science* (2000).
S. Fuller, *Knowledge Management Foundations* (2002).
M. Gibbons *et al.*, *The New Production of Knowledge* (1994).
A. Gouldner, *The Future of Intellectuals and the Rise of the New Class* (1979).
F. Hayek, "The Use of Knowledge in Society" (1945).
K. Knorr-Cetina, *Epistemic Cultures* (1999).
J.-F. Lyotard, *The Postmodern Condition* (1983).
F. Machlup, *The Production and Distribution of Knowledge* (1962–80).
P. Mirowski, *Machine Dreams: Economics Becomes a Cyborg Science* (2002).
W. Schaefer (ed.), *Finalization in Science* (1984).
A. Schutz, "The Well-Informed Citizen" (1964).
N. Stehr, *Knowledge Societies* (1994).

KUHN, POPPER AND LOGICAL POSITIVISM

"**K**uhn, Popper and logical positivism" refers to an intellectual trajectory from which philosophy has arguably exerted its greatest cross-disciplinary influence in the second half of the twentieth century. At the very least, Thomas Kuhn's *The Structure of Scientific Revolutions* is generally acknowledged as the most influential single book on the nature of science in this period. It continues to be popular with humanists and social scientists, although Kuhn thought he had nothing of interest to say to them, except that their knowledge pursuits failed to fit his cyclical model of normal and revolutionary science. (See SCIENCE AS A SOCIAL MOVEMENT.) Interestingly, Kuhn singularly failed to persuade the physicists in whose subject he was professionally trained and whose history provides the primary data for his model. Nevertheless, it must be admitted that *Structure* is a remarkably self-exemplifying text, since Kuhn correctly – if again unwittingly – identified the key psychosocial mechanism responsible for his own book's success.

If, as Socrates believed, the recognition of ignorance is the first step to wisdom, then *Structure* has proved to be an obstruction. The book did much to establish the relevance of the history of science to an understanding of contemporary science, but without encouraging its readers to check the accuracy or applicability of Kuhn's particular version. Readers claim to have found in Kuhn's account of paradigm formation a compelling model for their own disciplines. Typically these readers come to *Structure* with a rather patchy and personalized understanding of the histories of their own disciplines. More importantly, they have no other general account of the history of science with which to compare Kuhn's account or, when they do, the alternative account is a highly simplified and judgemental version of positivism that casts their own disciplines in a harshly negative light. Not surprisingly, they quickly embrace Kuhn and never look back.

Kuhn appeared to provide a salutary recipe for turning one's activities into a science. One only had to obtain agreement on a common theoretical and methodological framework within which permissible problems and their solutions are clearly defined: in a word, a paradigm. In contrast, positivism in its vulgarized form seemed to demand that a science also exercise instrumental control over some part of the natural world. This additional requirement proved to be a step too far for most humanists and social scientists. Not only did they lack the conceptual and material resources to render their enquiries "instrumental" in the relevant sense, but many also objected to the moral implications of such a worldview when applied to human beings. As it happens, the latter turns out to be not so far from Kuhn's own interest in defining PROGRESS in science by referring only to criteria that the scientists themselves have designed. To many of Kuhn's philosophical opponents, including such students of Popper as Imre Lakatos and Paul Feyerabend, this move smacked of RELATIVISM. However, it was made in the same spirit that had motivated the logical positivists to lay down principles of verification, falsification and operationalization. Despite their technical differences, these criteria and principles all presuppose that scientists define the rules of their own game, one that is insulated from the causes and effects of the larger reality in which they are embedded.

Kuhn and the logical positivists are often portrayed as holding diametrically opposed views. Basically, Kuhn defined science historically and sociologically, whereas the positivists defined it logically and empirically. However, this difference is relatively superficial *vis-à-vis* their commonalities. Indeed, the doyen of logical positivism, Rudolf Carnap, regarded the project of *Structure* as complementing his own. He had no problem including the book as part of the International Encyclopedia of Unified Science, positivism's collective American legacy. Moreover, Kuhn increasingly oriented his research towards technical problems in analytic philosophy of mind and language, which was how the positivist project flourished in the American academy. (See ANALYTIC SOCIAL EPISTEMOLOGY.)

Neither Kuhn nor the positivists ever fully acknowledged the technological dimension of modern science, where science most naturally interfaces with our pre-scientific understanding of reality. Even when Kuhn and the positivists wrote about scientific experiments, their focus remained fixed on the role of experiments in generating data or testing theories, not on their material character. Indeed, Kuhn and the positivists made a point of not asking whether the instruments used in experiments were inspired and/or applied in a military-industrial setting outside the experimental context. From a psychiatric standpoint, the accounts of science advanced by Kuhn and the logical positivists were what a Freudian would call "reaction formations" in response to traumas that had dealt severe blows to their normative ideals of science. The traumas were the twentieth century's two world wars. In their early 20s, Carnap had served in the First World War and Kuhn in the Second World War. Both began life as aspiring physicists, but physics failed them in wartime. The discipline that they understood to be natural philosophy by more exact means turned out to be a compliant accessory to mass destruction. In response, both promoted excessively idealized visions of science that were the opposite of the tendencies they rejected in the science of their day.

Carnap had been inspired by the Einsteinian revolution, in which science broke genuinely new philosophical ground by reconceptualizing the nature of space and time. However, he was disappointed by the ease with which, less than a decade later, the German physics community fell into line with the patriotic sentiments of practitioners of the inferior science of chemistry to enlist in the Kaiser's cause.

In response, Carnap attempted to justify physical knowledge without making any reference to its applications. His model was the successful attempt by mathematicians to declare disciplinary independence from physics and engineering in the nineteenth century by rediscovering their Euclidean roots in deductive proof theory. Here Carnap had been influenced by his old teacher Gottlob Frege and especially his fellow war veteran, Ludwig Wittgenstein, a self-loathing engineer who was heir to Austria's leading steel-making family. In the interwar years, Wittgenstein intermittently attended the meetings of the Vienna Circle in which logical positivism's tenets were crystallized.

Kuhn's original inspiration, interests and ultimate disillusionment were similar to Carnap's. Kuhn spent the Second World War jamming German radar signals in East Anglia and thereafter resolved not to pursue a career in physics once he completed his PhD. Physics in its nascent "big science" mode no longer held its original attraction, and so he moved to the history and philosophy of science. Not surprisingly, Kuhn eventually admitted that he was interested in the history of science solely as a sustained instance of pure enquiry (not, say, as an engine of wealth production or a bulwark of national defence). This was in response to a question about whether he ever felt compelled to change his model in light of the changes in the scale and scope of the physical sciences in the second half of the twentieth century. After all, virtually all of Kuhn's historical examples had been taken from the period 1620 to 1920, although Kuhn himself was professionally trained in more recent developments. Interestingly, Kuhn not only felt no need to revise his perspective but he equally felt no need to criticize contemporary science for failing to adhere to his account. It fell to others such as Jerome Ravetz and the German "finalizationists" to follow those leads, typically without Kuhn's support and sometimes with his active opposition.

Kuhn's successful disengagement from CRITICISM of science based on his work, and even the criticism that others made of his work, reflected his privileged academic position. This privilege was, in turn, rooted in his long-term mentorship under Harvard President James Bryant Conant, a major architect of US Cold War science policy and the person to whom *Structure* is dedicated. Conant enabled the disenchanted Kuhn to make the transition from physics to the humanities by finding him a job in the newly created General Education in Science programe, where *Structure*'s theses were honed. For Conant, the scientific idealism of Kuhn and other disenchanted young physicists (e.g. Gerald Holton) was a key ideological component in the appeasement of non-scientists, in an age when science was to play an increasingly formidable role in public affairs. Kuhn's refusal to back self-declared Kuhnians who denounced science's complicity in the military-industrial complex may be plausibly read as tacit endorsement of Conant's "dirty hands" image of a politically compromised science as nonetheless a stabilizing force in a world on the brink of nuclear war.

The differences between Kuhn and his positivist forebears lie in their specific reaction formations. Carnap and his fellow logical positivists retreated to mathematical formalism, while Kuhn and most of the current generation of SCIENCE AND TECHNOLOGY STUDIES practitioners have had recourse to historiographical (see HISTORIOGRAPHY) purism. The clearest symptom of this purism is a studied refusal to involve present-day judgements in accounts of past science. Before Kuhn, it had been common to narrate the history of science in terms of a mix of obstacles and breakthroughs that eventuate in today's knowledge, which, albeit imperfect, is presumed to be the best yet. After Kuhn, however, one tells the history entirely from the standpoint of the original agents, without passing judgement on the long-term significance of their actions. Indeed, for Kuhn, a proper understanding of a science's significance is possible only once its major disputes have been resolved, and the historian arrives on the scene as a spectator, not a participant. In the annals of Kuhn criticism, this reaction formation has been philosophized as the incommensurability thesis. While this thesis has helped to undermine the sorts of triumphalist Whig histories that scientists have told to raise funds and exert influence, it has carried an important cost: historical understanding would seem to require the abandonment of one's own worldview. Kuhn himself compared the switching back and forth between the past and the present to bilingualism. (See TRANSLATION.)

The incommensurability thesis operates also at a deeper level that helps to explain *Structure*'s success. For Kuhn, the ability to understand the world through two radically different paradigms is not only a skill imparted to fledgling historians of science, but also a mental capacity that was originally present in such scientific revolutionaries as Galileo and Einstein. Kuhn's interesting and controversial point here is that very few scientists actually have this capacity because it is not part of their normal training. Consequently, the main cause of revolutionary change in science is that subsequent generations are taught only the new and not the old paradigm. This process does not happen overnight, but its implications are clear. Argumentation in science sways uncommitted spectators, especially if they are young or newcomers to the field. It does not change the minds of the scientific principals themselves. The sheer fact that newcomers have not yet personally invested in the old paradigm is typically sufficient to make them open to a radical change in direction. From that perspective, matters of tradition, track record, accumulated wisdom and presumption are myths perpetuated in scientific textbooks to indoctrinate the young in the dominant paradigm. However, as Kuhn points out, these myths need to be reinvented after each scientific revolution, as in the periodic rewriting of history recounted in Orwell's *1984*.

When considering the technically false versions of their collective history that scientists promote among themselves and in the larger public – a version that the logical positivists largely rationalized – Kuhn adopted an attitude similar to Freud's towards his patients. Kuhn did not denounce scientists for their self-serving historiography but rather tried to understand its function as a coping mechanism for a practice whose maintenance requires the violation of its avowed principles. After all, science advertises itself as the epitome of rationality, which at the very least implies that people will change their minds in the face of logic and evidence. However, if scientists literally acted on such scruples, then the research frontier would change too often for any clear sense of progress to be registered. New ideas in their initial formulation can rarely survive critical scrutiny, so it becomes important that people sympathetic to those ideas are given an opportunity to develop them. (See FREE ENQUIRY.) Scientific revolutions ultimately occur because the minds of *different* people start to matter. Colleagues resistant to new ideas eventually retire, while the younger, more receptive colleagues take over the field. Such intergenerational change implies that very few people ever really need to change their minds for major conceptual change to occur in science. Although Kuhn confined his own development of this insight to the cognitive processes by which new recruits acquire a paradigm, the idea that new lines of enquiry require new personnel pointed towards a more biologically inspired, even Darwinian-selectionist, model of scientific change. In effect Kuhn has helped to erase a traditional mark of the human in the animal kingdom, namely, that our ideas can live and die in our stead. (See EVOLUTION.)

Kuhn's great nemesis, Karl Popper, strenuously objected to the profoundly pessimistic vision of human rationality depicted in *Structure*. While Popper granted that revolutionaries such as Galileo and Einstein were more the exception than the rule in the history of science, he interpreted what Kuhn benignly called "normal science" as a moral failure, not a successful adaptation strategy. Unfortunately, 40 years later, Kuhn has had the last laugh. The story of *Structure*'s reception in the philosophical community is a tale of two halves, which together provide a striking confirmation of his own generation-based account of intellectual change. The first twenty years consisted of an array of negative responses, ranging from Popperian high dudgeon to more pedantic charges of ambiguity and inconsistency. In the past twenty years, however, a new generation has come to dominate science and technology studies. They take *Structure* as the unproblematic foundation for their enquiries, as if the original criticisms had never been made. Certainly Kuhn never answered those criticisms, and the current generation is sufficiently indebted to *Structure*'s conceptual framework not to want to revive the criticisms.

In their "Kuhnified" state, philosophers of science are prone to see themselves as "underlabourers", who clarify and defend but never question the dominant paradigms, unless the scientists themselves have done so first. The general philosophy of science pursued by Popper, the positivists and even Kuhn himself has given way to multiple philosophies of the special sciences. Overriding concerns about RATIONALITY and progress have been replaced by more technical analyses of the relationship between evidence and inference in particular fields. Even today's overheated turf battles between philosophers and sociologists of science in the SCIENCE WARS turn on little more than who is more properly immersed in the scientific practices under investigation. Does taking a few science courses measure up to spending a few months observing a laboratory? The old idea that an outsider might criticize science for failing its own publicly avowed standards is virtually unthinkable today. For those who have inherited Kuhn's Cold War belief that normal science is a bulwark in a volatile world, then it is only to be expected that philosophers today will be quicker to criticize creationists for violating evolutionary strictures than evolutionists for violating more general scientific criteria of proof and explanation, an activity for which Popper and the positivists had been notorious.

In sum, *Structure* has enabled institutionally threatened disciplines to legitimize themselves as "sciences", at the cost of deflecting discussion from the larger normative questions surrounding science's place in contemporary society. In this sense, Kuhn may be said to have had a repressive effect. But it is an effect that can be detected only if we retain the pre-Kuhnian idea that intellectual life harbours a collective memory (see COMMON SENSE VERSUS COLLECTIVE MEMORY) that is sustained across generations, often in spite of what most individuals find convenient to believe. After all, the social psychology that underwrites a Kuhnian paradigm is none other than the experimental demonstrations of group conformity that were in vogue during the Cold War.

FURTHER READING

A. J. Ayer, *Language, Truth and Logic* (1936).
S. Fuller, *Thomas Kuhn* (2000).
S. Fuller, *Kuhn vs Popper* (2003).
M. Hacohen, *Karl Popper* (2000).
J. Kadvany, *Imre Lakatos and the Guises of Reason* (2001).
T. S. Kuhn, *The Structure of Scientific Revolutions* (1970).
T. S. Kuhn, *The Essential Tension*. Chicago (1977).
I. Lakatos & A. Musgrave (eds), *Criticism and the Growth of Knowledge* (1970).
J. Ravetz, *Scientific Knowledge and Its Social Problems* (1971).
G. Reisch, *How the Cold War Transformed the Philosophy of Science* (2005).
R. Sassower, *Popper's Legacy* (2006).
W. Schaefer (ed.), *Finalization in Science* (1984).
W. Shadish & S. Fuller (eds), *The Social Psychology of Science* (1994).
S. Toulmin, *Human Understanding* (1972).

MASS MEDIA

The idea of mass media originated with *propaganda*, a sixteenth-century Latin word for the Jesuits' counter-Reformation ideological campaign. Propaganda is a steady stream of consistent information from a credible source to a mass audience. It emerged from the classical epistemic basis for RHETORIC, namely, that truth is insufficient to convey import. In addition, a message must be conveyed frequently, or at least regularly, to appear reliable. (See TRUTH, RELIABILITY AND THE ENDS OF KNOWLEDGE.) The Protestants had been able to undermine the authority of the Roman Catholic Church simply by contradicting Catholic doctrines – in many different ways – without having to present a united front. For their part, the Catholics initially either ignored or dealt with the Protestants in a local fashion, but in either case without getting across the consistency and reasonableness of their own doctrine. The need to appear reliable through repeated airing of the same message served another function. We often forget that when the Bible was taken seriously as a historical document reporting unique events of lasting significance, the deterioration of the quality of evidence over time (through the inevitable mistranslations and textual corruptions) always created a demand for demonstrations of ancient truths by contemporary means that enable new audiences to re-enact for themselves the ideas that originally animated, say, the Old Testament Patriarchs, the Apostles or the Church Fathers. (See RELIGION and TRANSLATION.)

Jesuit propaganda aimed to address all of the above concerns, often by incorporating Protestant CRITICISM, typically in the form of converting a difference in kind to a difference in degree: moral absolutes and doctrinal allegiances became decisions taken under conditions of uncertainty between alternatives the truth of which only God knew for sure. In the history of propaganda theory, this is sometimes called *inoculation* because weaker strains of a potentially threatening influence – in this case, Protestantism – are promoted to those who would be harmed by stronger strains. Thus, in modern electoral politics, mainstream liberal and conservative parties repackage watered-down versions of, say, pro-ecology or anti-immigration politics to mitigate the effects of extreme versions of these views in democratic debate. At the same time, they stereotype those from whom they have borrowed as "unrealistic" and hence not worth taking seriously on their own terms. To be sure, inoculation, although undeniably manipulative, need not be sinister. Indeed, it is characteristic of the public intellectual as someone sufficiently secure in social status to present a reasoned version of an exceptionally unpopular point-of-view. Moreover, often it is only once the inoculating intellectual *qua* scapegoat has left the scene that public opinion comes round to accepting the content of her message, albeit expressed in a different form. (See **EXPLAINING THE COGNITIVE CONTENT OF SCIENCE**.)

The growth of mass media in the modern era is most directly tied to the value placed on the sheer quantity of people – voters, consumers, viewers – whose opinions matter to achieve some desired social effect. It is natural to think about this development in terms of activating the masses to assume a level of responsibility previously left to elites speaking on their behalf. A crucial transition, triggered by the eighteenth-century Enlightenment, came when responsibility for message content was shifted from producers to consumers. Thus, when not threatened with foreign invasion, modern states have preferred educating citizens to censoring publishers. While in this context it is natural to think about the emergence of national school and **UNIVERSITY** systems, an increasingly decisive role has been played by the establishment of the broadcasting media of radio, television and, most recently, the internet. These media, with which citizens are in contact not merely in youth but throughout their lives, have enabled unprecedented levels of experimentation and manipulation in the transmission of thought, the effects of which have been subject to intense statistical scrutiny with the advent of market research and public opinion polling in the 1920s. While the history of broadcasting has been, generally speaking, a matter of states trying to regulate, if not control, privately owned means of transmission, an early precedent was set by the British Broadcasting Corporation (BBC), which in 1927 had already nationalized wireless communication with the aim of "informing, educating and entertaining", a dedication to the audience's cognitive improvement that future broadcasters throughout the world have had to match, at least nominally.

As the mass media came to mediate all aspects of social life in the twentieth century, they also came under increasingly serious political and ethical scrutiny. However, the attempts at prescription and regulation have done surprisingly little to dampen the pace of technological **PROGRESS** that has driven developments in this domain, which by the 1960s had prompted the Canadian critic Marshall McLuhan to declare, "The medium is the message". Here we may distinguish a set of *modernist* and *postmodernist* (see **POSTMODERNISM**) worries about the mass media. Modernist concerns centre on the prevalence of entertaining over informing and entertaining, as well as the mass media's failure to present a balanced range of perspectives in its coverage. In contrast, postmodernist worries are focused on the blurring of the three seminal BBC functions, not least through the outright promotion of ideological conflict, even in areas where it might otherwise not thought to have existed. If the modernist worries that the mass media might lull audiences into a false consensus (see **CONSENSUS VERSUS DISSENT**), the postmodernist worries that they might manufacture discontent that generates unnecessary public involvement, simply in order to boost audience ratings.

Interestingly, this so-called postmodernist worry had been already voiced in the 1920s by the US journalist Walter Lippmann, and a decade later by the Viennese phenomenologist Alfred Schutz. For them, the sensory immediacy of the emerging mass media (i.e. radio, newsreels and tabloid newspapers) provided a false sense of empowerment, as people were too easily persuaded that they knew much more about the increasingly complex world of politics and economics than they really did, which in a democratic environment made them vulnerable to the flattery of demagogues. Read in light of the history of propaganda, Lippmann effectively offered a counter-Enlightenment (cf. counter-Reformation) approach to the mass media that stressed the communication skills of political leaders and other opinion-makers (or pundits like himself) to pacify mass audiences with sober, measured (if perhaps deceptive) accounts of current affairs that exuded an EXPER-TISE worthy of trust. However, it is worth observing that the staged exaggeration of differences in opinion for purposes of motivating judgement is not unique to the mass media, nor need its effects be as deleterious as Lippmann suggests. (See EPISTEMIC JUSTICE.) Indeed, a low-tech version is a staple of the dialectical method characteristic of liberal arts education, which perhaps survives most intact in the philosophy curriculum.

Perhaps the most epistemologically salient, yet controversial, phenomenon associated with the mass media in the twentieth century was what Elisabeth Noe-lle-Neumann called the "spiral of silence": a process that explains consensus formation as a largely unintended consequence in mass democracies. Noelle-Neumann's guiding insight was that people not only have opinions about various things but also opinions about the social environments in which such opinions are formed. This second-order knowledge takes on added significance in societies that regard themselves as free and open, and where public opinion is regularly sampled and reported. Noelle-Neumann's evidence base was drawn from Germany. A crucial but underrated feature of modern German history is its combination of very free-ranging discussions of democratic politics with relatively little legally sanctioned political participation, that is, until the 1920s, when the Weimar Republic provided Germans with their first taste of constitutional democracy.

The Weimar Constitution enacted a proactive policy of democratzation, licensing mass demonstrations and generally encouraging the organization of what would now be called special interest groups and identity politics. To be sure, this led to legislative gridlock, opening the door to Hitler's appeal to a German cultural identity that transcended internecine differences. This surprising result was made possible by a generally held second-order belief that any opinion not expressed was simply not held. This belief was based on the sound democratic principle that in an egalitarian public sphere, peers express themselves openly, be it for or against other expressed opinions. It follows that opinions not openly opposed are perceived as at least tolerable if not tacitly endorsed by the public. Such a spiral of silence was instrumental in the rise in Hitler's credibility. Critics of Nazism from academia and the intelligentsia often refrained from commenting directly on its outlandish racialist proposals for solving Germany's economic problems, regarding them as beyond serious political consideration. However, as Nazi support increased steadily over successive polls in the dozen years to Hitler's ascendancy, this silence apparently left the impression that the logic of the Nazi argument was unassailable but that politicians lacked the will to take it forward.

There are many lessons here for **SOCIAL EPISTEMOLOGY**, although only Fuller's version has pursued them at all. The main one is that intellectuals who officially endorse free speech and **FREE ENQUIRY** need to be more mindful of the democratization of judgement that inevitably results from such freedoms. Weimar intellectuals grossly overestimated their own authority once the populace were allowed to judge for themselves, not only in the voting booth but perhaps more importantly in public opinion polls. In particular, the intellectuals incorrectly presumed a **COMMON SENSE** of the true and the false, the plausible and the implausible, about Germany's plight after its defeat in the First World War. (This miscalculation was also formative in Karl Mannheim's **SOCIOLOGY OF KNOWLEDGE**, which specifically stressed the role in worldview of differences in generation and class.) Here one also needs to consider the role played by the right-wing media mogul Alfred Hugenberg, who deliberately boosted Hitler's public profile, which entailed the inclusion of Nazi views, despite their initially marginal status, among those regularly canvassed in surveys. Thus, people receptive to Nazi proposals but concerned about the lack of respectable public endorsement were encouraged by the opportunity that the pollsters provided for the expression of such views. This gives a new spin to the idea of the "silent majority", a phrase popularized by Richard Nixon in 1969 for those Americans who supported the Vietnam War but lacked an opportunity to express it. The difference is that the success of Nazism suggests that any of a number of majorities may be latent in a population, capable of being socially constructed (see **SOCIAL CONSTRUCTIVISM**) over time, once people are provided with an opportunity to express and develop a given set of opinions.

FURTHER READING

J. Franklin, *The Science of Conjecture* (2001).
S. Fuller, *Social Epistemology* (1988).
S. Fuller, *Knowledge Management Foundations* (2002).
S. Fuller, *The Intellectual* (2005).

S. Fuller & J. Collier, *Philosophy, Rhetoric and the End of Knowledge* (2004).
J. Habermas, *The Structural Transformation of the Public Sphere* (1989).
S. C. Jansen, *Censorship* (1991).
W. Lippmann, *Public Opinion* (1922).
K. Mannheim, *Ideology and Utopia* (1936).
E. Noelle-Neumann, *The Spiral of Silence* (1982).
A. Schutz, "The Well-Informed Citizen" (1964).
W. Shadish & S. Fuller (eds), *The Social Psychology of Science* (1994).
S. P. Turner, *Liberal Democracy 3.0* (2003).

MULTICULTURALISM

Multiculturalism is of special interest to **SOCIAL EPISTEMOLOGY** because it escapes the usual philosophical and sociological conceptions of knowledge. Multiculturalism is more than simply the recognition that there are distinct cultures, which would amount to little more than a "separate but equal" doctrine for the human condition. It further implies that these cultures stand in certain relationships to each other that may change as those relationships unfold in time and space. The epitome of this critical sense of multiculturalism is the political and legal debate surrounding affirmative action. (See **EPISTEMIC JUSTICE**.)

From a strictly historical standpoint, humanity has had little trouble tolerating the coexistence of diverse practices in one place, as well as the movement of people between places. Yet, our taken-for-granted notions of "culture" presuppose that such fluidity in the human condition is aberrant, if not pathological. Rootedness is presumed to be the norm. But this is to get matters exactly backwards. It is only by heightening levels of societal scrutiny and accountability – via capitalist expansion, on the one hand, and nationalist reaction, on the other – that the demand was created for people to behave uniformly over space in one time (universalism) and over time in one space (relativism). Double-entry bookkeeping and mandatory grammar classes symbolize this dual intensification. Such complementary demands had been salient during the period of European global hegemony, roughly, from 1760 to 1960, but are declining in importance in the twenty-first century. The sociohistorical relativity of our conception of culture – its "meta-relativist" status – has been overlooked, largely because we misinterpret the sociological character of philosophical distinctions such as **UNIVERSALISM VERSUS RELATIVISM**. They do not represent spontaneously recurring divisions in human thought, but rather the verbal residues of major attempts to arrest the flow of human activity.

Unfortunately, much of what passes for multiculturalism today is really better seen as *hyperculturalism*: an exaggerated – perhaps even essentialized – sense of cultural difference that tends unwittingly to incapacitate the people on whose behalf its advocates speak. Hyperculturalism has the following six characteristics:

1. Cultures correspond to geographical regions that only came into being with European colonial expansion. The result is a syncretistic conception of a region's cultural identity that combines practices that probably have never been part of any single individual's life. Talk of "Hindu nationalism" and "Afrocentrism" that presupposes the ontological integrity of "India" and "Africa", respectively, fall under this category.

2. Cultures have a strong sense of continuous identity over time. Not surprisingly, a culture's "Occidentalism" is often judged by the degree to which historical change is constitutive of its identity. The core Western cultures are defined as having exhibited a kind of directed change, or PROGRESS, which leaves behind most elements of cultural identity. However, to the hyperculturalist, this mark of "civilization" is a negative, not positive, feature of the West.

3. There are clear criteria for distinguishing one culture from another, and especially membership in a culture. These criteria usually presuppose that cultures are geographically discrete "homelands", with cultural identity determined by the birth of oneself and one's parents, and perhaps their progenitors.

4. Cultural differences are logically prior to differences in either class or gender. Such a homogeneous sense of cultural identity neglects any internally generated hierarchies. For example, the culture's external representatives may be those few who have received formal training in writing, a skill restricted to men of a certain class whose local power is then unwittingly reinforced in cross-cultural communication.

5. The historical authenticity of a cultural practice underwrites its relevance to the life circumstances of the current members of that culture. The adjective "indigenous" is often used in this context, especially when explaining failed attempts to integrate Western technologies in non-Western contexts. However, this talk reifies concrete power relations between the West and non-West into abstract epistemological distinctions between inherently Western and non-Western ways of knowing.

6. Only natives of a culture are authorized to speak on its behalf. Anyone else's voice is regarded as suspect because they have not immersed themselves in the life of that culture.

It is worth noting that, taken together, points 3 and 4 constitute the residue of *race* in the hyperculturalist's conception of culture. Nevertheless, hyperculturalism gains its initial plausibility as *relativism*, the second half of the dialectic with *universalism* that has dominated post-Kantian epistemology. Relativism remains lodged in the minds of both friends and foes of multiculturalism. The problems with this conception tend to arise during attempts to test non-Western knowledge claims by the empirical methods dominant in Western culture. Hyperculturalists are prone to pre-empt the testing process so that only accredited members of the relevant culture can pass judgement on the validity of one of its knowledge claims. While such assertions of autonomy – "You have your knowledge, we have ours" – play an important role in constructing a voice for traditionally suppressed (or *subaltern*) groups, to tie one's academic politics exclusively to the maintenance of this voice is to court two undesirable prospects. In a liberal culture, it invites the familiar pattern of academic cooptation: say, a "Centre for Black Studies" that coexists peacefully with all the other departments, which themselves remain unchanged. In a more reactionary culture, it reinforces prejudices that (in this case) blacks are beyond redemption by Western ways of knowing and should therefore be cut off entirely.

To avoid being boxed into this rhetorical corner, multiculturalists must realize that any "test" of their claims need not be one-sided. If "non-Western" forms of knowledge do not appear valid by "Western" methods, then that could just as easily reflect poorly on the testing methods as on the knowledge claims being tested. In other words, Western methods may be not simply inappropriate (as a relativist might claim) but wrong (as a universalist might claim). Fuller's version of social epistemology aims to replace the relativist picture of culture with a more "interpenetrative" one that allows for this kind of mutual CRITICISM and a subsequent reconstruction of testing as a consensual form of social interaction. Rather than claiming to possess radically autonomous forms of knowledge, multiculturalism would do better to adopt FEMINISM's *standpoint* line that the West's neglect of the subaltern's epistemic perspective reflects a substantial flaw in the West's own mode of knowledge production.

Multiculturalism is typically defended as enabling cultural minorities to develop their own voices in the wider society. What is not sufficiently stressed is multiculturalism's role in re-educating cultural *majorities*, causing them to change their fundamental beliefs, even about a form of knowledge as seemingly universal as natural science. *Pace* hyperculturalists, epistemic credibility is less to do with the authenticity of cultural origins than the autonomy of critical perspective. However, the latter requires resources that are distributed much less equitably than the former. The main problem with, say, Karl Marx and Max Weber criticizing India or Ashis Nandy and Aijaz Ahmad criticizing Europe is not that they should mind their own business or are talking about things of which they have only second-hand knowledge. Rather, it is because their views end up assuming disproportionate significance because there are so few competing perspectives. That in itself reveals the depth of cross-cultural power asymmetries. It follows that the relationship between the Western enquirer and the non-Western enquired about becomes more *ethical* than strictly epistemological, that is, enquiry is no longer an asymmetrical relation between an active knower and a passive known. Rather, each is rendered accountable to the other, as "knower" and "known" are recognized as roles performed by both parties simultaneously. (The mutual responsibility of scientific enquirers in a Popperian polity as both conjecturers and refuters is a model here.)

To appreciate the difference between Fuller's perspective and that of mainstream multiculturalism, consider Charles Taylor's 1992 essay, "The Politics of

Recognition". Taylor argued that the recognition of a subaltern culture is, in the first instance, the introduction of a new voice in the global conversation but not necessarily a marker of that culture's ultimate value for world culture, which may remain small, even once it becomes familiar. Taylor is clearly trying to disentangle issues of emancipation and epistemic merit that are often fused together under the rubric of *political correctness*: for example, that principles of proportional representation or affirmative action should guide the composition of the curriculum. Yet, Taylor neglects that the diminished status of a subaltern culture is integrally connected to the enhanced status of the dominant one. Indeed, the institutionalization of epistemic value in the curriculum may be itself the main vehicle by which subalternation is achieved and reproduced. In other words, the "common standards" embodied in a canon of great art, philosophy or science do not exist prior to this institutionalization but are themselves the products of it. In this respect, the concept of political correctness serves as a reminder of the deeply constructed character of multiculturalism. (See **SOCIAL CONSTRUCTIVISM**.)

The father of Indian cultural studies, Ashis Nandy, has remarked on how Westerners have played both sides of the dialectic of subalternation. Consider the **RHETORIC** surrounding the transfer of scientific knowledge as part of development aid. On the one hand, applications of science that de-legitimize indigenous knowledges and generally immiserize the natives are blamed on the agents of application: profit-driven technologists, unscrupulous local politicians and insensitive global policy-makers. If science itself shares any responsibility, it is only by virtue of its perversion. The implication is that were science not itself rendered subaltern, it would develop as a universally beneficial force. Yet, given the 500-year history of science's supposedly subaltern status (i.e. from the start of European colonial expansion), Nandy wonders when science's subaltern state simply becomes its authentic form. On the other hand, reflecting on the very same history, Westerners have equally argued that scientific knowledge travels so much better cross-culturally than other forms of knowledge because it conveys truths of universal scope. Clearly, this reading of the history of science presupposes that science's development has *not* been perverted. Moreover, it fails to recognize that science's generalizability – especially when regarded as a performance standard for all forms of knowledge – may merely express imperialist imperatives at a higher level of abstraction, in terms of which local sources of epistemic authority are unsurprisingly found wanting. (See **EXPLAINING THE NORMATIVE STRUCTURE OF SCIENCE**.)

Of course, certain deadly diseases have been virtually eliminated, astronauts have flown in space and atomic bombs have caused untold damage. However, the bone of contention is the *explanation* given for these achievements, which may affect the ultimate value assigned to them. It is little more than secular superstition to suppose that Western science has some special explanatory purchase on widely used technologies, simply because its theories were the ones that first provided legitimacy for such technologies. (See **EXPLAINING THE COGNITIVE CONTENT OF SCIENCE**.) Natural scientific theories generally played a relatively minor role in technological design until the second half of the nineteenth century. Only then, technology started to be the product of large-scale industrial processes, the planning of which was predicated on scientific principles. Yet, the superstition of an undifferentiated "technoscience" persists among those who would claim that a technological innovation "implicitly instantiates" scientific principles that were discovered far in time and space from the site of the original innovation.

Thus, an important charge of multiculturalism is to show how these technologies – in so far as they deserve global diffusion – can be explained and appropriated with the help of theories ("alternative sciences", if you will) generated from outside the dominant cultures, even if those cultures originated the technologies. Among scholars of **SCIENCE AND TECHNOLOGY STUDIES**, Donna Haraway has been most articulate in arguing that the real heroes of multiculturalism (and feminism) are those who can appropriate, say, cyberspace for their own purposes, *not* those who refuse to engage with the new information technologies because they are seen as irrevocably tied to Eurocentric, masculinist forms of knowledge. In contrast, to make such a tight connection between science and technology, and between both of these and a particular culture, is to betray multiculturalism's potential for providing an emancipatory standpoint that transcends the stereotypes of the **UNIVERSALISM VERSUS RELATIVISM** debates.

An interesting concept in relation to multiculturalism's capacity as a critical vehicle for universalism is the *relative advantage of backwardness*. This phrase, coined by the economic historian Alexander Gerschenkron, characterizes the capacity of latecomers to leapfrog ahead of leaders by capitalizing on two aspects of their backward status: (i) latecomers count on the leaders to try out certain ideas first and hence reveal sources of error and waste from which latecomers are often well-placed to benefit; (ii) latecomers can innovate by either outdoing the efficiency of the leaders in existing markets or creating new markets in which they have a comparative advantage over the leaders. In this way, the industrial ascendancy of Germany, the United States, Japan and Russia have been explained.

The relative advantage of backwardness is interesting for its insight into the nature of innovation. Three points stand out:

- It implies that an initial liability may turn out to be a source of hidden strength – and vice versa. Being first is not always good, and being second is not always bad.

- It suggests a sense of cosmic justice (or *theodicy*) whereby the leaders are compelled to spend some of their advantage in committing to a course of action that latecomers would find too costly. Thus, what the leaders are forced to treat as a largely irreversible policy, the latecomers have the luxury of treating as a falsifiable experiment.
- It gives a specific meaning to the slogan "Necessity is the mother of invention": namely, that the appropriate response to the "path-dependency" of innovation may be to find a new path and not simply go down the old one. In that sense, the originator may set an example that is to be *avoided*. Thus, the concept may be seen as opposed to both sides of the Marxist logic of uneven development. On the one hand, it opposes "stage theories" that presuppose that all societies must undergo the same path of development as the Western leaders in order to make progress. On the other, it refuses to accept that the West's early development forces the rest of the world to adapt in ways that create enduring patterns of dependency.

Specifically, the relative advantage of backwardness returns to David Ricardo's *principle of comparative advantage*, which explains how producers secure their autonomy in a global market. According to the principle, people should not necessarily produce what they have traditionally produced, nor even what they produce best, left to their own devices. Rather, they should produce what no one else can produce as well, *even if that turns out to be their second- or third-best product*. In effect, Ricardo has provided a recipe for universalism by what might be called "reverse relativism", since a producer's sense of identity emerges from learning what he or she can do that others cannot. It is easy to see how this scheme would generate global interdependency, especially once others come to esteem the thing that one does better than they. A good example of a product of backwardness that became a source of comparative advantage is the UNIVERSITY. Its status as an autonomous corporation largely reflected a lack of uniform clerical and imperial control in medieval Europe. Self-governance was legally ceded in return for minimum loyalty to the church and local secular rulers. In contrast, Islam had no need for this legal innovation because its political and ideological control was more secure over a larger territory. Consequently, unlike Christendom, Islam's political and intellectual ends had no need to be pursued independently of each other. Its original advantage discouraged institutional innovation, which gradually metamorphosed into intellectual stagnation and political repression, on which a secularized Christendom eventually capitalized.

FURTHER READING

A. Ahmad, *In Theory* (1992).

S. Fuller, *Science* (1997).

S. Fuller, *The New Sociological Imagination* (2006).

D. Haraway, *Simians, Cyborgs, Women* (1991).

S. Harding, *Whose Science? Whose Knowledge?* (1991).

Z. Sardar, *Postmodernism and the Other* (1997).

C. Taylor, *The Politics of Recognition* (1992).

NATURALISM

The exact implications of naturalism depend on whether the natural sciences are considered an orthodox or heterodox form of knowledge. In the former case, after W. V. Quine, writing in the 1960s, naturalism is often defined as the conversion of philosophical questions to ones in the natural sciences. This sort of naturalist addresses problems of knowledge by looking into the composition of the brain, and problems of morals by examining humanity's biological heritage. Philosophers thus serve, as John Locke described his relationship to his friend Isaac Newton, as "under-labourers" who clear the conceptual obstacles to a properly scientific understanding of the world. When analytic social epistemologists (see ANALYTIC SOCIAL EPISTEMOL-OGY) such as Alvin Goldman and Philip Kitcher describe themselves as "naturalists", they mean to accord the natural sciences this level of epistemic privilege.

However, "naturalism" had first been used polemically three centuries earlier against Spinoza to refer to his heretical interpretation of the Bible, which implied that God is one with material reality, and that Creation is simply the self-realization of this single unified substance. However, Lessing, Goethe and other leaders of the eighteenth-century German Enlightenment gave "naturalism" a more positive spin, which made humanity the intellectual vanguard of nature's EVOLUTION. This perspective was enthusiastically adopted in the nineteenth and early-twentieth centuries by Ludwig Feuerbach, Karl Marx, Ernst Mach and the pragmatists. It is also present in Fuller's version of social epistemology.

Two interrelated lessons can be drawn from this longer history of naturalism: (i) naturalism is primarily opposed to "supernaturalism" in the sense of a theory of knowledge that postulates mental faculties or objects of knowledge that go beyond ordinary human capacities, which is then used to legitimize a stratified society based on competence or expertise; (ii) naturalism is rooted in critical-historical theology that by the early-nineteenth century had secularized Christianity's positive mission in terms of SOCIAL SCIENCE (e.g. Marx) and by the end of that century had warned against the natural sciences themselves becoming institutionalized as a new state RELIGION (e.g. Mach). From this perspective, the philosophy of science known as "realism", especially when used to justify accepted theories, may be seen as a secular descendant of supernaturalism.

The relevance of the long history of naturalism to social epistemology is three-fold. Each aspect discussed below challenges a tenet associated with the tradition of classical epistemology originating with Descartes, who upheld a supernatural view of God (contrary to the common pedagogical practice of lumping together Descartes and Spinoza as "rationalists"):

- *A commitment to a common nature, or metaphysical monism.* The naturalist does not presume that enquiry begins with the mind alienated from an external reality that it must then try to grasp. No hard distinction is drawn between the objects or methods of the natural and the human sciences. Whatever distinctions we see result from a historical process of institutional differentiation that has obscured the real and potential degree of interpenetration between the two sets of fields. Natural things can be (and have been) subject to interpretive methods (as was common in geology and biology when they were still considered branches of "natural history"), just as much as human things can be (and have been) subject to experimental methods. The organization of human beings is just as essential for the conduct of physics as the mobilization of physical space and material things is essential for the conduct of social life. Once such interpenetration is granted, a thoroughgoing naturalist cannot accept the simple idea that the human sciences are "ultimately" reducible to the natural sciences, since the natural sciences, as currently constituted, suffer just as much as the human sciences from their common history of reinforced segregation.
- *A commitment to theorizing* in medias res. The theorist always comes encumbered with prejudices she needs to articulate, transform and often discard before reaching a desired conclusion. Popper turned Descartes on his head by claiming that we were born with *false a priori* ideas, for which regular exposure to new experience was the only available antidote. Sometimes the source of a fixed idea's error is subtle, in that we can survive quite nicely without realizing the idea's limitations – or, more precisely, how the idea limits our possibilities for action. For example, Western culture flourished for two millennia before the geocentric theory of the universe was systematically challenged. Thus, special situations are required to enable people to have the relevant experiences that reveal the error. This critical function is performed by the design and execution of experiments in science. Only in the ontology of games is there such a thing as pure thought that moves from first principles to a conclusion in the fewest number of steps possible.
- *A commitment to a reflexive understanding of the natural sciences.* The natural sciences must be understood not as detached observations of nature, but as specific products of collective human endeavour over the course of history. This perspective does not deny the unprecedented power of the natural sciences. Rather, it demands that the success of the natural sciences be explained, not as a miraculous coincidence with reality, but as the result of processes that can then function in explanations of other endeavours undertaken by the same people. So, if a scientist or a formation of scientists is said to be "rational",

the term must refer to qualities that the scientist displays on other occasions or can be said to apply to a similar formation of other workers. In short, "science" will be characteristic more in terms of its quantitative features (such as its scale and scope) than in its qualitative ones (such as its rationality or progressiveness).

In short, social epistemology's naturalism amounts to the idea that knowledge cannot be *about* the world unless it is clearly situated *in* the world. Even when the logical positivists formally distinguished the contexts of "discovery" and "justification", they were precisely in this frame of mind. (See **KUHN, POPPER AND LOGICAL POSITIVISM**.) Thus, they regarded any original formulation of an idea – including its original published expression – as an alloy of blindness and insight whose decontamination must precede its evaluation. The positivists' chosen form of decontamination was logical translation, to which Popper famously objected, claiming that what was required was a specific kind of epistemic community, one governed by the interplay of conjectures and refutations. Social epistemology attempts to flesh out the institutional context – a "civic republican" science polity – that is required for the realization of Popper's ideal. (See **FREE ENQUIRY**.)

Whatever epistemic **PROGRESS** humanity has made is not due to divine dictate or permission, but to the organization of human beings into social wholes whose knowledge is greater than that of the sum of the individuals constituting them. The legal category of *corporation*, which refers to social entities whose ends transcend those of its current members, captures the diversity of these wholes, including universities (see **UNIVERSITY**), churches, states and firms. From this perspective, the teleologies of Hegelian historicism, Comtean positivism and Peircean pragmatism are attempts to simulate supernaturalism naturalistically by specifying a process by which higher-order human knowledge (or "science") has been generated from a systematic critique of lower-order human knowledge (or "consciousness"). Accordingly, progress is made by trying to achieve standards of our own making that nevertheless enable us to exercise greater control over reality as a whole. This, in a nutshell, is the naturalistic theory of **RATIONALITY**.

Naturalism implies a dynamic and open-ended vision of the relationship between human beings and their environment, based on the following insight: the price of acquiring any knowledge at all is that it will be somehow distorted by the conditions of its acquisition. Thus, **CRITICISM** is the only universally reliable method, which means that the naturalistic enquirer is engaged in a perpetual project of self-transcendence. The view is compatible with both **SOCIAL CONSTRUCTIVISM** and materialism, if "matter" is understood as a kind of raw material out of which reality is under continual construction. The signature scientific practice of hypothesis-testing, which combines the dialectical tradition of RHETORIC with the deductive tradition of logic, should be understood as the formalization of this endless critical process. Thus, from a naturalistic point of view, a theory of knowledge is doomed to failure if it aspires to a universality that ignores its own contingent origins as a corrective hypothesis.

FURTHER READING

C. Degler, *In Search of Human Nature* (1991).
S. Fuller, *Philosophy of Science and Its Discontents* (1993).
R. Giere (ed.), *Cognitive Models of Science* (1992).
A. Goldman, *Epistemology and Cognition* (1986).
P. Kitcher, *The Advancement of Science* (1993).
M. Mandelbaum, *History, Man and Reason* (1971).
W. V. Quine, *Ontological Relativity and Other Essays* (1969).
P. Singer, *A Darwinian Left* (1999).
D. Sperber, *Explaining Culture* (1996).

NORMATIVITY

Social epistemology's normative impulse – signalled most clearly in its preoccupation with CRITICISM, EPISTEMIC JUSTICE, KNOWLEDGE POLICY, PROGRESS and RATIONALITY – returns to a nineteenth-century idea of philosophers intervening in order to improve knowledge production. In the twentieth century, this case was most pressed by the logical positivists in their Viennese phase, but ultimately to greater effect by that renegade positivist Karl Popper and his students, Imre Lakatos and Paul Feyerabend, all of whom operated with an appropriately wide scope for understanding the role of knowledge in the human condition, without assuming that science is as it ought to be. (See EXPLAINING THE NORMATIVE STRUCTURE OF SCIENCE.) Originally, philosophical interventions ran the gamut of philosophers advising scientists on matters of conception and interpretation (e.g. William Whewell *vis-à-vis* Michael Faraday and Charles Darwin), laying out the steps by which a fledgling discipline might become a science (e.g. Auguste Comte and John Stuart Mill *vis-à-vis* the social sciences), and recovering minority dissents from the history of science to which the dominant paradigm has yet to respond adequately (e.g. Ernst Mach *vis-à-vis* Newtonian mechanics, an instance of "Tory history": see HISTORIOGRAPHY).

Social epistemology's normative concerns largely reflect the bureaucratic context of modern resource-intensive "big science". It situates the points of critical intervention not in the laboratory, but in the policy forums where research is initially stimulated and ultimately evaluated. Part of this shift is due to the gradual demystification of scientific work that has attended the rise of SCIENCE AND TECHNOLOGY STUDIES. What had previously been taken to be properties of scientific geniuses are now better seen as properties of the networks associated with their names. Another part of the story is the increasing realization that bodies of knowledge can be evaluated, not merely in terms of their conception, but also in terms of their consequences. Given the increasing access to resources that science commands, research has become – if it was not already – both an investment opportunity and a public trust. It needs to be evaluated as such.

Fuller's version of social epistemology adopts the normative perspective of the *interested non-participant* in the knowledge system. This is diametrically opposed to the *disinterested participant* of ANALYTIC SOCIAL EPISTEMOLOGY, which aims to acquire knowledge first-hand above all else. It also contrasts with POSTMODERNISM, which tends to adopt the standpoint of the *interested participant* (a.k.a. situated reasoner). Thus, Fuller's interest in knowledge policy is grounded in the idea that, generally speaking, the *prescribers* and *evaluators* (or, respectively, *legislators* and *judges*) of knowledge production are not the same – in terms of identities or interests – as the first-order knowledge producers. Knowledge serves as a means to other human ends (which themselves may be epistemic), but one's participation in the knowledge process is usually confined to the meta-level of enquiry, that is, the design and evaluation of knowledge-production regimes that *others* carry out. These regimes encompass issues of fiscal and employee management and social responsibility, as well as specifically process- and product-based forms of quality control.

Accordingly, the social epistemologist is less interested in what we ought to think and do than in the conditions for deciding such things. She is less *connoisseur* than *constitutionalist*. In these postmodern times, when "serious" academics recoil from issuing clear value judgements, it is not just pedagogically useful, but even intellectually impressive, to offer judgements about the past, present and future of some aspect of social life. To be sure, then, connoisseurship is in short supply. However, to avoid the charge of being a disguised elitist or tyrant, the social epistemologist needs to create some conceptual distance between her personal judgements and the framework (or "constitution") within which she would have final judgements on these matters be delivered. To take a current US example, a social epistemologist may believe (on what she regards as very good grounds) that creationism should not be accorded the same status as EVOLUTIONary biology in science courses, while at the same time granting that the final decision should be taken by the local educational authorities, to whom the social epistemologist would argue her case as vigorously as possible but ultimately accept whatever judgement they reach. Hopefully, under such a democratic regime, any judgements reached by the local authorities should be in principle reversible at some later time, depending on their consequences. (See FREE ENQUIRY.)

Thus, the social epistemologist's normative position is, generally speaking, *rule-utilitarian*: if the people subjected to an epistemic regime can live well with its consequences, then that is success enough. The difficult question is how long and widely should such a regime be in effect before its consequences are evaluated and its continuation questioned. Little more than Kuhnian (see KUHN, POPPER AND LOGI-CAL POSITIVISM) superstition allows a scientific paradigm to continue indefinitely until it self-destructs, so track records are a prerequisite to the rational comparison of alternative research trajectories. This is Lakatos's old question of when a "problemshift" is "progressive", but now rephrased to give it more political bite. Accordingly, knowledge policy improves over time by removing obstacles both to the expression of epistemic interests and knowledge of the results of actions taken on the basis of those interests. A progressive knowledge regime institutionalizes both the exploration and the criticism of alternative research trajectories. In democratic political theory, such matters are normally discussed in the context of *elections*, a topic conspicuous by its absence from treatments of "theory choice" in the philosophy of science. (Competing research programmes are like political parties vying for office, where "crucial experiments" correspond to voting.) Nevertheless, whatever progress there is in science occurs at this meta-level of the increasing inclusiveness and transparency of decision-making processes, not at the object level of approximating some transcendental goal of enquiry that remains fixed over time, be it called "truth" or "welfare". (See EXPLAINING THE COG-NITIVE CONTENT OF SCIENCE).

Unfortunately, the normative judgements issued in recent times (i.e. since logical positivism's transatlantic migration) have been more in the spirit of a schoolmaster giving marks than of the policy-maker trying to improve the conduct of enquiry. Thus, philosophers of science tell us that it was good to choose Copernicus over Ptolemy by Galileo's day, and that it would have been better to have made the choice sooner, but they say precious little about what line of research we ought to pursue *next*. While many philosophers cheerfully accept these limits, their prescriptions are rendered idle if they are not ultimately aimed at guiding the course of present and future enquiry. This point might be better recognized if philosophers realized just how close their current schoolmasterly mode places them to literary criticism and art connoisseurship, two disciplines whose practices have become increasingly alienated from their putative objects of evaluation. Contrary to eighteenth- and nineteenth-century hopes, the judgements of critics typically do not feed back into the creation of better art or even better publics for the reception of art. What is produced, instead, is a self-sustaining body of scholarly literature and journalism that bears fortuitously on its objects. This tendency may be even more pronounced in the philosophy of science.

However, almost in spite of themselves, philosophers have been pushed towards social epistemology by the increasing resistance of scientists and their sociological investigators to norms of enquiry that presuppose reasoners who are either too perspicuous or too selfless. How are philosophers to deal with the embarrassing fact that scientific reasoners typically fail to manifest the requisite cognitive virtues? Wayward scientists simply no longer feel the guilt and remorse they did when positivists found fault with their practices. But instead of either castigating scientists or (worse) excusing their behaviour as virtue in disguise, social epistemology proposes a twofold strategy for tackling the inevitable discrepancy between philosophical norms and scientific practice: either (i) the norms really pertain to some form of group interaction or computer android, but not to the activity of any individual human being, or (ii) the norms could govern the activity of individual human beings, provided that the individuals are instructed or, in some way, motivated to adopt the norms. To appreciate what hangs in the balance, consider the difference in psychologies implied by the following ways in which the Popperian norm of falsificationism may be instantiated in science: either (i) each scientist is expected to offer her own bold conjectures, but to rigorously refute her neighbour's; or (ii) each scientist is expected both to boldly conjecture and to rigorously refute her own claims. A credit to his training in educational psychology, Popper realized that the first option is psychologically more realistic than the second. If falsificationism is essential for the growth of knowledge, science would seem to be – for all practical purposes – an irreducibly social activity.

Alternatives such as the ones above drive home the key difference between Fuller's position and that of analytic social epistemology. For Fuller, the normative mission of social epistemology goes beyond simply constructing a conceptually satisfying model of how enquiry ought to proceed (e.g. definitions of knowledge that require the enquirer to seek only "justified true beliefs"). On the contrary, that is the easy part. The hard part is to determine the units to which the norms are likely to apply and then the means by which those norms may be instantiated or institutionalized in those units. (See **PHILOSOPHY VERSUS SOCIOLOGY**.)

Virtually all the norms of enquiry proposed by modern philosophers of science – including formulations of inductive logic (Carnap), the falsification principle (Popper), paradigms (Kuhn), disciplines (Stephen Toulmin), research programmes (Lakatos), and research traditions (Larry Laudan) – are better seen as governing some supra-individual unit of enquiry than the behaviour of any particular enquirer who might be part of that unit. The founder of pragmatism, Charles Sanders Peirce, anticipated this point a century ago when he observed that the rationality of induction as a method of science presupposed a potentially infinite and continuous community of enquirers. The exact dimensions of that supra-individual unit – how many people, what sort of interactions, over what chunk of spacetime – is open to empirical determination, specifically by comparative historical and experimental social psychological studies of science.

To presume that the norms of enquiry could be straightforwardly instantiated in a particular scientist or that a scientific community is typified by any one of its members (a "normal scientist") is to court what logicians call the *fallacy of division* or what sociologists dub the "oversocialized" individual. From the standpoint of social epistemology, it would be more productive to presume that variation in individual behaviour should be indicative of a statistically normal pattern of differences within the social organism rather than deviations from an ideal typical individual. But suppose a philosopher managed to construct an ideal individual reasoner, one who routinely implements whatever the epistemologist thinks is the formula for producing reliable knowledge. How should we understand its status in a social context of enquiry that is dominated by imperfect human reasoners? I have in mind a computer android – or *expert system* (see **EXPERTISE**) – programmed to execute the reasoning required of formalized scientific norms (e.g. Bayesian inductive logic) better than any group or individual human being could.

On the one hand, if there is sufficient interest in applying the norms governing the machine's performance, then the community may prefer to cut the risk of human error by deferring to the machine's authority on the relevant occasions. On the other hand, there may be background normative commitments to any of the following: individual accountability to the group, the maximum employment of human beings in intellectually challenging tasks, or the intrinsic value of approximating a norm regardless of one's ultimate success. Such commitments would divert the machine's human co-workers from the path of least resistance – that is, let the computer do what it does best – by encouraging them to approximate the norms embodied in the machine. Exactly how to negotiate this situation is the social epistemologist's toughest assignment, as it requires the skills of both policy-maker and pedagogue. Moreover, this situation is "normative" in the strictest sense, as it concerns the foundations of government: to what standards can people's actions be legitimately held, and under what circumstances may they legitimately resist the imposition of such standards?

Here the social epistemologist is reflexively implicated as a social agent in which questions of knowledge and power are fused. Put more exactly, "knowledge" and "power" are revealed to be alternative RHETORICs for treating the same matters. If it already seems that people are heading in a normatively desirable direction, it will appear that all the social epistemologist needs to do is to remove whatever few obstacles remain. A task of this sort trades on the *knowledge-rhetoric* of telling people what will enable them to pursue their own goals more effectively. However, if it seems that people are adrift or heading away from a normatively desirable direction, *power-rhetoric* enters the picture. In that case, the social epistemologist will need to flag a proposed change in course with incentives and sanctions designed to get people to do other than they normally would.

FURTHER READING
S. Fuller, *Social Epistemology* (1988).
S. Fuller, *Philosophy of Science and Its Discontents* (1993).
S. Fuller & J. Collier, *Philosophy, Rhetoric and the End of Knowledge* (2004).
I. Lakatos & A. Musgrave (eds), *Criticism and the Growth of Knowledge* (1970).
L. Laudan, *Progress and its Problems* (1977).
R. Proctor, *Value-Free Science?* (1991).
J. Rouse, *Knowledge and Power* (1987).
S. Toulmin, *Human Understanding* (1972).
S. P. Turner, *The Social Theory of Practices* (1994).
S. P. Turner, *Brains/Practices/Relativism* (2002).

PHILOSOPHY VERSUS SOCIOLOGY

S ocial epistemology straddles the philosophy/sociology disciplinary boundary, one of the most heavily policed zones of academia of the past century. Historically this is rather puzzling. Émile Durkheim and Max Weber had grounded the discipline of sociology in matters of ontology and epistemology, respectively, by developing possibilities left open by the leading philosophies of their day. Moreover, psychology, a discipline of the same late-nineteenth-century vintage founded on similar considerations, has managed to make its peace with philosophy after a half-century of charges and counter-charges of "psychologism". In the past generation, the mutual respect between these two fields has evolved into several joint teaching and research programmes in cognitive science, where the empirical and normative dimensions of thought are once again fruitfully studied together. No such similar trend characterizes the current relationship between sociology and philosophy. "Sociologism" is still something that most philosophers and even some sociologists wish to avoid.

The troubled relationship between philosophy and sociology is most clearly marked in introductory logic textbooks. It is epitomized in the informal fallacies, popularly called red herrings, that purport to establish a conclusion on the basis of logically irrelevant premises. On closer inspection, these fallacies consist of explanatory strategies frequently found in sociology. Cognitive scientists would call them "heuristics", namely, conceptual frameworks whose *prima facie* informativeness trades off against hasty generalization. Below is a list of these *argumenta* in their canonical Latin guises, alongside an explication that brings out their latent sociological content:

- *Ad origines*: The origins of a claim are relevant to determining its validity.
- *Ad verecundiam*: The authority backing a claim is relevant to determining its validity.
- *Ad baculum*: The force of threat behind a claim is relevant to determining its validity.
- *Ad populum*: The popularity of a claim is relevant to determining its validity.
- *Ad hominem*: The kind of person making a claim is relevant to determining its validity.
- *Ad misericordiam*: The emotional response elicited by a claim is relevant to determining its validity.
- *Ad consequentiam*: The consequences of a claim are relevant to determining its validity.

All of these *argumenta* assume that the circumstances surrounding the production and reception of a knowledge claim are material to assessing the claim's validity. To social researchers, these are reasonable opening moves that then need to be tested, modified and perhaps even overturned in light of further empirical enquiry. Yet, the philosophical force of calling the *argumenta* "fallacies" is to discourage their use in the first place. Philosophers often presume that sociologists reduce, say, Plato's thought when they embed Plato in a richer historical and sociological context than philosophers normally do. But this charge could also apply to the equally selective but rather more charitably interpreted readings that canonize Plato in the philosophy curriculum. Is it not equally reductive to abstract arguments from distinctive philosophical texts in order to construct positions in perennial dialectical struggle? It would seem that, strictly speaking, *both* philosophers and sociologists can be charged with *either* contextual or reductive readings of philosophy. However, the contextual–reductive distinction masks a deeper contrast in philosophical and sociological sensibilities towards philosophical texts, which is captured by Paul Ricoeur's famous distinction between the hermeneutics of *trust* and *suspicion*, respectively. At stake is whether one treats the canon "philosophically" as a benign legacy bequeathed by our worthy ancestors (i.e. trustingly) or "sociologically" as a Trojan Horse left by a treacherous past, fraught with danger to the naive interpreter (i.e. suspiciously). Are philosophers too uncritical or sociologists too critical in their reading of texts? (See CRITICISM and TRANSLATION.)

The red herring fallacies only start to make their way into Anglophone logic textbooks in the late-nineteenth century and perhaps the most important of these, the *genetic fallacy* (*argumentum ad origines*), appears only in the 1930s. The Latin naming of these fallacies was an Oxbridge anachronism that did scant justice to the ancients' own more probing, proto-sociological attitudes towards the relationship between thought and the conditions of its production and reception. Aristotle's *Rhetoric* and *Sophistical Refutations* can be read as early exercises in the SOCIOLOGY OF KNOWLEDGE because of their acute analyses of the conditions under which people are moved to action in a democracy. In contrast, the red herring fallacies have erected an impassable barrier between philosophy and sociology that may be usefully regarded as a pincer attack on the value of empirical research into the human condition. The first prong appeals to truths whose intuitive validity can be grasped without further consultation, the second to truths whose counterintuitive validity requires intellectual powers beyond the normal demands of social life. It would seem that from the standpoint of philosophy, humanity is an object either much more banal or much more profound than can be reached by systematic empirical enquiry. These attacks on empirical social research can be considered from, so to speak, below and above.

On the one hand, the red herring fallacies were a rearguard response to the ascendancy of utilitarianism and evolutionism (see EVOLUTION). These two intellectual movements had come from outside the academy to become the standard-bearers of NATURALISM. In 1903, G. E. Moore canonized philosophical anti-naturalism as the *naturalistic fallacy*, that is, the mistaken inference of "ought" from "is". A tendentiously Platonic reading of David Hume enabled Moore to conjure up a domain of objects – "intuitions" – that were presumed to have normative import yet were accessible only to pure philosophical enquiry. Intuitions are objects whose universal character is immediately apparent through introspection without need for further investigation. Thus, for Moore, knowledge of "the good" is a self-certifying experience that does not require knowledge of origins or consequences, or any other material conditions. Not surprisingly, the studiously anti-empirical cast of Moore's philosophical vision was originally criticized for aestheticism. However, once Moore became the academic orthodoxy, his vision was praised for its down-to-earth appeals to common sense (see COMMON SENSE VERSUS COLLECTIVE MEMORY) and ordinary language in the face of jargon-toting experts in the nascent social sciences. (See FOLK EPISTEMOLOGY.) Moore's legacy is felt in the retarded development of the SOCIAL SCIENCEs in the UK *vis-à-vis* continental Europe and the USA.

On the other hand, the red herring fallacies encourage the exclusive identification of philosophical activity with a kind of virtual, or transcendental, sociology: specifically, an intertextual understanding, which Richard Rorty, following Michael Oakeshott, has personified as "the conversation of mankind". Here philosophers are portrayed as addressing each other across the centuries on topics of perennial concern. To be sure, these concerns are social but in the broadest possible sense. It is precisely by saying things whose true meanings lie beyond the assertion's material conditions that philosophers make their most distinctive contributions to this conversation. In Leo Strauss's extreme formulation, the tension between the demands of the quotidian and the perennial is normally so great that philosophers must write in code to address both temporal horizons at once. That code is metaphysics. In effect, philosophers inhabit two social worlds: the sociologically real but philosophically virtual world that transpires on the surface of metaphysical discourse and the philosophically real but sociologically virtual world that transpires beneath the surface. As a result, metaphysics simultaneously provides a secular cosmology for the pious and a political blueprint for the cunning. Philosophers since Plato have engaged in this doubletalk, if not doublethink, as an exercise in self-restraint, since only elite enquirers are capable of grasping esoteric truths of universal significance without succumbing to the temptation to demystify a world whose stability is founded on mass illusion.

Moore's appeal to common sense and Strauss's appeal to secret codes conspire from opposite directions to immunize philosophical accounts of the human condition from empirical social enquiry. The form of this immunity involves an elision in reasoning that makes the red herring fallacies appear more persuasive than they otherwise would. Indeed, to regard these characteristically sociological forms of argument as fallacies is itself to commit a version of the *modal fallacy*: in this case, to slide from arguing that something is not always the case to arguing that it is never the case. Take the genetic fallacy as an example. While it is certainly true that the origins of a claim do not always bear on its validity, it hardly follows that they *never* bear on its validity. Yet, philosophers tend to interpret the genetic fallacy in just this stronger sense. Nevertheless, concerns about committing the genetic fallacy are not supposed to preclude consideration of an idea's origins from an assessment of its validity. Rather, they are meant to shift the burden of proof to those who would claim that, say, Einstein's Jewish origins are *automatically* relevant to an evaluation of relativity theory. These origins *may* be somehow relevant, but simply revealing them does not clinch the argument. One would need to explain exactly how Einstein's Jewish background predisposed him to propose a false physical theory that comes to be widely accepted only once others have been contaminated by the Jewish mindset. To be sure, given what we know today, it is unlikely that such an enquiry would confirm the hypothesis, but clearly the enquiry would be sociological. (See **EXPLAINING THE COGNITIVE CONTENT OF SCIENCE**.)

Because Einstein's Jewish origins were taken seriously by racially oriented sociologists in the 1930s as a potential contaminant to his physics, anti-racist philosophers (the **LOGICAL POSITIVISTS**) tried to prohibit on logical grounds what would otherwise have remained an empirically open question. These philosophers had good reason to suspect the objectivity and policy import of research done by racialists. They reasoned as follows: if you believe that Einstein's Jewishness does not bear on his physics, but you also do not trust the people who are likely to study the matter empirically, then you could try to demonstrate the inappropriateness of the entire line of enquiry. It would seem, then, that the genetic fallacy is a residue of a past generation's sense of political correctness. In other words, the fallacy was introduced as a well-meaning attempt to pre-empt prejudiced empirical enquiries on behalf of those potentially under investigation. Yet, over a half-century after the fall of Nazi Germany, perhaps the genetic fallacy – and indeed the entire category of red herring fallacies – has outlived its usefulness.

The **SOCIOLOGY OF KNOWLEDGE** is probably the branch of sociology that has most fallen foul of the red herring fallacies. Shortly after the publication of the English translation of Karl Mannheim's *Ideology and Utopia*, logic-based attacks began in the guise of the "problem of imputation". Mannheim was read as having argued that the validity of a set of ideas (or knowledge claims) is relative to its capacity to legitimize a particular social order. But how does one "impute" this capacity? Implied in this question were two complementary challenges to Mannheim's thesis: (i) are specific ideas so integral to a social order that the social order would lose its legitimacy without those ideas; (ii) must specific ideas have the capacity to legitimize a social order in order to lay claim to validity? Challenge (i) harks back to the original problem of imputation that the Austrian economist Carl Menger posed to Marxist labour theories of value at the end of the nineteenth century. Here the problem was how to determine the contribution made by various factors of production to the overall value of a good. Menger argued that labour's contribution is not the actual work performed by a labourer but the hypothetical cost of the labourer's replacement (by other labourers or technology) in manufacturing a good that would satisfy human needs. Menger's calculation of value from the standpoint of consumer demand rather than producer supply amounted to a "Copernican revolution" in economic thought, one that put *Marxisant* thinkers such as Mannheim on the intellectual defensive for most of the twentieth century.

Once transferred to the sociology of knowledge, Menger's analysis yields the following type of argument. Say that the Protestant ethic was historically instrumental in animating the capitalist spirit. Nevertheless, capitalism certainly has not required Protestantism for its survival, extension or legitimacy. Other ideas have functioned just as adequately – if not more so – in this capacity. In what sense, then, is Protestantism "capitalist ideology", since it seems eminently replaceable by other ideas? Moreover, and this introduces challenge (ii) to Mannheim's thesis, Protestantism's primary frame of reference is not political economy but humanity's relationship to the deity. Therefore, Protestantism's validity should be judged principally in terms of the adequacy of that relationship, which, depending on circumstances, may or may not have some bearing on the legitimacy of specific social orders. Taken together, challenges (i) and (ii) dismember the grounds for the sociology of knowledge, as social orders are portrayed as appropriating ideas opportunistically, while ideas exist in a realm of their own that is arbitrarily related to the social orders temporarily housing them. While this conclusion neatly divides the work of sociologists from that of philosophers, it has exacted a heavy toll on contemporary social thought.

For example, the most influential work in political theory of the past half-century, Rawls's *A Theory of Justice*, is a thinly veiled justification of the welfare state, written when its attractiveness as a model for the just society was at its peak. This coincided with the achievements of concrete welfare states – not least the "Great Society" launched by Lyndon Johnson in Rawls's USA – in reducing inequality and expanding opportunity through a policy nowadays derided as "tax and spend". However, Rawlsians were keen to detach the fate of their political philosophy from that of particular political regimes, especially given the Janus-faced character of what Alvin Gouldner dubbed America's "welfare–warfare state". After all, over the next two decades Rawlsians found themselves in the rhetorically unenviable position of defending principles that are supposedly necessary conditions for the possibility of a just society against the empirical evidence of countries that had democratically rolled back, if not outright rejected, policies based on those principles. Consequently, they provided ineffectual, if any, resistance to the dismantling of welfare states. Had these philosophers taken more seriously the empirical sources of the intuitions behind Rawls's principles of justice, they would have regarded the fate of their philosophy as more intimately bound with that of the welfare state regimes under attack in the Reagan–Thatcher era and its "Third Way" aftermath.

That Rawls remains a major text in contemporary social and political thought even in our "post-welfarist" era speaks only to the relative autonomy – or perhaps alienation – of philosophical merit from practical politics. To draw the more hopeful conclusion that it demonstrates the transcendence of philosophy from its social conditions is to make a virtue out of a liability, an instance of what Jon Elster calls "sweet lemons": the mirror image of "sour grapes". But there is a specifically logical difficulty here as well. Philosophers have been so averse to empirical defences of their normative (see **NORMATIVITY**) claims that they are vulnerable to the *deontic fallacy*, which trades on the equivocal meaning of "necessary" in English. The fallacy consists in arguing that something is the case because it is necessarily the case, when the sense of "necessarily" is merely that of legal or moral obligation rather than strict logical or physical necessity. Instead of simply admitting that one's preferred normative order has failed to materialize, one appeals to a deeper reality that declares the empirical situation to be itself a transient, self-correcting error. In this respect, the deontic fallacy is the converse of Moore's naturalistic fallacy, as it would now have us derive "is" from "ought". Thus, philosophy becomes sociology in the subjunctive. But philosophy could be much more, were its disciplinary identity not so closely tied to immunity from empirical social enquiry.

In conclusion, we can envisage four possible strategies for establishing a productive relationship between philosophy and sociology, each of which has precedent in the histories of the two fields. They are listed below, along with the relevant social theorists. *Social epistemologists* (see **SOCIAL EPISTEMOLOGY**) occupy positions (1) and (2): *social ontologists* (3) and (4).

1. *Philosophy relates to sociology as form to matter.* If philosophy articulates the idea of the good society, sociology establishes the conditions under which it

can be realized. Philosophy first guides but is then superseded by sociology. This view is most strongly associated with Marx, with earlier resonances in Hegel and Comte. Fuller's social epistemology is sympathetic with this position, which sees philosophy and sociology as two overlapping stages in what is essentially the same enquiry.

2. *Philosophy relates to sociology as rational to irrational.* There is a division of labour between the two disciplines, which still gives sociology much to do, since most of social life regularly falls short of the rational ideals articulated by philosophers and officially espoused by social agents. The standard-bearer for the sociology side is Vilfredo Pareto, although Mannheim's sociology of knowledge is probably the best-known variant. On the philosophy side, this position was explicitly occupied by logical positivism and more implicitly by today's ANALYTIC SOCIAL EPISTEMOLOGY. (See RATIONALITY.)

3. *Philosophy relates to sociology as metaphysics to physics.* Here philosophy underwrites the validity of much, most or all empirical social research by demonstrating the existence of a domain of reality towards which social enquiry is directed. This demonstration is characteristically "transcendental", in that it proceeds from the assumptions that social research could not take place at all if reality were not constituted in a certain way. This is how Durkheim originally carved out a niche for sociology in French academia, and "critical realists" following the lead of Roy Bhaskar continue to justify a normatively inspired structural Marxism

4. *Philosophy relates to sociology as conscious to unconscious.* Here sociology articulates the logic of everyday practices that constitute the social order, which are not normally dignified with comment, much less codification. On this view, the forms of reasoning of traditional interest to philosophy constitute merely the linguistic surface of social life. In this respect, (4) turns (2) on its head. Accordingly, ethnomethodologists and symbolic interactionists transform Max Weber's original interest in the meanings that agents attach to their actions into a source of hidden semantic competence out of which all of social life is constructed, including "local knowledge" and "situated reasoning", which philosophers have traditionally dismissed as trivial or irrational. In recent years, feminists and multiculturalists (see FEMINISM and MULTICULTURALISM) have turned this perspective into a general account of identity formation in subaltern groups. (See SOCIAL CONSTRUCTIVISM.)

FURTHER READING
R. Aron, *Main Currents in Sociological Thought* (1965).
R. Bhaskar, *Scientific Realism and Human Emancipation* (1987).

K. Burke, *A Grammar of Motives* (1969).

L. J. Cohen, *The Dialogue of Reason* (1986).

R. Collins, *The Sociology of Philosophies* (1998).

J. Elster, *Sour Grapes* (1984).

S. Fleischacker, *A Short History of Distributive Justice* (2004).

S. Fuller, *Social Epistemology* (1988).

S. Fuller, *Kuhn vs Popper* (2003).

A. Gouldner, *Enter Plato* (1965).

A. Gouldner, *The Coming Crisis in Western Sociology* (1970).

K. Mannheim, *Ideology and Utopia* (1936).

K. Popper, *The Open Society and its Enemies* (1945).

R. Proctor, *Value-Free Science?* (1991).

J. Rawls, *A Theory of Justice* (1971).

P. Ricoeur, *Freud and Philosophy* (1972).

R. Rorty, *Philosophy and the Mirror of Nature* (1979).

L. Strauss, *Persecution and the Art of Writing* (1952).

S. Toulmin, *Return to Reason* (2003).

POSTMODERNISM

Postmodernism emerged in the late 1970s to capture the changed character of the sciences in the twentieth century, which called into question the idea that the organized pursuit of knowledge has a unique and natural course of development that can provide the basis for the general improvement of humanity, typically in the form of rational statecraft. This "modernist" ideal had gone under a variety of names, from *positivism* in philosophical circles to simply PROGRESS in more popular ones. However, far from denying the fundamental importance of knowledge, they hold that knowledge is constitutive of social and individual identity. (See KNOWLEDGE SOCIETY and SOCIAL CONSTRUCTIVISM) Instead, what they deny is that knowledge functions in some situation-transcendent capacity as a goal or regulative ideal in terms of which progress may be measured. In this respect, postmodernism is a revolt against the NORMATIVITY of knowledge. Michel Foucault's stress on the embodied and self-disciplining character of knowledge is indicative of this position. Generally speaking, social epistemology attempts to reconstruct knowledge's normativity, given the features of our epistemic predicament that Jean-François Lyotard originally called the "postmodern condition".

The term "Enlightenment" is often used for the tendency in the history of Western thought that postmodernism is said to oppose, if not undermine. However, principled opponents of postmodernism such as Jürgen Habermas generally mean by the term something rather different from the movement's eighteenth-century originators, such as Voltaire, Diderot, Hume and Kant. Indeed, in certain important respects, the eighteenth century Enlightenment was very much like contemporary postmodernism: (i) both bemoaned the role of the universities in legitimizing the status quo; (ii) both broke with scholastic conventions of intellectual expression by turning to irony, satire, shock and ridicule; (iii) both celebrated the plurality of cultures, especially when they provided critical distance from taken-for-granted European customs; (iv) both were resolutely sceptical in demeanour, often confounding any positive foundation for social and intellectual order, as in the case of the signature Enlightenment project, *L'Encyclopédie*, in which cross-referenced entries often contradicted each other, so as to force readers to make up their own minds.

The temporal ambiguity of postmodernism is reflected in a variety of associated "end" states, all of which include an ironic twist, whereby the future turns back into the past:

- *End of science.* As science gets more specialized and technical, it also requires a larger outlay of material and human resources, which then reopens the door to greater public scrutiny and, increasingly, scepticism about the rate of return on investment. Consequently, high-tech science may return – via computer simulation – to the status of an art that aims to model nature, rather than predict and control it. This also opens the door to a revival of the typically low-tech "alternative" sciences promoted by **MULTICULTURALISM**.

- *End of economics.* As capitalist economies increase productivity so as to eliminate most forms of material scarcity, new scarcities emerge that reflect one's relative deprivation of such immaterial, or status-based, goods as credentials, of which one can never have enough, as long as others are trying to acquire them as well. These are often called "positional goods", precedents for which can be found in feudalism. (See **SOCIAL CAPITAL VERSUS PUBLIC GOOD**.)
- *End of politics.* As more people acquire the right to vote, the value of voting diminishes, so much so that the interactive character of the public sphere in advanced democracies dissolves into, on the one hand, **MASS MEDIA** presentations and, on the other, customized consumption patterns. The internet symbolizes this apolitical future, although it has also been used for developing post-public "lifestyle politics", perhaps the most substantial of which are associated with such pre-modern sources of meaning as **RELIGION** and the natural environment.
- *End of history.* If all possible forms of social organization have been tested at some point in human history, and liberal democracy seems to be most robust, what more needs to be done than to ensure that we do not backslide? This was the question that Nietzsche originally posed of Hegel's progressive vision, which seemed to reduce the "last men", the most advanced in the species, to mere caretakers. In response, Francis Fukuyama's influential *The End of History and the Last Man* (1992) offered a syncretistic vision of the future that aimed to reintroduce the Athenian craving for honour into capitalism's endless drive towards innovation.

Postmodernism is perhaps most precisely captured as a set of replies to the following question: what happens to the project of the Enlightenment, once you deny the inevitability of its success? Notice that the question does not presume that the Enlightenment has failed, only that it has met obstacles, which may or may not be surmountable. It is also left open whether the Enlightenment project has been given a fair run for its money over the past 250 years. Thus, there are four logically possible answers:

1. The Enlightenment has been given a fair run, so it is time to move on to something else.

2. The Enlightenment has been given a fair run and merits continued pursuit.
3. The Enlightenment has not been given a fair run but deserves to be.
4. The Enlightenment has not been given a fair run – and for good reason!

1. The Enlightenment has been given a fair run, so it is time to move on to something else. This is the most familiar postmodernist attitude, one closely associated with Lyotard himself and Richard Rorty. According to Lyotard, systematic enquiry has become increasingly bold and free, yet the result has not been the coherent and unified worldview that the Enlightenment promised. Rather, one finds a scattering of cross-cutting perspectives that collectively subvert each other. At the very least, this result undermines the UNIVERSITY as a place devoted to a common universe of discourse. For Rorty, the persistence of the Enlightenment vision is responsible for inflated public expectations of what science can deliver, the failure of which then only serves to trigger an antiscientific backlash. Thus, beyond recognizing the endless proliferation of specialties, Rorty would urge that each specialty be sufficiently modest in its aims that it can survive in an expectant world.

2. The Enlightenment has been given a fair run and merits continued pursuit. This position, shared by Stephen Toulmin and Jacques Derrida, holds that a sustained pursuit of the Enlightenment project ironically leads to just those consequences most indicative of the postmodern condition. One can then adopt a "postmodern ethic" and learn to accept these consequences. Toulmin locates the dawn of postmodern science in the pursuit of the Newtonian paradigm to the point of self-destruction (or self-deconstruction), with the triumph of relativity theory and quantum mechanics in the early twentieth century. Scientific enquiry had traditionally been a spectator sport, since the dimensions of reality one sought to understand did not implicate the position of the enquirer. However, once physics began to make sense of the very small and the very fast, it became clear that the enquirer's presence (or frame of reference) participated in constituting the object of enquiry. For Derrida, instead of physics, reason itself is engaged in an act of self-subversion. Derrida notes that only wishful thinking has guided the idea that the relentless application of critical reason will ultimately reveal indubitable foundations for thought. More likely is one of two scenarios: Either criticism is arrested at an arbitrary point, so that what remain become the *de facto* foundations for thought; or criticism is allowed to proceed uninterrupted, thereby issuing in a corrosive scepticism. Hume and Kant, in rather different ways, developed the first option, while Derrida notoriously pursued the second option by showing how language's capacity for representation breaks down when it tries to represent itself. Apparently transcendental conditions for the possibility of thought appear, on closer reflection, to be little more than the limitations of writing as the medium by which speech is represented.

3. *The Enlightenment has not been given a fair run but deserves to be.* Here are all the "critical theorists" (the Frankfurt School) and "critical rationalists" (the followers of Popper) who disagreed among themselves but jointly regard the postmodern condition as cause for redoubling efforts in pursuit of the Enlightenment ideal. These modernists believe in the critical power of reason to cut through the myths and ideologies of our time. Not surprisingly, today's leading critical theorist, Habermas, was explicitly targeted by Lyotard. For Habermas, the information explosion points to the mutually alienated character of the different branches of learning, such that each body of knowledge represents a part dismembered from the "totality" of reality. However, a unified sense of enquiry remains implicit in the persistence of such institutions as the university, the public sphere and even "science", understood as the overarching commitment to openly critical communication. (See SCIENCE AS A SOCIAL MOVEMENT.) Critical rationalists uphold the same ideals but diagnose our current malaise differently, namely, as a failure of actual practice to match normative ideals. Thus, in response to Kuhn's famous account of scientific change, Popper argued that only during its rare "revolutionary" phases has science rallied from the herd mentality dominant in other forms of social life to live up to the ideals of principled criticism. From the postmodern standpoint, Habermas and Popper are purveyors of "grand" or "master" narratives who refuse to accept the irreducible diversity and fragmentation of contemporary knowledge enterprises. (See DISCIPLINARITY VERSUS INTERDISCIPLINARITY.) Indeed, their ideals are so removed from reality that Lyotard claimed they could be realized only by imposing a totalitarian regime that paradoxically coerces some principled sense of "openness" in the face of spontaneously self-constituting disciplines. The precedent for Lyotard's nightmare scenario is the Enlightenment-inspired Reign of Terror that followed in the wake of the French Revolution of 1789 – and, of course, the Soviet Union. Notwithstanding Lyotard's reservations, SOCIAL EPISTEMOLOGY sides with the forces of CRITICISM.

4. *The Enlightenment has not been given a fair run – and for good reason!* Here stands Bruno Latour and others in SCIENCE AND TECHNOLOGY STUDIES who argue that "we have never been modern" because the Enlightenment has never been more than an ideological smokescreen behind which scientists and their philosophical well-wishers have hidden the mundane sociological character of scientific practice. Notwithstanding modernist rhetoric of positivism and PROGRESS,

the sciences have never been in a position to govern the rest of society. In that sense, postmodernism is an unneeded cure for a nonexistent disease. Accordingly, the special qualities that Enlightenment thinkers have attributed to science are treated much as these thinkers originally treated the special qualities attributed to religion. Both are demystified. To be sure, as with religion, the ideology surrounding science's exceptional epistemic status need not be conscious or even dysfunctional. Following Kuhn, heroic tales of historical progress may be required to motivate both the average scientist's limited routines and a larger society that would otherwise find such routines alien to their concerns. However, Latour overlooks that the Enlightenment's defenders have usually treated it as a project that has yet to reach completion, not a description of the world as it is. The relevant question, then, is whether the project is worth our continued pursuit, given its failures to date.

FURTHER READING

T. Adorno (ed.), *The Positivist Dispute in German Sociology* (1976).
A. Ahmad, *In Theory: Classes, Nations, Literatures* (1992).
J. Derrida, *Of Grammatology* (1976).
S. Fuller, *Kuhn vs Popper* (2003).
I. Hacking (ed.), *Scientific Revolutions* (1981).
T. S. Kuhn, *The Structure of Scientific Revolutions* (1970).
I. Lakatos & A. Musgrave (eds), *Criticism and the Growth of Knowledge* (1970).
B. Latour, *We Have Never Been Modern* (1993).
J.-F. Lyotard, *The Postmodern Condition* (1983).
R. Rorty, *Philosophy and the Mirror of Nature* (1979).
Z. Sardar, *Postmodernism and the Other* (1997).
S. Toulmin, *Return to Reason* (2003).

PROGRESS

The capacity to make progress is the most basic feature of **RATIONALITY**. An adequate conception of progress requires a goal and clear criteria for moving towards and away from the goal. This, in turn, defines an agent as, respectively, more and less rational. The goal may be specified as a dimension, such as income per capita or the ratio of true beliefs, in which increases and decreases can be registered over time. Crucially, in the course of its pursuit, the goal of progress must either be fixed or else changed explicitly. The problem with most conceptions of progress is that they meet neither of these conditions. Rather, goals are subtly shifted as they are pursued. Often substantially different (or *incommensurable*) goals are discussed in largely the same terms, so that the shifts are not readily apparent. This gives rise to instances of *adaptive preference formation*, whereby people come to adjust their goals to match their expectations: they come to want what they are likely to get. Fuller's version of social epistemology has consistently drawn attention to this feature of collective memory (see **COMMON SENSE VERSUS COLLECTIVE MEMORY**), which appears especially in acts of **TRANSLATION**, in which people from the past are interpreted as having said things that justify current orthodoxies as the most advanced stage towards goals that have always been pursued. This is the basis of Whig history. (See **HISTORIOGRAPHY**.) Unsurprisingly, the goals of progress tend to be defined in terms such as "wealth", "truth", "freedom" and "equality", which have been subject to various, often conflicting, interpretations. (See **TRUTH, RELIABILITY AND THE ENDS OF KNOWLEDGE**.)

For example, if Aristotle were transported to today, would he say that science has made progress over the past 2500 years? On the whole, Aristotle would probably say no, because he would question the wisdom of the endless production and consumption of goods without concern for ultimate consequences. Of course, Aristotle would grant a trivial sense of progress in terms of our improved ability to measure things, but these would be things that he did not want to have measured. Readers who dismiss this counterfactual thought experiment must consider the exact legitimizing work done by the concept of progress. If the concept is supposed to show that we can now better address issues that those in the past found significant, then it is appropriate to ask how a relevant ancestor would judge today's science. The only remaining question is *who* counts as a relevant ancestor. If Aristotle lived too long ago, then perhaps Newton or Darwin would prove a more appropriate judge of today's achievements. However, the closer that the historical judge's original home is to the present, the more self-serving the judgements of progress will appear.

These first two paragraphs may appear controversial because we think of progress as involving endless productivity, regardless of its measurement. The mere fact that we have a more detailed knowledge of more of reality than ever before – in part because we have more people specifically devoted to producing knowledge than ever before – is *ipso facto* a mark of progress. However, to believe this is to be captive to the military–industrial metaphor of enquiry. This metaphor draws attention to two countervailing conceptions of progress that are often conflated: on the one hand, progress is approximation to a goal or target (hence military); on the other, it is tantamount to increased productivity (hence industrial). In measurement theory, one speaks of "intensional" and "extensional" magnitudes, respectively; the former is about degrees of truth, the latter about number of truths. The upshot is that we tend to interpret the positive reinforcement we receive from our current activities (i.e. industrial) with our being drawn closer to some desired end state (i.e. military). Consequently, no clear distinction is made between, say, genuine progress towards solving some standing problems in physics and a simple addiction to doing physics. "Doing more" is simply equated with "getting better".

As a historical concept, progress presupposes that differences among human societies can be arranged in a hierarchy that over time will be eliminated as those on the bottom catch up with those on the top. Industrial capitalism has usually been implicated as the motor of greater productivity that will result in more wealth for all. Indeed, when Count Saint-Simon coined "socialism" in the early-nineteenth century, this was precisely what he had in mind. However, a strong but controversial undercurrent in the history of the concept of progress has argued that progress also requires *redistribution*, as societies on the top have overshot the ideal of human existence, typically by exploiting those on the bottom. (See **EPISTEMIC JUSTICE**.) Such theorists of progress as G. W. F. Hegel, Auguste Comte, J. S. Mill and Karl Marx shared this belief, and supported rather different institutional innovations to make the requisite redistributions. Fuller's version of social epistemology is sympathetic with this entire line of thought, which sees progress as an attempt to redress the mutually alienated state of humanity in its diverse conditions. (See **FEMINISM**.) However, the postmodern condition (see **POSTMODERNISM**) has complicated this situation, by observing that people not only presuppose different goals but also different understandings of humanity's location relative to those goals. In particular, phenomena previously regarded as negative now appear in a more positive light. Thus, underdevelopment has been reinterpreted as indigenous knowledges, mass consumption revalorized as consumer choice. (See **MULTICULTURALISM** and **UNIVERSALISM VERSUS RELATIVISM**.)

The default sense of human history in virtually all societies is cyclical. It has been considered natural for societies to experience short-lived periods of material wealth followed by political corruption and decline. The idea of irreversible human progress was first tied to Christianity as a proselytizing RELIGION whose benefits would be more fully realized through universal inclusion. During the Enlightenment, this attitude was secularized, with science replacing Christianity as the motor of universal progress, whose aim was then often seen (e.g. by Jean-Baptiste Lamarck) as the perfection of the biological species. A key feature in this transition was the idea that human suffering does not reflect divine fate but human ignorance, which is to be remedied by science. However, the relevant sense of "science" had more to do with the spread of technologies for economizing effort and increasing productivity than the sort of theory-driven scientific discoveries associated with twentieth-century conceptions of scientific progress. In this respect, SOCIAL SCIENCE – as envisaged, say, by Comtean positivism or Marxian socialism – was the ultimate aim of science.

The difference here between the Enlightenment's science-led social progress and scientific progress, in the strict sense, is subtle but important. By the end of the First World War, the British historian J. B. Bury famously argued that the idea of progress had come to an end. Bury meant that science's Baconian drive to place nature under human control was no longer a reliable route to social progress, given the mass destruction wreaked by science-driven military operations. Starting in the 1920s, Bury's pessimism was countered by two strategies designed to salvage the concept of progress. On the one hand, social scientists influenced by Darwin turned progress into the latest phase of biological evolution. This served to magnify the timescale of progress into millions of years, causing the "recent" cyclical patterns of human history to pale into insignificance when compared with the static and decidedly inferior existences of earlier species. On the other hand, philosophers – especially the logical positivists – argued that scientific progress was still demonstrable, even if social progress was not. Scientific progress was theory-driven, or paradigm-driven, as Kuhn (see KUHN, POPPER AND LOGICAL POSITIVISM) would later say. Thus, one could speak of progress in terms of a science's ability to solve the problems it sets for itself. In this spirit, a seventeenth-century "scientific revolution" – as distinct from the Renaissance – came to be identified as the mythical origin of this "pure" sense of scientific progress. (See DISCIPLINARITY VERSUS INTERDISCIPLINARITY.)

The model for the philosophical vision of science as autonomous from technology was mathematics's successful nineteenth-century campaign to recapture its autonomy from physics. In the Enlightenment, mathematics had become essentially a handmaiden to engineering, resulting in a preference for heuristics over formal proofs. However, by 1900, David Hilbert was able to list twenty-three problems distinctive to mathematics that set the field's research agenda for the coming century. Indeed, the twentieth century witnessed instances of pure mathematics anticipating their physical applications, most notably Einstein's use of non-Euclidean geometries in the formulation of relativity theory. Inspired by this precedent, the logical positivists proceeded to reconstruct the foundations of all the sciences as if they had always been aiming for what Hilbert called "formalization". Even Kuhn, whose account of science placed greater emphasis on laboratory practice, nevertheless confined himself to the branches of the physical sciences where mathematics constitutes the "symbolic generalizations" that underwrite paradigm-based research. The philosopher Imre Lakatos and the sociologist Randall Collins offer a common explanation for mathematics's suitability as a model of scientific progress: it is distinctive among academic disciplines in making the rational reconstruction of its own history – that is, the explicit derivation of new discoveries from old ones – its primary subject matter. Of course, within SCIENCE AND TECHNOLOGY STUDIES, this image of science has been largely replaced by that of *technoscience*, in which progress is purely a matter of extensional magnitudes, as in "big science".

FURTHER READING

J. B. Bury, *The Idea of Progress* (1956).
R. Collins, *The Sociology of Philosophies* (1998).
S. Fuller, *Science* (1997).
I. Lakatos, *Proofs and Refutations* (1976).
L. Laudan, *Progress and its Problems* (1977).
M. Mandelbaum, *History, Man and Reason* (1971).
D. Noble, *The Religion of Technology* (1997).

RATIONALITY

In most contemporary accounts, rationality is "always already" implicit in what we do. (See **PHILOSOPHY VERSUS SOCIOLOGY**.) In contrast, Fuller's version of **SOCIAL EPISTEMOLOGY** holds that rationality is normally alienated from our epistemic practices. It exists as an external standard to which we hold ourselves and others accountable. Indeed, this standard may be embodied in a book or a machine that attracts widespread agreement. Nevertheless, there remains the problem of how make good on the definition, or "instantiate the ideal", as Plato might put it. Philosophers tend to make life easy for themselves by claiming that we are "always already" rational. In practice, this might amount to an endorsement of the scientific establishment or a retreat to Kantian transcendentalism. (See **EXPLAINING THE NORMATIVE STRUCTURE OF SCIENCE**.) But in either case, any radical sense of **CRITICISM** is rendered virtually impossible. For its part, **SCIENCE AND TECHNOLOGY STUDIES** treats the divergence of scientists' rationality talk from their day-to-day practice as a *de facto* falsification of the rationality talk as an account of the norms governing their practice. While accepting this divergence as an empirical fact, perhaps most social epistemologists, including Fuller, would claim that rationality talk remains valid as long as the scientists would have themselves be judged by the standards embodied in that talk.

As a point of historical reference, consider that before the Treaty of Utrecht (1713), the set of laws that should be used for trying non-citizens was an open question. Sometimes the jurisdiction of the alien's declared legal home was applied, other times natural law was invoked. Kant's categorical imperative clearly harks back to the pre-Utrecht era, before the territorial sovereignty of the law became fixed. The same may be true of scientists' rationality talk, especially if the scientists envisage themselves as citizens of a republic that transcends the sites where the science and technology studies researcher encounters them. In that case, it is a mistake to presume that rationality talk is designed to bind action in a fixed location, such as a scientific laboratory. That would reduce the normative (see **NORMATIVITY**) character of science to statistically normal behaviour. However, we still have not addressed the tricky question of which, if any, institutions are capable of backing the scientists' rationality talk with normative force. Social epistemology's concern with **KNOWLEDGE POLICY** focuses precisely on this issue, especially as it relates to **EPISTEMIC JUSTICE**.

A principle of rationality must meet two conditions, the first common to most theories of rationality and the second a mark of social epistemology's concern with epistemic justice: (i) the principle must describe a regularly efficient means towards some end; and (ii) the efficiency of the principle is preferably increased, but certainly not decreased, as it becomes more widely known.

Condition (i) simply says that instrumental rationality is the only form of rationality, a view that social epistemology shares with positivism, utilitarianism, pragmatism and other forms of NATURALISM. John Dewey captured the full import of this position when he spoke of the "continuity of means and ends": Rationality is not only a matter of judging the adequacy of the means to their purported ends but also the adequacy of the ends as means to still other ends. In other words, unlike such traditional consequentialists as Aristotelians and Thomists, instrumentalists deny the existence of intrinsic or ultimate ends. However, it is common even among those who do not wish to return to Aristotle and Aquinas to conclude that instrumental rationality epitomizes the impoverished state of reason in today's world. The canonical source for this verdict is the founding text of the Frankfurt School of "critical theory", Adorno and Horkheimer's *The Dialectic of Enlightenment* (1947), which popularized a sharp distinction between instrumental and critical rationality. Whereas the former seeks the most efficient means to a given end, the latter calls the end itself into question, thereby subverting any straightforward sense of efficiency. However, this distinction mixes logical types. Instrumental rationality is a specific form of thought that may be either "critical" or "uncritical", depending on when, where and by whom it is deployed. In contrast, "critical rationality" does not refer to a specific form of thought, but to the oppositional relationship in which one form of thought stands in relation to the dominant form of thought.

The Frankfurt School distinction fails to acknowledge the historically variable role of instrumental rationality in Western culture. In the Enlightenment, instrumental rationality was invoked to criticize the inefficiency of religious and aristocratic practices by treating them as merely one of many alternatives forms of social organization that may be compared along a variety of dimensions: are the advertised benefits delivered by the established practices and, if so, at the right cost? Thus "anthropological" evidence was periodically adduced for the superiority of non-European cultures (e.g. Montesquieu's *The Persian Letters*, 1721). This critical appeal to instrumental rationality perhaps ended with Thorstein Veblen's critique of "conspicuous consumption" of nouveau riche capitalists (*The Theory of the Leisure Class*, 1899). While the rich may complain that they deserve to enjoy the fruits of their labour, Veblen wanted to hold them to the logic of capital, which regards excessive time off as wasteful, not only for workers but for anyone encompassed by the capitalist system. Thus, the best producers will be the most efficient consumers, in short, a professional class of "engineers", whose ascetic devotion to production will supersede an increasingly idle class of "businessmen".

However, after the First World War, instrumental rationality was increasingly seen as an uncritical form of thought. For the first time natural scientists had been mobilized in great numbers to design technologies of mass destruction without ever calling into question their ends. The Weimar Republic, which bred the Frankfurt School, staged the first great backlash against institutionalized science. This backlash was felt not only in the rise of outright irrationalism (e.g. Oswald Spengler, Martin Heidegger) but also in the distancing of instrumental rationality from more theoretical or substantive forms of rationality. In this respect, the logical positivists and the Frankfurt School were in common cause against Dewey's pragmatism, which (perhaps because of the US victory in the First World War) continued with diminishing rhetorical (see RHETORIC) success to connect instrumental and critical rationality. (POSTMODERNISM marks the final separation of the two conceptions.) Perhaps the last major philosopher to defend the connection was Karl Popper (see KUHN, POPPER AND LOGICAL POSITIVISM), although Fuller's social epistemology follows in that tradition.

Condition (ii) incorporates several considerations normally absent from philosophical theories of rationality:

- *The Hegelian point that certain principles work only because people have not had an opportunity to reflect on the conditions of their efficacy.* Provided with such an opportunity, the principles may become self-defeating. For Popper and Friedrich Hayek, this proves that rationality is not reducible to blind social or historical laws. A deliberate plan to do something may be among the least efficient means of bringing about that outcome, in which case more indirect means may be necessary. Freud radicalized this point as a justification of psychoanalysis: all seemingly rational actions ultimately fail to survive self-consciousness, as one comes to realize the hidden needs served by the actions and the costs they incur.

- *The Marxist point that certain principles work only because an elite are in a position to apply them.* Such principles are pseudo-rational ideologies whose primary function is to stratify the population. These ideologies lose their efficacy as more people try to apply them for their own purposes. Thus, welfare economists distinguish between merely *positional* and genuinely *public goods*. (See SOCIAL CAPITAL VERSUS PUBLIC GOOD.) Rationality aspires to be a public good, but actual instances typically turn out to be positional goods. This is true even in science. Consider a rational principle common to Aristotle and Newton: "To expedite the growth of knowledge, pick theories that explain the most effects by the fewest causes". This principle works only if there is prior agreement on the effects that need to be explained and few alternative sets of causes available to explain them. This agreement will typically have been among scientific elites, though without it, the principle would invite babble.

- *The pragmatist point that rationality is the mark of human, as opposed to mere animal, intelligence.* As heirs to Darwin, both pragmatists and behaviourists accept that animal intelligence is a function of largely automatic responses that enable an organism to adapt to its environment. In contrast, human intelligence involves a delayed response, which reflects the conversion of the stimulus into a problem. Defining the problem consists of transforming the stimulus – typically by supplying a context for it – and then generating a suitably novel response. In supplying a context for the problem, human beings take into account the presence of other things and persons in their environment. As both B. F. Skinner and Herbert Simon have noted, this more complex stimulus may be itself made a stable part of the environment as "cues" that remind others of previously efficacious responses to the stimulus, what phenomenologists would regard as a "technological transformation of the life-world" and Donald Norman has more recently popularized as "smart environments" (see **INFORMATION SCIENCE**). In that case, one implicitly builds on these embedded responses to determine the information conveyed in a new stimulus. This is *bounded rationality* of the sort associated with a Kuhnian paradigm.

Fuller's concern with bounded rationality begins by treating Paul Feyerabend's self-styled "epistemological anarchism", developed in *Against Method* (1975), as an extreme version of instrumental rationality applied to scientific enquiry. In other words, Feyerabend's notorious methodological advice – "Anything goes!" – simply means that the optimally rational scientist realizes that there is no method that *in the long run* will issue in the truth, or whatever is taken to be the ends of enquiry. (See **TRUTH, RELIABILITY AND THE ENDS OF KNOWLEDGE**.) Every method has failed at some point, and this situation is unlikely to change in the future. Even a computer capable of retrodicting all the actual theory choices made in the history of science – an aspiration of Herbert Simon in his later years – at best only captures decisions that were good enough to get science to the next point when another decision had to be taken. This observation led Feyerabend to what many regard as a counter-intuitive conclusion with regard to Galileo: although most of Galileo's theory choices were not justified by the standards of his day, Feyerabend still approved of Galileo's actions because they served to transform the decision-making environment so that, *in the long run* (especially after Newton), they turned out to have been well-grounded choices. Thus, the optimally rational Feyerabendian scientist is a risk-seeker, much like the entrepreneur who first needs to manufacture a demand for his novel product before he can expect to yield a profit.

Unsurprisingly, the scientific establishment has largely recoiled from Feyerabend's challenge. While granting the fallibility of all proposed standards of rationality, we tend *not* to take this fallibility seriously when making *our own* decisions. In one breath, we wonder how the experts were unable to see the revolutionary import of Galileo's work; yet, in the next breath, we use our current EXPERTISE to rule on theories that are potentially of equal revolutionary import. This "boundedness" in our own conception of rationality is typically expressed as Whig history. (See HISTORIOGRAPHY.) Whig history manipulates COLLECTIVE MEMORY by: (i) showing the inevitability of the current research trajectory; (ii) insinuating counterfactually that alternative trajectories would have involved a high risk and/ or relatively low benefit; and (iii) reconstructing the preferred trajectory's past so that its errors are minimized (or excused) and respectable scientists pursuing alternative trajectories appear as having been implicitly on the right trail. The key element of the RHETORIC of bounded rationality is that trade-offs must always be made between competing intellectual, material and social demands when deciding on a line of research. While no doubt true, this point then excuses a self-serving presentation of one's own position as having been the only reasonable one under the circumstances.

In conclusion, reflecting on the intertwined history of rationality as instrumental, critical and bounded, the social epistemologist engages in a kind of *science accounting* that weighs the costs and benefits of pursuing alternative epistemic trajectories. This activity can be conceived as happening either retrospectively (i.e. what would have been the respective costs and benefits of past alternatives) or prospectively (i.e. what would be the respective costs and benefits of present alternatives). Four *accountability conditions* can be identified that pertain to terms on which scientists can be held accountable for their actions:

- *Discernibility*: The ends are known to the social accountant, mainly because the accountant chooses them, or participates in their construction. The ends are not mysterious, or accessible only to some undefined entity. In this respect, science accounting is both constructive and reflexive.
- *Transcendence*: The ends are more than the sum of the immediate ends of the individuals whose actions are being held accountable.
- *Responsibility*: The ends are not idiosyncratic to the social accountant, but are ends to which the accountable individuals would reasonably consent.
- *Revisability*: The ends may change, even quite radically, as the knowledge or identity of the social accountant changes.

FURTHER READING

T. Adorno (ed.), *The Positivist Dispute in German Sociology* (1976).

S. Fuller, *Social Epistemology* (1988).

S. Fuller, *Philosophy of Science and Its Discontents* (1993).

S. Fuller & J. Collier, *Philosophy, Rhetoric and the End of Knowledge* (2004).

I. Lakatos & A. Musgrave (eds), *Criticism and the Growth of Knowledge* (1970).

L. Laudan, *Progress and its Problems* (1977).

P. Mirowski, *The Effortless Economy of Science?* (2004).

D. Norman, *Things that Make us Smart* (1993).

L. Popper, *Objective Knowledge* (1972).

F. Remedios, *Legitimizing Scientific Knowledge* (2003).

P. Roth, *Meaning and Method in the Social Sciences* (1987).

H. Simon, *The Sciences of the Artificial* (1977).

RELATIVISM VERSUS CONSTRUCTIVISM

Relativism and constructivism should be understood as equally opposed to the view philosophers call *scientific realism* but from complementary perspectives. Scientific realism involves two distinct claims, each of which can be denied separately:

- A scientific account is universally valid. Therefore, if scientific theory, T, is true, it is true everywhere and always. The denial of this claim is *relativism*. It implies that reality may vary across space at any given time.
- A scientific account is valid independently of what people think and do. Therefore if T is true, it is true even if nobody believes it. The denial of this claim is *constructivism*. It implies that, for a given place, reality may change over time. The particularist orientation of relativism opposes realism's claim to universality, whereas constructivism's reliance on the contingent actions of knowers undermines realism's claim to necessary truth.

It follows that philosophical criticism targeted at constructivism may miss its mark by taking issue with relativism. For example, the constructivist slogan "the rational itself is constitutively social" is meant to deny any clear distinction between what is rationally and socially acceptable. This view is compatible with *either* a relativist or a universalist epistemology. (e.g. Fuller's version of social epistemology is a *constructivist* UNIVERSALISM.) All that it implies is that rationality is to be explained sociologically. In principle, the relevant sense of "social" may be common to all societies. It certainly need not be limited to the relativist's clearly bounded, self-contained social worlds that are grist for paradoxes about the impossibility of standing both inside and outside one's world at the same time. Indeed, constructivists do not accept the idea that worlds (social or otherwise) have such clear insides and outsides, as these boundaries are themselves the product of social construction, not the cause of them.

Clearly, then, relativism and constructivism are compatible only under certain conditions. However, from Parmenides onwards, the Western philosophical tradition has tended to obscure this point, as necessity and universality, on the one hand, and contingency and particularity, on the other, have been associated together. Good examples include the longstanding distinction between *a priori* and *a posteriori* knowledge, or the kind of knowledge one can acquire from deduction versus induction. To be sure, there have been attempts – such as Kant's synthetic *a priori* or Hegel's concrete universal – to forge intermediate forms but they have generally been regarded with suspicion. The presumption has been that difference – be it defined in terms of sheer variety (à la relativism) or restless change (à la constructivism) – is always a deviation from a fixed norm that needs to be disciplined by either explanatory subsumption (i.e. theoretically) or social control (i.e. practically).

Had the West instead taken its marching orders from Heraclitus, we might now be operating in a philosophical universe where relativism and constructivism are clearly distinguished, but scientific realism exists only as an unstable hybrid. Thus, we would be puzzled about the idea of truths that remain invariant across all possible worlds without first having broken down the boundaries separating those worlds. (In other words, can universalism be anything other than imperialism?) For, in the Heraclitean universe, knowledge claims would be either contingently universal or necessarily particular. The presumption here would be that the maintenance of a consistent identity is an ongoing, and only locally successful, struggle in a world engulfed in endless flux.

As it turns out, the Heraclitean starting-point is the one adopted by SCIENCE AND TECHNOLOGY STUDIES. However, science and technology studies is not alone in deferring to Heraclitus. The literature surrounding "globalization" routinely supposes that we are living through a struggle between "the network society" and "the power of identity", to recall the titles of the first two volumes of Manuel Castells' magnum opus, *The Information Age*. In each binary, the former term refers to an unbounded constructivism and the latter to a resistant relativism. But we can reach back further to one of sociology's founding dualisms, what Ferdinand Toennies called *Gemeinschaft* and *Gesellschaft*. To be sure, the classical sociologists regarded the flow of history rather differently from today's globalizationists. They saw *Gesellschaft* as a rationalization of *Gemeinschaft*, usually through the mediation of the state, whereas globalization theorists would have *Gemeinschaft* emerge as a spontaneous reaction against *gesellschaftlich* practices that are no longer under state control.

The clearest case of non-relativist constructivism is free-market capitalism, in which the value of goods is determined entirely by negotiated exchanges among interested parties. No preferences or beliefs are so fundamental as to be exempt from such negotiations, to which there is no "natural" outcome. Indeed, it is this inherent volatility that unites relativists and realists against constructivists. Indeed, the prototype of the modern relativist position – the "culture" that affixes a worldview to a particular group – was introduced in Germany to stave off the universalizing ambitions of the commercial ethic emanating from Britain in the early-nineteenth century. Moreover, before the advent of POSTMODERNISM, most anthropologists were probably relativists but *not* constructivists. To believe that truth is culturally relative has usually implied that there are "facts of the matter" (about tribal history, geography and perhaps even biology) about which knowledge claims are true for which cultures. Anthropologists such as E. E. Evans-Pritchard did not suppose that the natives negotiated their epistemic practices as they went along. That would have rendered a science of anthropology virtually impossible, a point that postmodernists gladly admit. Instead, anthropologists regarded native practices as *ceteris paribus* instances of normal behaviour in the societies where they occurred. The difficult task was establishing the scope of these practices: when and where did the natives tend to behave this way? But, in principle, this task was no different from establishing the boundary conditions under which an empirical regularity applied in the physical world.

It is often forgotten that the radical "otherness" with which anthropologists classically regarded the natives contributed to the idea that native cultures enjoyed a kind of epistemic independence from the anthropologist. (See MULTICULTURALISM.) Thus, to a constructivist, anthropology's relativism amounted to a realism about multiple social worlds. (See SOCIAL CONSTRUCTIVISM.) However, anthropology has suffered from its original non-constructivist relativism, typically by underestimating interaction effects: the ease with which native practices can be altered by alien intrusion and aliens can be fooled by native irony and deceit. Unsurprisingly, then, the turn to constructivism in anthropology began with a reflexive realization that the anthropologist was *in* the very world she was trying to write *about*. From the standpoint of constructivism, the "otherness" of relativism turned out to be a form of self-deception whereby anthropologists were discouraged from observing their own participation in the imperialist project. In that sense, a reflexive relativism *is* constructivism.

In a much shorter time, science and technology studies has largely repeated anthropology's sequence of relativist consolidation and constructivist dispersion, as recently epitomized by, respectively, David Bloor and Bruno Latour. Together they illustrate an instance of what appears in Table 2 as *The Heraclitean Dialectic of Sociology*. As suggested by the row "Principle of social change", it is possible to regard relativism and constructivism as complementary positions, for example, if social functions are reproduced across generations by redistributing properties previously possessed by one group of individuals to another group. However, this neat macro–micro picture starts to crack once the redistributive process is seen as a source of emergent properties that alter the character of the reproductive process, such as when women come to fill roles previously filled by men. At this point, constructivism breaks free from relativism.

In the English intellectual tradition from Hobbes to Spencer, "war" and "commerce" often appeared as alternating historical phases. War unifies a people against

Species of anti-realism	Relativism	Constructivism
Fundamental process	Identification	Differentiation
Image of the social	Bounded groups	Interactive networks
Scope of the social	Finite and invariant	Infinite and variable
Source of value	Intrinsic to society	Defined in exchange
Principle of social change	Reproduction at the macro-level	Redistribution at the micro-level
Classical sociological image	Customs (*Gemeinschaft*)	Contracts (*Gesellschaft*)
Defining social practice	War	Commerce
Political extreme	Totalitarianism	Imperialism
Biological version	Racialism	Adaptationism
Science and technology studies version	Group-grid theory	Actor-network theory
"Return of the repressed"	"Revolution"	"Ecology"

Table 2. The Heraclitean dialectic in sociology.

a common foe, whereas commerce encourages people to forge networks that extend beyond tribal borders. Indeed, this attitude has permeated science policy thinking well into the twentieth century, given the cycles of mobilization and redeployment of scientific effort that have marked the periods before and after wars. According to this model, the threat of war stabilizes society, which over time may intensify into a totalitarian mindset, whereby individual differences are completely submerged into a single cultural identity. The removal of external threat opens the door to a more outwards policy that by acquiring cumulative advantage over many exchanges may evolve into imperialism. No imperialist pretends that, say, Christian values are "natural" to non-Western cultures, only that these cultures are likely to benefit by adopting them. Whether this is because Christianity satisfies a standing need or induces such a need by virtue of its associated consequences is a matter of indifference to the imperialist.

In the science and technology studies literature, actor-network theory, most closely linked with Latour, canonizes the imperialist's indifference as constructivist research methodology. Thus, constructivists tend to be insensitive to pre-existent (structural or historical) power relations between the parties to an exchange that may overdetermine the outcome of the ensuing negotiations, as in British imperial encounters with African natives in the 1930s and 1940s. In contrast, group-grid theory, as adapted by Bloor from Douglas, is explicitly concerned with the conditions under which social identity is stabilized. Consequently, "outsiders" only figure as candidate insiders, not as potential subsumers of the entire social order. Here, then, are the complementary weaknesses of constructivism and relativism that appear as the "repressed" sides of their positions. Constructivists are haunted by the idea of a social and/or material limit to "free exchange", which nowadays is often expressed as the need to incorporate "ecology" into social theory. For their part, relativists face the prospect of their normative orders imploding as anomalies accumulate without formal resolution. This situation is captured by the Kuhnian (see **KUHN, POPPER AND LOGICAL POSITIVISM**) concept of "revolution" in science.

FURTHER READING

D. Bloor, *Knowledge and Social Imagery* (1976).

M. Castells, *The Information Age* (1996–8).

S, Fuller, *Social Epistemology* (1988).

S. Fuller & J. Collier, *Philosophy, Rhetoric and the End of Knowledge* (2004).

M. Hollis & S. Lukes (eds), *Rationality and Relativism* (1982).

B. Latour, *Science in Action* (1987).

B. Latour, *The Pasteurization of France* (1988).

B. Latour, *We Have Never Been Modern* (1993).

Z. Sardar, *Postmodernism and the Other* (1997).

D. Sperber, *Explaining Culture: A Naturalistic Approach* (1996).

S. P. Turner, *Brains/Practices/Relativism* (2002).

RELIGION

It is difficult to characterize "religion" as a form of knowledge because the set of practices with which the term is normally associated share little more than the capacity to maintain complex social relations over large chunks of space and time without a need for the modern nation state. In this respect, religions are the original non-governmental organizations (NGOs). As for the existence of some unique religious experience, William James had already put paid to that idea in 1902 by demonstrating that suitably "numinous" experience could be reliably induced by pharmaceutical means. (Given the cross-cultural prevalence of drug use, the so-called "world religions" would then seem to cover social practices that valorize the drug-free induction of numinous experience.) As for a belief in God, some religions, like Buddhism, are formally atheistic, while others, like Hinduism, treat God and nature as coextensive. (See **NATURALISM**.)

Not surprisingly, then, the canonical list of world religions came into being in the second half of the nineteenth century, as sociologists and anthropologists sought criteria to mark the transition from traditional to modern society. Perhaps the least prejudicial definition of religion – one that neither demeans nor mystifies its cognitive character – is that it is the systematic social embodiment of a metaphysical worldview. In this respect, *any* set of beliefs becomes a religion once they constitute the medium through which people live their lives. This led Kenneth Burke to regard religion as the most sublime form of **RHETORIC**. The distinction often drawn between prophetic and wisdom religions, which corresponds to religions that do and do not descend from the Old Testament, may be thus seen as capturing the temporal direction in which people live: the prophetic religions live in *anticipation* (of what might happen) whereas the wisdom religions live in *adaptation* (to what has already happened). Of all the grammatical constructions associated with religion, the adverb "religiously" captures religion's core idea best, namely, its lived character.

Perhaps the most influential attempt to give a positive empirical account of religion as a form of knowledge was undertaken by the comparative philologist Max Müller in the 1860s. He identified religion as the original seat of culture because through the rituals surrounding its sacred texts, language use came to be standardized. In this respect, religion provided the most fundamental expression of worldviews whose residues remained even after the nation state took control of the propagation and regulation of language use. Generally speaking, the world religions were divided into two or three language groups, all of Asian origin. Müller's most famous dichotomy – between Aryan (Indian) and Semitic (Near

Eastern) languages – was based on the idea of alternative origins of civilization in the Sanskrit and Hebrew scriptures. For example, it underwrote Matthew Arnold's popularization of the word "culture" in the English language, via his distinction of "Hellenic" (cf. Aryan) and "Hebraic" (cf. Semitic) sensibilities. (See MULTICUL-TURALISM.)

The Aryan root flowed through Greece to become the basis of aristocratic culture, what Nietzsche called the "master ethic", with its emphasis on hierarchical modes of organization, as reflected in the Hindu caste system and "hypotactic" grammatical forms, whereby a prefix or suffix may transform a word's meaning, and even its logical status, so that the whole is greater than the sum of its parts. This is characteristic of the dialectical forms of reasoning at which the Hindus and Greeks excelled. In contrast, the Semitic root flowed through Protestant Christianity to underwrite egalitarian culture, Nietzsche's "slave ethic", with its concern for the weak, which is supposedly mirrored in its paratactic grammatical forms, which treats all words on the same logical plane. As more was learned about Chinese religion, language and culture, the Semitic root came to be seen as the hybrid of the Aryan root and a more fundamental Sinic root, which approximated an ideal that Leibniz originally associated with Chinese ideograms, namely, the universal language of thought, whereby each sign stands for one and only one idea, such that the whole is logically reducible to the sum of the parts, an ideal approximated by modern symbolic logic.

Müller was also responsible for a theory of religious PROGRESS that made it continuous with scientific progress. While the distinction between polytheistic and monotheistic religions had been long accepted, Müller argued that polytheism in practice was a matter of belief in one god *at a time*, while monotheism implied a belief in one god *all the time*. Polytheists were in effect the original devotees of RELATIVISM, which helped to explain why cultures attached to this perspective failed to develop a sense of "universe" that is presupposed by modern science, as exemplified by Newton, which assumes that reality can be understood as a system closed under a set of knowable principles. Polytheists lacked a supreme deity whose workings are sufficiently intelligible to human beings to enable them to resolve whatever conflicts might exist among lesser deities. From that standpoint, science flows directly from the secularization of monotheism, as humanity replaces the supreme deity as the vehicle for the ultimate realization of whatever design the deity might have intended. It is associated with what the historian David Noble has pejoratively called the "religion of technology", and explains the intimate connection between the projects of systematically understanding and radically transforming nature, to which SCIENCE AS A SOCIAL MOVEMENT has been dedicated in the West.

This characteristically "modernist" turn in religious thought began in earnest in the eighteenth-century Enlightenment, when such pioneers of biblical CRITICISM as John Toland and Gotthold Lessing identified the three great monotheistic religions – Judaism, Christianity and Islam – as jointly engaged in the emancipation of humanity from its child-like dependency on secular authority. Often this project was counterposed to Roman Catholicism, whose various layers of noble and clerical mediation were held to inhibit humanity's capacity for self-realization. Indeed, the Catholic Church's lavish symbolic displays and mystifying propaganda amounted to idolatry, which played on human susceptibility to sensationalism, a residue of our animal natures. (See CONSENSUS VERSUS DISSENT and MASS MEDIA.) In contrast, monotheism in its pure form stood for an unmediated and abstract spirituality ("Unitarianism") that by the nineteenth century – in the historicisms of Auguste Comte, Hegel and Marx – had come to be divested of nearly all biblical traces. This turn was indicative of the rise of SOCIAL SCIENCE as a distinct body of knowledge dedicated to humanity's dominion over nature without human beings exerting dominion over each other, the secular TRANSLATION of the biblical idea that all human beings are equally created in the image and likeness of God. In terms of this trajectory, Darwin's theory of EVOLUTION by natural selection marked a return to a pagan sensibility that treated humanity as simply a transient phase in a self-sustaining nature, where the circulation of genetic material scientifically updates the doctrine of karma.

FURTHER READING

R. Aron, *Main Currents in Sociological Thought* (1965).
P. Berger, *The Sacred Canopy* (1967).
H. Bergson, *The Two Sources of Morality and Religion* (1935).
K. Burke, *A Grammar of Motives* (1969).
J. A. Campbell & S. Meyer (eds), *Darwin, Design and Public Education* (2003).
R. Collins, *The Sociology of Philosophies* (1998).
S. Fuller, *Science* (1997).
S. Fuller, *The New Sociological Imagination* (2006).
J. Hecht, *Doubt* (2003).
M. Mandelbaum, *History, Man and Reason* (1971).
T. Masuzawa, *The Invention of World Religions* (2005).
J. Milbank, *Theology and Social Theory* (1990).
D. Noble, *The Religion of Technology* (1997).
J. M. Robertson, *A History of Free-Thought in the Nineteenth Century* (1929).
M. Weber, *The Sociology of Religion* (1965).
B. Wilson, *Rationality* (1970).
R. Wuthnow, *Discourse Communities* (1989).

RHETORIC

Rhetoric is the art of rendering things public, or *res publicae* (see FREE ENQUIRY). In other words, things that might otherwise be simply taken for granted or ignored are turned into resources that one may use to move an audience to action. William Fusfield has usefully distinguished ideals of rhetorical practice. On the one hand is *demonstration*, a relatively short and focused speech; on the other, *declaration*, a complex piece of writing. According to Fusfield, this distinction was crucial to the German idealist understanding of the distinction between ancient and modern modes of communication. This theme recurs in the leading schools of contemporary continental philosophy, including the Frankfurt School and French poststructuralism. (See RATIONALITY.)

Demonstration invites an immediacy and explicitness of response that is common to both face-to-face encounters in the public sphere and logical proofs. It presupposes that consensus (see CONSENSUS VERSUS DISSENT) is the goal of communication, either because the appeal to reason is purportedly universal (logic) or because the exigency is common to all within earshot of the speech (politics). In contrast, declaration presupposes that the goals of communication are diverse because audiences are diverse, as symbolized by the different places where people would read a written text, not all gathered in the classroom or the forum. Whereas demonstrativists aspire to convergence on a set of propositions or even a common course of action, declarativist wish to stimulate the reader positively in many different ways, but perhaps all in opposition to a common orthodoxy. Not surprisingly, equivocation is valued in declarative rhetoric, but despised in demonstrative rhetoric. Conversely, clarity is often regarded with suspicion by declarativists, whereas demonstrativists take it as necessary for communication.

Those who see rhetoric and science as opposed, rather than complementary, deny the rhetorical character of demonstrative rhetoric and the scientific character of declarative rhetoric. Even partisans fall victim to these blindspots. Thus, demonstrators may fail to mention that the steps of their argument may be self-evident only to those they wish to persuade, while declarers may not wish to admit that their oblique expression has been compelled by the complexity of reality. From the Greeks onwards, the paradigm of demonstration has been geometry because all of its premises are explicit; it is measured in tone; it aims at consensus. Whereas demonstration is guided by method, declaration is led by wit. Its message is conveyed obliquely, in several registers at once, typically inviting the audience to participate in the completion of the message, which may vary according to the context of utterance. This was the view championed by the Sophists, who, much to Socrates' dismay, refused to draw a sharp, principled distinction between science and rhetoric. Science might simply be a form of rhetoric that aims to overturn a presumption held by most people in favour of one that will enable them to cope with the world more effectively. This would unite the Sophists' interest in "making the weaker argument appear the stronger" with, say, Popper's falsifiability principle.

To illustrate the demonstrativist and declarativist approaches to rhetoric, how would each explain the paradigmatic status of Darwin's theory of **EVOLUTION** in biology? The demonstrativist would point to the truth of Darwin's fundamental claims, which enables their fruitful application in various theoretical and practical settings. In contrast, declarativist would say that Darwin's theory is sufficiently open textured to justify a variety of things said and done. The former would explain early resistance to Darwin in terms of the cognitive deficiencies of either Darwin himself or his audiences, the latter in terms of difficulties audiences had in making the theory do something useful for them.

This difference in emphasis points to alternative understandings of the pragmatic dimension of language. The demonstrativist follows a line close to most analytic philosophy, whereby the content of Darwin's theory – its semantics – is fixed prior to its communication, which is itself regarded as an application of the theory's content. In contrast, the declarativist treats the content of Darwin's theory more hermeneutically, that is, as only partially formed in the pages of *On the Origin of Species*. The text's reception history then tracks the process by which Darwin's argument is continually constituted and reconstituted by the book's readers. It is only in light of this reception history that a canonical version of Darwin's theory can be abstracted retrospectively. Not surprisingly, the three most celebrated scientists of the modern era – Newton, Darwin and Einstein – all benefited from powerful rhetorical intermediaries (John Locke, Thomas Henry Huxley and Max Planck) who not only translated formidable technicalities but also contributed catchy images that epitomized the master's work.

In the case of scientific theory choice, the demonstrativist presumes that the moment of decision is always appropriate and what matters are the relevant arguments and evidence. Behind this view is the belief that science has its own internal rhythm: no major change in research trajectory occurs before its time. In contrast, the declarativist wonders why the moment of decision occurs at one point in time rather than some other. After all, had the moment been a bit earlier or later, the relative standing of the parties to the dispute – not to mention the actual composition of the parties – may have been quite different. A slight change in context and the weaker argument may have turned out to be the stronger. In short, those who control *when* the decision is made control *what* decision is made. Thus, for the declarativist, knowledge of rhetoric is necessary for knowing when to *start* and *stop* arguments that would otherwise continue *ad infinitum*. In a classic application of the declarativist approach to the rhetoric of science, Paul Forman argued that the German physics community's shift to an indeterminist interpretation of quantum mechanics in the interwar years was due more to political expedience than the balance of technical arguments and evidence, which had remained largely unchanged.

Modern science has increasingly questioned the demonstrative–declarative distinction. To be sure, scientists continue to attach overriding significance to demonstrations of reasoning and evidence. However, the scale and scope of modern science make it impossible for every scientist to witness – or recreate – the relevant demonstrations. Consequently, the scientific journal article has come to evince a declarative rhetoric that Steven Shapin calls "virtual witnessing", whereby readers are persuaded that the author is a reliable witness who argues in good faith, that is, without fabricating evidence or reasoning. Such rhetoric is declarative because scientific journal articles do not typically provide sufficient information for evaluating the research they report. The reader must make additional assumptions about the author, the research environment, the mastery of techniques and so on. But often these assumptions turn out to be false.

In recent years, concerns about professional scientific rhetoric have been raised following a rise in the detection of fraud in published research that was costly to do and substantial in impact. Some **SCIENCE AND TECHNOLOGY STUDIES** scholars have responded with a declarativist's sense of scepticism that scientists could ever write so as to enable a foolproof evaluation of their research. Indeed, unlike the humanities, where the close reading of texts is a normative desideratum, the natural sciences typically treat texts as a mere means to other ends, such as the design of new experiments and the acquisition of funds. Thus, the history of scientific journal writing exhibits successive innovations to streamline the reading process. Nowadays the scientific text is divided into modules of "theory", "method", "data" and "discussion" to enable scientific readers to appropriate relevant sections for their own purposes, and to ignore (*not* criticize; see **CRITICISM**) the rest. What would strike humanists as sheer negligence – namely, to read only selected sections of an article – appears crucial to the consolidation and cumulative growth that distinguish knowledge in the natural sciences from knowledge in the humanities and the social sciences. Whereas a highly cited article in the natural sciences is usually exemplary in only one or a few respects, a comparably cited article in the social sciences or humanities might be regarded more ambivalently, but also in its entirety.

The production and consumption cycles of texts in the natural sciences turn out to be like those of the **MASS MEDIA**. From patterns discerned in the *Science*

Citation Index, the "harder" the science, the more its research specialties resemble fads in their lifecycles. In contrast, research specialties in the "softer" sciences have long half-lives, so that it is unclear when – or even if – they definitively go out of fashion. This general phenomenon probably reflects the similarities in the size and shape of today's scientific enterprise and the mass media. In both cases, invisible colleges and opinion leaders structure the reception and appropriation of texts. Fuller's version of social epistemology treats this state of affairs as not inevitable but pathological (see **INFORMATION SCIENCE**). It requires recovery of science's lost rhetorical dimension, which involves disaggregating overall scientific tendencies to the specific decisions taken to express and interpret things in certain ways. (See **EXPLAINING THE COGNITIVE CONTENT OF SCIENCE**.)

The steady decline of science as an object of rhetoric begins with the English coinage of "scientist" by William Whewell in the 1830s to designate someone academically qualified and paid to pursue science on a full-time basis, not a mere inventor or naturalist who works in his spare time. Whewell spawned his own rhetoric, normally called "philosophy of science", that aims to demarcate genuine scientists from those now deemed "pseudoscientific" practitioners of what had become a profession. In previous generations, amateurs with sufficient time and money had made the bulk of the contributions to science. Newton the salaried academic was the exception, whereas Darwin the leisured gentleman was the rule. However, there had been a kind of moral obligation to the leisured pursuit of science, based on Aristotle's injunction at the opening of the *Metaphysics*, where he presents the search for knowledge as the ultimate form of self-actualization. This was still true of the American founding fathers Benjamin Franklin and Thomas Jefferson, who regarded scientific pursuits as integral to republican citizenry as much as property ownership. (See **KNOWLEDGE MANAGEMENT**.)

Before Whewell's semantic innovation, science was not conceptualized as a technical specialty that would have disqualified public discussion of its means and ends. Of course, such discussion remained restricted, but only because very few people (men, more precisely) enjoyed the requisite leisure to pursue science, not because the subject matter itself precluded more public involvement. Before the extension of citizenship rights to all adult males in the nineteenth-century West, "public" and "elite" were perfectly compatible terms. During this period, "technical" most naturally meant – as it did in ancient Greece – an art closely tied to particular manual skills.

Reflecting on this history, it might seem that "rhetoric of science" is a contradiction in terms. Science is supposedly much too technical for rhetoric to play a constructive role; at most rhetoric may function as a kind of public relations for science. However, this assessment is misdirected. For Aristotle to be convinced that today's scene precludes rhetoric from science, he would need to be shown that what we call "science" is primarily driven by skills that are so contextually specific that only those expert (see **EXPERTISE**) in them can say anything sensible about how, where and why those skills are used. But to admit this (according to Aristotle) would also be to deny that what we call "science" has universal cognitive purchase. Of course, most science and technology studies scholars concede this point, typically as part of a more general postmodern scepticism (see **POSTMOD-ERNISM**) about the very idea of "universal cognitive purchase".

Nevertheless, it remains open to rhetoricians to defend the classical view that scientific discourse must allow public participation to live up to its universalist (see **UNIVERSALISM VERSUS RELATIVISM**) aspiration. One strategy is for rhetoricians to demystify scientific jargon and introduce considerations that force scientists to address a wider audience than their discourse would otherwise allow. This may involve revealing hidden disagreements among experts who would otherwise provide a united front to the public. Science's rhetorical status is most easily seen by observing that science most frequently enters public debate over problems whose solution transcends any given scientist's expertise. (See **SCIENCE WARS**.) While science's increased division of intellectual labour has often been used to license the kind of "anti-rhetoric" of science associated with the philosophy of science, which stresses science's technical and specialized character, this division in fact supports an opening up of the sphere of deliberation. Because each new specialty tends to be defined in relation to already existing specialties rather than a free-standing social problem, lay ignorance (which tends to be experientially richer) and expert specialization (which tends to be experientially poorer) turn out to be rhetorically equivalent positions from which to argue for a democratic approach to **KNOWLEDGE POLICY**. In short, rhetoric is necessary for science because each scientist knows more and more about less and less. This fact forces her back more quickly to the position of a layperson, especially when it comes to science's increasingly general and uncertain impacts on society. (See **SCIENCE AS A SOCIAL MOVEMENT**.)

FURTHER READING

T. Adorno (ed.), *The Positivist Dispute in German Sociology* (1976).
C. Bazerman, *Shaping Written Knowledge* (1987).
K. Burke, *A Grammar of Motives* (1969).
J. A. Campbell & S. Meyer (eds), *Darwin, Design and Public Education* (2003).
L. Ceccarelli, *Shaping Science with Rhetoric* (2001).
M. De Mey, *The Cognitive Paradigm* (1982).
P. Forman, "Weimar Culture, Causality, and Quantum Theory" (1971).
S. Fuller, *Science* (1997).
S. Fuller & J. Collier 2004. *Philosophy, Rhetoric and the End of Knowledge* (2004).

W. Fusfield, "To Want to Prove it ... is ... Really Superfluous" (1997).

N. Gilbert & M. Mulkay, *Opening Pandora's Box* (1984).

J. Habermas, *The Structural Transformation of the Public Sphere* (1989).

W. Keith, *Democracy as Discussion* (2007).

R. Macksey & E. Donato (eds), *The Structuralist Controversy* (1970).

J. S. Nelson, A. Megill & D. McCloskey (eds), *The Rhetoric of the Human Sciences* (1986).

S. Shapin & S. Schaffer 1985. *Leviathan and the Air Pump* (1985).

S. Toulmin, *Return to Reason* (2003).

C. A. Willard, *Argumentation and the Social Grounds of Knowledge* (1983).

SCIENCE AND TECHNOLOGY STUDIES

S cience and technology studies (STS) is the interdisciplinary field concerned with the study of science and technology mainly, but not exclusively, in contemporary society. The field's preferred methods are associated with SOCIAL CONSTRUCTIVISM, although most of its leading practitioners were originally trained in the natural sciences and engineering but subsequently came to be disenchanted with how science's material entanglements compromised its normative integrity. In STS, SOCIAL EPISTEMOLOGY appears as a NORMATIVE approach to science and technology policy.

STS characteristically treats science and technology as a composite entity, *technoscience*, which is thoroughly integrated in all social processes. Within STS, a "low church" and "high church" can be distinguished, depending on whether the focus is on turning STS into, respectively, a movement aimed at transforming the role of science and technology in society or an academic discipline pursued for its own sake. (See SCIENCE AS A SOCIAL MOVEMENT.)

Low church STS harks back to the original use of "technoscience" in the 1960s as a synonym for what C. Wright Mills called the "military-industrial complex", in which the trajectory of scientific research was being shaped according to the imperatives of capital expansion and Cold War strategy. This became noticeable in terms of scientists' employment patterns, which reflected a scaled-up, specialized and targeted research culture, the fruits of which could have immediate impact on ordinary lives, be it as goods or weapons. The British physicist John Desmond Bernal had already observed this pattern in the 1930s as part of the proletarianization of science, the solution to which (according to Bernal) lay in the constitution of scientists as a "class" aligned with the workers' revolutionary movement. However, Bernal's pro-Soviet politics rendered his views unpalatable during the Cold War. Nevertheless, a milder version of the same thinking flourished among educators interested in having scientists acquire a critical appreciation of the various social and political contexts in which their work would increasingly figure. In the late 1960s, the Edinburgh Science Studies Unit – canonically treated as the original institutionalization of STS – was founded with this aim in mind. In the same period, the US witnessed a proliferation of "science and society" programmes designed to raise consciousness about science's involvement in warfare, exploitation and environmental despoliation.

High church STS derives from the Science Studies Unit's abiding interest in moving beyond "service teaching" for scientists to an autonomous research programme. In this aspiration, the unit was influenced by the writings of Thomas Kuhn, Michael Polanyi and the anthropologist Mary Douglas, all of whom stressed the importance of insularity (what Douglas called "purity") to the conduct of enquiry. In 1970, the unit's director, David Edge, founded what remains the main STS journal, *Social Studies of Science*. In this setting, STS defined itself against philosophical defences of the normative structure of science that did not stand up to empirical scrutiny. (See **EXPLAINING THE NORMATIVE STRUCTURE OF SCIENCE**.) Originally this anti-philosophical stance was made in the spirit of demystification, explicitly modelled on the **SOCIOLOGY OF KNOWLEDGE**. (See **CRITICISM**.) However, high church STS has increasingly lost any interest in reconstructing the normative structure of science in the wake of its demystification. Instead, the field has become preoccupied with providing an empirically adequate account of technoscience, as judged by its own social constructivist strictures, leaving the policy implications of such an account completely open. This acritical perspective explains two features of recent STS that are epitomized by Bruno Latour's influence. On the one hand, in the ongoing **SCIENCE WARS**, STS's official stance is that the field simply describes without prescribing for science, so that the messenger should not be blamed for the bad news it might deliver about the state of science. On the other hand, in our budget conscious **KNOWLEDGE SOCIETY**, STS can be a very useful policy instrument in recording exactly how scientists spend their time and money for purposes of evaluating their performance (a.k.a. **KNOWLEDGE MANAGEMENT**).

Roughly corresponding to high church and low church STS are two distinct attitudes to the scientific enterprise. Some STS researchers appear satisfied that the training of scientists ensures that they know what they are doing, and should continue doing it, largely without the misguided commentary of philosophers and other outside scrutinizers. Yet, other STS researchers are less satisfied, taking their own success in penetrating the inner workings of science to imply that non-specialists should have more of a say about which science is done, and how. The first viewpoint, tied to the high church, is called "deep science"; the second, tied to the low church, is called "shallow science". Fuller's **SOCIAL EPISTEMOLOGY** adopts a form of **KNOWLEDGE POLICY** aligned to shallow science that aims to infuse the high church with low church spirit.

Deep science is a largely non-verbal craft that requires acculturation into long-standing disciplinary traditions and is best studied by a detailed phenomenology of scientific practice. Opposed to this image is that of shallow science, a largely verbal craft that consists of the ability to negotiate the science/society boundary to one's own advantage in a variety of settings; it is best studied by deconstructing the seamless **RHETORIC** of scientists so as to reveal the clutter of activities that such rhetoric masks. Typical students of deep science are the many historians of experiment, who follow Michael Polanyi in devaluing the role of theorizing in everyday scientific practice. Students of shallow science include most social constructivists and discourse analysts. Unlike most other members of this camp, Fuller holds that a robustly normative approach to science is compatible with – indeed, even facilitated by – shallow science. That most prescriptive of normative enquirers, positivist philosophers, originated the shallow science perspective by searching for an all-purpose methodological trick (a.k.a. demarcation criterion) to enable non-scientists like themselves to hold science accountable for its activities. By contrast, students of deep science tend to be purely descriptive in their aspirations, tacitly presuming that science works as long as the scientists do not complain. Not surprisingly, deep science tends to be concentrated in laboratories, whereas shallow science is spread diffusely across society.

These two images – deep and shallow science – define polar attitudes towards the cognitive powers of the individual scientist. At the deep end is the idea that scientists are especially well-suited, in virtue of their training, to represent the nature of reality. At the shallow end is the idea that scientists are no better suited than laypeople to represent reality, an idea that is rarely appreciated not only because scientists share with laypeople basic limitations in their ability to scrutinize their own practices, but also because the epistemic cost of admitting the fallibility of scientific judgement is especially dear: how would engineering be possible if the judgements of physicists were not well grounded? Yet, it is precisely this easy relation between science and technology that the shallow science perspective has endeavoured to challenge. The basic problem with deep science is that its conception of the social is unbecoming to anyone who wishes to hold science accountable to anyone other than the scientists themselves. It is a conception that provincializes society into jurisdictions of local knowledge, or EXPERTISE, the authority of which is taken on trust, regardless of its potential consequences for those outside a given jurisdiction. (See MULTICULTURALISM.)

STS has both significantly advanced and retarded our understanding of science and technology. It has certainly compelled a more nuanced conception of the *content* of science. Philosophers traditionally identified the content of science with the normative potential of scientific work, that is, the ability of laboratory activities, especially experiments, to produce well-founded propositions. In contrast, STS has taken at face value scientists' own tendency to identify the content of science with the technical character of their work, relatively little of which is ever distilled into a system of testable propositions. Whereas philosophers profess to offer a purified vision of science that is continuous with the philosophical search for truth, STS has given voice to a view held by many, especially non-theoretical, scientists; namely, that philosophy abstracts from the linguistic surface of science, and then judges scientific practice against this abstraction (a.k.a. RATIONALITY). Moreover, in so doing, STS has appealed to proponents of the main anti-philosophical strains in twentieth-century philosophy, notably Ludwig Wittgenstein, Gaston Bachelard and

Martin Heidegger, all of whom, in strikingly different ways, argued that philosophical theories were superfluous accretions on locally grounded practices. Consistent with this approach, STS has adopted a *grounded theory* methodology, whereby the STS researcher limits her conceptual apparatus to what the people under study use to account for their own behaviour. As Latour puts it, the researcher simply follows the actors, recording their actions, but offers no resistance to their activities in the form of second-order theoretical claims that scientists systematically misrepresent, if not misunderstand, their own practices.

STS's grounded theory methodology probably puts it most at odds with modern philosophy of science, including **KUHN, POPPER AND LOGICAL POSITIVISM**. Despite their other differences, these philosophers all agreed that scientific enquiry is *by definition* constrained by theories and value commitments. STS assumes no such constraints unless clearly demonstrated in the scientists' practice.

In any case, it does not generally apply this point to its own enquiries. It reflects the professionalization of the field: a "good fences make good neighbours" policy that renounces any critical interrogation of the social dimensions of disciplinary boundary construction and maintenance (a.k.a. knowledge policy). Instead, STS adopts a much more object-centred stance, in which the STS researcher begins only with her client's frame of reference, unencumbered by a position of her own towards the actors she studies. This has been a source of concern for more critical STS researchers, such as Donna Haraway. It is epitomized in the contrast in metaphors for knowing. There is, on the one hand, the fixed standpoint of, say, Marxism or **FEMINISM**, which is necessary for an independent critical perspective. On the other hand, there is STS's explicitly nomadic character, which befits a field whose activities are increasingly given over to client-driven, contract-based research. In the transition from the former to the latter metaphor, STS seems to have abandoned the interest in social responsibility that had motivated its low church.

The concept of technoscience, now used in many fields, probably provides the greatest source of conceptual and practical difficulties for STS. Philosophically speaking, these tensions pull along the **UNIVERSALISM VERSUS RELATIVISM** divide. "Technoscience" signifies the undifferentiated character of science and technology in contemporary society. It is meant to oppose the strong science–technology distinction that became increasingly prominent in twentieth-century philosophies of scientific **PROGRESS**, precisely the time when technology became increasingly integral to the conduct of science, and this scaled-up "big science" merged with the material infrastructure of society. However, STS conceptualizes this transformation rather differently from, say, Marxist political economy. Instead of seeing science and technology as integrated into the capitalist mode of production, STS regards technoscience as a principle of self-organization that reproduces the rest of society as objects for its own study and control. The great heroes of technoscience are thus people such as Louis Pasteur and Thomas Edison, who accomplished with science and technology what politicians could not do with mere words.

While perhaps flattering to scientists, and especially engineers, this image of technoscience ignores underlying and often longstanding power relations that give certain technoscientific innovations forward momentum, quite independently of their intrinsic merit or the intentions of their originators. At the same time, STS tends to cast technoscience in very particularistic terms, namely, as an extended actor-network. That a society might appropriate science or technology for its own cultural purposes without becoming involved in the formative actor-network turns out to be a point of contention between Western and non-Western STS researchers. (See MULTICULTURALISM.) This point was aired in the first global cyberconference on the public understanding of science, organized under the auspices of the UK's Economic and Social Research Council in 1998. In spite of resistance from non-Westerners, Western STS researchers appeared keen to treat the success of "Japanese science" or "Islamic science" as more a matter of the *hybridization* of local knowledges than the *appropriation* of universal knowledge. Whereas "hybridization" draws attention only to the non-Westerners' creative efforts, "appropriation" implies that they also had to wrest control of relevant knowledge from Westerners who might not otherwise have shared it. From the standpoint of social epistemology, STS's preference for the language of hybridization over appropriation arguably points to the field's abdication of its own responsibility for the course of science and technology by refusing to implicate the knowledges of the peoples it studies in the wider epistemic universe of which STS is itself a part.

FURTHER READING

J. D. Bernal, *The Social Function of Science* (1939).
S. Fuller, *The Philosophy of Science and Technology Studies* (2006).
S. Fuller & J. Collier, *Philosophy, Rhetoric and the End of Knowledge* (2004).
N. Gilbert & M. Mulkay, *Opening Pandora's Box* (1984).
B. Glaser & A. Strauss, *The Discovery of Grounded Theory* (1967).
D. Haraway, *Simians, Cyborgs, Women* (1991).
S. Harding, *Whose Science? Whose Knowledge?* (1991).
B. Latour, *Science in Action* (1987).
B. Latour, *The Pasteurization of France* (1988).
B. Latour, *Pandora's Hope* (1999).
B. Latour & S. Woolgar, *Laboratory Life* (1986).
P. Mirowski, *The Effortless Economy of Science?* (2004).
A. Pickering (ed.), *Science as Practice and Culture* (1992).
M. Polanyi, *Personal Knowledge* (1957).
J. Ravetz, *Scientific Knowledge and Its Social Problems* (1971).

SCIENCE AS A SOCIAL MOVEMENT

S cience is perhaps most interesting as a kind of social movement. We being by considering four common understandings of science, and then define a fifth, by contrast.

1. *Science as a style of reasoning that pervades just about everything in the modern era.* It is epitomized in Max Weber's process of "rationalization": the inexorable replacement of local folkways and traditions with formal administration. While this conception correctly stresses science's historical tendency towards global colonization, it obscures the uneven and reversible ways in which scientific styles of reasoning have become implicated in social processes.

2. *Science as common sense rendered self-conscious,* which, over the course of evolution, has enabled human beings to flourish in an ever wider variety of environments. This view is associated with the American pragmatists, especially John Dewey. While correctly stressing science's aim at controlling – and, indeed, remaking – the natural environment, it overestimates the naturalness of this way of being in the world (to the point of rendering it "biological") and hence obscures the historical contingency of our world happening to become (and remain) a scientific one. From this perspective, positivistic vigilance in policing the precincts of science begins to make sense, regardless of the acceptability of specific positivist strategies for demarcating science from non-science.

3. *Science as the content of scientific beliefs,* which today spread faster than any other kind, often enjoying the authority previously reserved for religious beliefs. This point is most vividly illustrated today in the colonization of one's health by medical science, such that people now need to consult physicians in order to learn how they feel. This epidemiological side of science has been studied by the social psychologist Serge Moscovici. While correctly stressing how science can be an ideology held by scientists and non-scientists alike, it downplays science's distinctiveness, which is more in terms of procedures and methods than the content of its beliefs. Indeed, scientific beliefs are popular often because they are already rooted in political, religious and other traditionally non-scientific forms of thought. What matters, then, is whether those beliefs are subject to scientific scrutiny.

4. *Science as the ethos of the practising scientist.* Such are the norms of objectivity that scientists regularly say what they and their work stand for. For Robert Merton, **EXPLAINING THE NORMATIVE STRUCTURE OF SCIENCE** is tantamount to

such professions of faith. While this conception certainly captures the self-understanding of many scientists and often constitutes the public rhetoric that scientists use to legitimize their activities (typically the only exposure that the public has to science at all), it presupposes a simplistic notion of NORMATIVITY that fails to allow for how the same public rhetoric can legitimize widely divergent practices.

5. *Science as a set of principles for organizing imperfect reasoners* to enable them to make the world bend to their collective will so as to allow them to do more of the same in the future. Science, in this sense, is both rhetorical (see RHETORIC) and experimental: it aims to alter the behaviour of reasoners under specifiably changeable conditions. In this sense, science is a highly disciplined social movement, akin to a religious order in its dedication to, in Weber's memorable phrase, a "vocation".

Steve Fuller has argued that paradigms should be regarded as arrested social movements that have become captured, and hence "disciplined", by one or more interest groups. (See DISCIPLINARITY VERSUS INTERDISCIPLINARITY.) This lesson implies a reversal of the explanatory burden in SCIENCE AND TECHNOLOGY STUDIES. Following in Kuhn's footsteps, Ian Hacking, Bruno Latour and most of the leading science and technology studies researchers have studied how stability is gained and regained in scientific and technical practices over wide expanses of space and time. Such successive regimes of "normal science" are generally regarded as good things. In contrast, Fuller stresses how paradigms manage to arrest and contain intellectual and political dynamism. From this perspective, normal science is not such a good thing, as it depoliticizes the course of enquiry. This reversal of value-orientation informs the idea of science as a social movement. At the very least, this shows that judgements about the progressiveness (see PROGRESS) of science depend on when and where you begin the history you recount.

A good model for understanding science as a social movement is provided by the sociologist Robert Wuthnow, who has treated Christian religious change similarly (see RELIGION). The benchmark historical episode here is the Protestant Reformation of the sixteenth century, not the scientific revolution of the seventeenth century. Thus, the focus is more on recovering the spirit of Christianity from the letter and practice of Catholicism than establishing institutions such as the Royal Society, which insulated enquiry from religious controversy. (See CONSENSUS VERSUS DISSENT and CRITICISM.) Whereas the former stressed evangelism, gnosis and personal revelation, the latter relied on courtliness, method and mutual trust. With the sort of irony that only history can deliver, the so-called "Reformation" eventuated in the Thirty Years War that engulfed most of Europe, while the so-called "revolution" is often credited with, if not terminating the conflict, at least securing safe havens away from the fighting.

Movements and paradigms can be regarded as the first two of three stages through which organized enquiry pass in its career as a technology of social transformation. The third is ideologies. The sequence of movement–paradigm–ideology is depicted in Table 3. It consists of an endless cycle of overlapping phases of energization, consolidation and dissipation. In the first phase, ideas constitute the driving forces of social change at large (movement), then the ideas are captured by a group that embodies them and controls their subsequent dissemination (paradigm), and finally they become what Marxists used to call "superstructural", as they are absorbed by society at large (ideology).

The crucial relationship in defining these phases is between word and deed. Here the distinctions drawn by competing approaches to the mind–body problem in philosophy provide a useful precedent. (See **EXPLAINING THE COGNITIVE CONTENT OF SCIENCE**.) The mind–body problem arises, in part, because we can talk about our minds without making much reference to our bodies or the surrounding environment. Similarly, we can talk about the flow of ideas without making much reference to their socio-physical vehicles or contexts of reception. In both the narrowly psychological and more generally intellectual cases, we can ask whether this is a good thing. The three philosophical approaches that are highlighted in what follows – reductionism, functionalism and eliminativism – define the mind's relationship to the body in subtly different ways that can be treated as micro-models for a macro-level understanding of the generation and spread of ideas.

The reduction of mind to matter has had the explicitly normative aim of disciplining our language use, so that a kind of mental state always refers to the

Epistemic formation	Movement	Paradigm	Ideology
Politics of knowledge	Civic republican	Communitarian	Liberal
Word–deed relationship	Reductionism	Functionalism	Eliminativism
Temporal orientation	Future	Present	Past
Rhetorical function	Motivate	Perform	Legitimate
Science–politics relationship	Science and politics are co-produced	Politics is applied science	Science is polymorphously political
Implicit logic	Knowledge is necessary and sufficient for power	Knowledge is necessary but not sufficient for power	Knowledge is sufficient but not necessary for power

Table 3. The cycle of epistemic formations.

same kind of physical state. In practice, the reductionist project has been preoccupied with which sorts of behaviours or neuronal patterns are to be included and excluded from the relevant operationalization of a mental state. Presumably, it could then be determined whether one has formed, say, a "belief that there is a horse in the meadow" in an appropriate manner. More generally, movement discourse has exemplified the power of words by fixating on the link between theoretical concepts and generally observable empirical facts, so as to call for a uniform political response. Not surprisingly, movement discourse often has the character of judges disputing the interpretation of laws that have yet to be institutionalized: a sort of utopian hermeneutics. This would describe not only the Reformation's concern with the terms in which the Kingdom of God could be established on earth, but also the socialist movement, especially 1880–1980, when Marxism was the dominant discourse. In the latter case, it was thought that agreement on the appropriate analysis of "exploitation", "surplus value" or "class consciousness" would lay the groundwork for the revolution. Movements are inspired by reductionism in so far as they hold that conceptual clarity is necessary for focusing collective action, with linguistic regimentation (a.k.a. ontological levelling) providing the bridge between the two. In the modern period, this inspiration has been explicit, in the case of biological reductionism in late-nineteenth-century Germany, various forms of artistic and literary modernism in the early-twentieth century and, perhaps most notably, logical positivism (including its vulgarization by I. A. Richards as "practical criticism" and Alfred Korzybski as the General Semantics Movement).

According to the "functionalist" theory of mind, our ideas are systematically related to each other but only contingently related to particular brain states or physical events. As mentioned earlier, this point is apparent from ordinary language use. In more metaphysically inspired times, it led to dualism: the view that mind and body are radically different sorts of entities. Nowadays, functionalism is the philosophy that underwrites most cognitive science research. Paradigms presuppose a view of science analogous to the functionalist's view of mind. Without denying that science requires a political and economic substratum, the internal logic of scientific research need not refer to it (e.g. experimental work is stylized as theory-testing). From the standpoint of a paradigm, a movement aims to design concepts that dictate their entire range of practical application, whereas from a movement perspective, a paradigm attempts to divide the co-production of knowledge and power into a discrete sequence of science and politics. (See EPISTEMIC JUSTICE.)

Several episodes from the history of science that have been portrayed by Kuhn (see KUHN, POPPER AND LOGICAL POSITIVISM) and others as first-order paradigmatic struggles may be better understood as second-order disputes over the sort of epistemic formation science should be. (See **TRUTH, RELIABILITY AND THE ENDS OF KNOWLEDGE**.) Generally speaking, movement-oriented scientists have been attracted to phenomenological approaches that merge epistemic and practical interests (e.g. Joseph Priestley, Ernst Mach, Wilhelm Ostwald), whereas paradigm-oriented scientists have sought refuge in a more stratified ontology that sports a pecking order that sharply distinguishes between what Wilfrid Sellars called the "scientific" and "manifest" images (e.g. Antoine Lavoisier, Max Planck, Ludwig Boltzmann). According to Kuhn's theory of scientific change, the paradigm-oriented scientists always defeat (a.k.a. discipline) the movement-oriented ones, whose followers in turn either try to regroup as a paradigm with its own autonomous sphere of enquiry or dissolve into ideological formations across the wider society.

A Kuhnian legacy to science and technology studies is that it is difficult to explain, or even register, attempts to convert a paradigm into a movement. Consider, for example, the injection of "gene talk" into the public sphere, as well as the various attempts to read culture into science that have marked the ongoing "**SCIENCE WARS**". A Kuhnian would treat both of these cases as ideological devolutions of the dominant paradigms, whereby the experts come to lose control over the meanings of their words. The analogue position from the mind–body problem is "eliminativism", in which mental concepts are epiphenomenal on physical ones, which means that every act of thinking corresponds to some set of neural firings, but which set it is will vary from case to case. Thus, the turn to ideology renders the meanings of scientific terms diffuse and metaphorical. While appeals to, say, "**EVOLUTION**" or "complexity" in contemporary public debate is meant to confer some scientific legitimacy on the arguments made, one cannot easily tell the arguer's political orientation or even the relevance of scientific evidence to the argument. These uncertainties would be precisely the sorts of things that would be made explicit and turned into a matter of contestation by a movement approach. But here we should distinguish contemporary discourse formations surrounding "evolution" and "complexity" as instances of movement and ideology, respectively. Accordingly, a variety of cultural critics and postmodernists have taken "complexity" in rather different directions, which while vaguely counter-paradigmatic do not culminate in any pressing political or scientific disagreements. In contrast, the public controversy over evolution, especially in light of recent developments in biotechnology, is about tying the deployment of scientific concepts to specific, say, "eugenic", policies that at least in principle could affect the lives of many, if not everyone. As would be expected of a movement orientation to enquiry, here what is to happen both in and out of the laboratory are simultaneously at stake.

The series movement–paradigm–ideology constitutes a cycle of epistemic formations. How, then, does an ideology revert to a movement? The short answer is that the ideological appropriation of paradigmatic concepts presupposes an awareness of the tension involved in trying to limit knowledge of reality to a self-appointed group of experts. Thus, the ideology and movement phases correspond to self-consciousness about, respectively, the "universal" (see UNIVERSALISM VERSUS RELATIVISM) and the "knowledge" character of universal knowledge: knowledge confined to a paradigm is first dispersed to society at large and then re-grounded as a potential principle of governance. In its various historic inventions and re-inventions, the UNIVERSITY has been the institution most directly implicated in the conversion of ideologies to movements by providing a site for the incorporation in some systematic fashion of dispersed ideas by society at large. That site is the curriculum. Marxists typically dream of historic opportunities for organizing people into a self-conscious class, yet universities have always been available for that purpose, albeit only for an elite. Little surprise, then, that in their academic captivity Marxists have been among the chief defenders of the university's Enlightenment mission.

FURTHER READING

J. D. Bernal, *The Social Function of Science* (1939).

R. Bhaskar, *Scientific Realism and Human Emancipation* (1987).

J. A. Campbell & S. Meyer (eds), *Darwin, Design and Public Education* (2003).

R. Collins, *The Sociology of Philosophies* (1998).

E. Eyerman & A. Jamison, *Social Movements* (1991).

P. Feyerabend, *Science in a Free Society* (1979).

M. Foucault, *The Order of Things* (1970).

S. Fuller, *Thomas Kuhn* (2000).

R. Giere (ed.), *Cognitive Models of Science* (1992).

A. Gouldner, *The Future of Intellectuals and the Rise of the New Class* (1979).

T. S. Kuhn, *The Structure of Scientific Revolutions* ([1962] 1970).

B. Latour, *The Pasteurization of France* (1988).

R. K. Merton, *The Sociology of Science* (1977).

J. T. Merz, *A History of European Thought in the Nineteenth Century* (1964).

A. Pickering (ed.), *Science as Practice and Culture* (1992).

R. Proctor, *Value-Free Science?* (1991).

J. Ravetz, *Scientific Knowledge and Its Social Problems* (1971).

Z. Sardar, *Postmodernism and the Other* (1997).

T. Sorell, *Scientism* (1991).

R. Wuthnow, *Discourse Communities* (1989).

SCIENCE WARS

B efore the 1830s, when "scientist" began to refer to someone with specific professional qualifications, the pursuit of science had two countervailing qualities: on the one hand, it was expected only of those (few) with sufficient leisure;
on the other, the results of science were accorded universal validity, even if most
people remained ignorant or passive with regard to their production. This para-
dox persists today. Indeed, science appears to be sociologically unique as a form
of knowledge – certainly in contrast with RELIGION or even politics – in that most
of its believers have little specific knowledge of what it is they believe. Thus, there
is widespread cross-cultural agreement that Einstein was the premier intellect of
the twentieth century, but who in this consensus (see CONSENSUS VERSUS DISSENT)
can correctly express Einstein's estimable insights? If anything, greater knowledge
of science appears to be correlated with greater scepticism of science's goodness.
Not surprisingly, to this day the most effective critics of science have come from
within the scientific community, since there remains no widely institutionalized
means of soliciting public input into the conduct of science. In this respect, science
remains *for* – but not *by* – the people.

From Plato's *Republic* to Auguste Comte's positivist polity, the tension between
elitism and universality (see UNIVERSALISM VERSUS RELATIVITY) in the public understanding of science has inspired philosophers to imagine that a non-coercive social
order could be built by establishing clear patterns of deference to the appropriate
scientific authorities. However, as the chequered career of the expert witness in
law illustrates, the ability of scientists to function with such authority depends on
presenting a united front, with scientific agreement providing a basis for public
agreement. Unfortunately, the requisite level of agreement among scientists is
rarely achieved, even when defending science itself. Moreover, once the end of the
Cold War exposed scientists to a much more competitive funding environment,
they responded by campaigning for science as if its multifarious activities could
be justified as an extension of their particular research orientation.

For example, 1992 alone witnessed the publication of two distinguished works
of science advocacy: *Dreams of a Final Theory* by Steven Weinberg, a US theoretical
physicist, and *The Unnatural Nature of Science* by Lewis Wolpert, a UK experimental embryologist. Not surprisingly, Weinberg portrayed science as aiming for
"beautiful theories" whose internal coherence resists all attempts at falsification,
while Wolpert stressed the falsification of fixed ideas as the only guarantee that
one is actually doing science. The one tests his theories on instruments (i.e. particle accelerators) that have little clear application outside the immediate research

context, while the other conducts experiments in a medical school where applications are in the forefront of the researcher's mind. Yet, despite their radically different accounts of contemporary science, both lay claim to the 2500-year-old legacy of Western rationalism. How is that possible? Not surprisingly, **SCIENCE AND TECHNOLOGY STUDIES** has invoked such interpretive flexibility of the historical record to question whether such a legacy really underwrites today's scientific practices. This questioning has trigged the Science Wars.

The Science Wars entered the **MASS MEDIA** in 1996, when a disgruntled US physicist, Alan Sokal, published an article in a leading cultural studies journal that combined scientific nonsense and politically correct references. The "Sokal Hoax", as Sokal's old teacher Weinberg dubbed it, brought to mainstream public attention the contested nature of speaking for science. While sociologists had long known that science speaks in many voices, for scientists themselves this was a potentially damaging revelation, which (so they feared) would give policy-makers an excuse to cut science budgets or, perhaps even worse, channel resources towards unorthodox, even alternative, forms of enquiry that more directly satisfied both the spiritual and material needs of the populace. (See **KNOWLEDGE POLICY**.) It quickly became clear that scientists found it difficult to countenance a politics of science in which scientists "represent" our knowledge of reality in the same sense as a politician might represent her constituency.

As the Science Wars have progressed, two diametrically opposed strategies have emerged to protect scientists from the larger sense of public accountability implied by sociologists' accounts. On the one hand, some scientists have agreed with Weinberg that scientists virtually *own* science. Not surprisingly, then, every so often – as in the Sokal Hoax – they must catch trespassers who try to extract surplus cultural value from science without having first undergone the relevant training. On the other hand, others have followed Wolpert, who portrays scientists as modest toilers whose competence does not extend beyond the confines of the laboratory. They envisage scientists delivering a fully mapped human genome on the public's doorstep, but then quickly moving on to their next research project without involving themselves in the political implications of what they have done.

However, both strategies fail to get to grips with the overall tendency of which the Science Wars are merely a prominent symptom: the *secularization of science*. The end of the Cold War has witnessed a divestiture of public funding for research and education in science, which has led scientists to resort to many of the same strategies religions have used when church and state have been formally separated. Thus, there has been a rise of "science evangelism", whereby arguments in support of science are specifically oriented towards the satisfaction of human needs. The most obvious general trend is represented by the shift in intellectual and financial interest from high-energy physics and the space programme to the human genome project and new age medicine. Solving 2500-year-old conundrums about the nature of matter provides a much less persuasive basis for public science policy than the prospect of eliminating hereditary diseases in one's offspring.

If scientists fail to admit the secularization of science as the backdrop to the Science Wars, science and technology studies researchers are so fixated on the micro-level of the laboratory sciences as "stable material practices" that they ignore the rhetorical significance of these practices' commanding the relevant philosophical labels of "rational", "real", "objective" and so on. Command over this RHETORIC remains the primary mode of social legitimization in *all* the sciences. Otherwise, why *should* intelligent lay people see a connection between the stability of laboratory phenomena and the stability of everyday social life? How many people are familiar with the stages by which a laboratory finding is stabilized into a nugget of knowledge or a reliable technique? Were the numbers large, then science and technology studies would not have caused such a stir. In this respect, natural scientists concerned about the consequences of their fields being seen as "constructed" have had a better grasp of the SOCIOLOGY OF KNOWLEDGE informing their situation than their sociological opponents. Scientists are not just personally offended by SOCIAL CONSTRUCTIVISM: they are justifiably worried about the fate of their endeavours.

Thus, the social epistemology of science must ask how science is to be legitimized once social constructivist accounts are widely *accepted*. Can science, like religion, survive in a demystified form? Thomas Kuhn's legacy (see KUHN, POPPER AND LOGICAL POSITIVISM), which operates as a lingua franca in the Science Wars, ill equips us to address this question because practitioners of a scientific paradigm are licensed to discuss the overall ends of their enquiries only once they have started to fail on their own terms, and hence enter a "crisis".

There are two productive strategies for resolving the Science Wars. The first is the institutionalization of public participation in science policy decision-making. One clear proposal is to make *consensus conferences*, sometimes called "citizens' juries", a regular and binding part of the policy process, perhaps akin to the primary and convention season that precedes a general election in the US. In such settings, a sample of the general public engages in its own collective enquiry by sampling a range of relevant EXPERTISEs for purposes of drawing up legislative guidelines that then frame the terms of reference for political decision-making. The second issue involves the communicative process that joins scientists and their publics. As scientific research increasingly impinges on public concerns about health and safety, professional scientific bodies have called for the tightening up of procedures by which scientists and science journalists report to policy-makers and the public at large. At the same time, however, the spread of graduate programmes in "science communication" points to the emergence of a new field that conceptualizes "public understanding of science" as not merely good public relations for science but a mechanism for making scientists publicly accountable along the lines that investigative journalism has made politicians more publicly accountable.

FURTHER READING

H. M. Collins & T. J. Pinch, *The Golem* (1993).

S. Fuller, *The Philosophy of Science and Technology Studies* (2006).

P. Gross & N. Levitt, *Higher Superstition* (1994).

S. Harding, *The Science Question in Feminism* (1986).

S. Harding, *Whose Science? Whose Knowledge?* (1991).

A. Irwin, *Citizen Science* (1995).

P. Mirowski & E.-M. Sent (eds), *Science Bought and Sold* (2002).

A. Ross (ed.), *Science Wars* (1996).

A. Sokal & J. Bricmont, *Fashionable Nonsense* (1998).

T. Sorell, *Scientism* (1991).

S. Weinberg, *Dreams of a Final Theory* (1992).

L. Wolpert, *The Unnatural Nature of Science* (1992).

SOCIAL CAPITAL VERSUS PUBLIC GOOD

The expression "social capital", first popularized by Harvard political scientist Robert Putnam in 1970s, is used to characterize the cultural differences between economically advanced and backward (or developed and developing) regions. Social capital captures the voluntary associations whose knock-on effects increase the general welfare of those involved in them. Moreover, these knock-on effects may be produced more efficiently than, say, a state that administers to the needs of everyone as isolated individuals. Social capital thus testifies to the power of positive feedback: we are vindicated by, and hence trust, others who have made decisions similar to ours about which groups to join. Ideally this would attenuate the state's need to provide tax relief or investment subsidies as incentives for collective risk-taking. In many developing countries, people depend on the state to compensate for their mutual distrust, which then places a prohibitive moral and financial burden on the state.

Compare social capital with a concept that captured the imaginations of social scientists and policy-makers in the previous generation: public good. The US economist Paul Samuelson invented the concept in the 1950s for goods that the state had to provide because they would never be provided efficiently in a pure market environment. These goods turned out to be the ones that would come to epitomize the welfare state over the next twenty years: healthcare, education, utilities and transport systems. The defining feature of a public good is that it would cost more to restrict access to the good to just those who paid for it than to allow everyone access to it. Not surprisingly, no purely self-interested economic agent would want to produce public goods, although all such agents would clearly want *someone* to do so. That someone, then, turns out to be the state, which has the power to extract taxes from the egoists so as to provide the capital required to produce and maintain public goods. SOCIAL EPISTEMOLOGY treats knowledge as a public good in this strict sense (see KNOWLEDGE POLICY), which explains its concerns with explicit construction and maintenance of the *res publica* (literally, the public thing) for the promotion of EPISTEMIC JUSTICE, including its clearest institutional realization, the UNIVERSITY.

The decline of the welfare state and the corresponding rise of neo-liberalism have effectively allowed the concept of public goods to be replaced by that of social capital. There is a subtle side to this transition that is especially relevant to social epistemology. Public goods are usually portrayed as knowledge-based, with knowledge presumed to be something that flows freely unless deliberately arrested. For example, however much it may have cost to provide the education, facilities and salaries for the medical scientists who develop a technique for treating a deadly disease, it would cost society more to restrict access to the treatment to just those who could pay market-driven prices for it than to distribute the cost across the entire society through taxation so that the treatment is free at the point of delivery.

The rise in the popularity of social capital over the past generation testifies to a profound change in our conception of who and what matters in the social order, which is reflected in a change in what knowledge is valued for. Neo-liberalism has broken with the welfare-state assumption that full employment is necessary for efficient economic growth. This, in turn, has diminished the urgency with which new knowledge should be made available to everyone. Indeed, knowledge is now defined divisively as whatever it takes to gain a market advantage over competitors (see KNOWLEDGE SOCIETY). Thus, the state now assigns a lower priority to the maintenance of the infrastructure for public goods, as is evidenced in the decline in schools, hospitals and roads. A society (so it is thought) may prosper, even if many of its members lag behind the market leaders. Indeed, the *res publica* comes to be reduced to a space of contestation without the overarching sense of solidarity associated with citizenship in republican polities (see FREE ENQUIRY). But this then generates a new problem: the market leaders may find it more convenient to pool their resources with people outside their own societies. To halt this potential evacuation of money and talent, social capital is invoked to encourage a form of economic protectionism that does not require a full-blown welfare state.

The exact appeal of social capital depends on where you live. Social capital offers the poor in the developing world an oasis of economic self-determination by pooling resources with family and friends in what would be otherwise a desert of deregulation or outright lawlessness: a world where civic republicanism has never taken root. In contrast, in the developed world, social capital satisfies a longing for an integrated lifestyle in these centrifugal POSTMODERN times: the promise of higher profits from deeper socializing, or "playmates as workmates". Here it may constitute a spontaneous form of economic protectionism to counterbalance the neo-liberal tendency to see only trade-offs between engagement in the local community and the potentially long-distance pursuit of economic self-interest. According to social capital theory, a region may make and keep its own wealth if the inhabitants see each other as potential customers or business partners. This point, in the guise of "civil society", originally impressed Alexis de Tocqueville in the 1830s as the secret to America's success. "Democratization" was more than simply the removal of privilege but an invitation to multiple overlapping collaborations or, in sociological jargon, "dense social networks" that cover everything from business ventures to marriages.

Nevertheless, social capital is ultimately about competitive advantage: specifically, the return to investors in a suitably dense social network *vis-à-vis* non-investors. In this respect, social capital is an example of what the economist Fred Hirsch originally called a "positional" good, that is, a good whose value is principally tied to the exclusion of specific consumers: the exact opposite of a public good. Thus, education has increasingly shifted its status from a public to a positional good, as it both becomes subject to direct payment (as opposed to tax subsidization) and used as source of job certification.

This point has ramifications throughout society. On the one hand, it justifies cooperative businesses that charge preferential prices to investors. On the other, it encourages stronger informal links between academia and industry that result in jointly owned inventions or companies that are protected by intellectual property legislation. (See **KNOWLEDGE MANAGEMENT**.) The perniciousness of these set-ups may not be immediately apparent but may become so in the long term, if they exacerbate existing social inequalities. (This is the import of Pierre Bourdieu's related expression, "cultural capital", used primarily in **CRITICISM** for the cumulative effect of economic class differences *vis-à-vis* access to other social resources, such that, generally speaking, the richest people also tend to be regarded as the most influential and exhibiting the best taste. It may be also seen as underwriting Robert Merton's "principle of cumulative advantage", which is used in **EXPLAINING THE NORMATIVE STRUCTURE OF SCIENCE**.) In more moralistic times, this intimate linking of social and economic interests so valorized by social capital thinking had a special, albeit now unfashionable name: corruption.

Social capital is interesting to social epistemologists because it shifts the source of ignorance that needs to be overcome to satisfy welfare needs. Public goods theory presupposes that everyone faces the same challenges to their survival, regardless of their individual ability to overcome them. However, these challenges (e.g. personal health) are of an inherently uncertain nature, and so it makes sense for the state to collectivize the risk that everyone faces in the form of a wealth redistribution scheme that provides a generic safety net. In contrast, social capital theory does not presume that these challenges come from outside society. Rather, they come from the failure of individuals to constitute themselves properly as a society in the first place. From that standpoint, concerns about health reflect less the threat of invasive microbes than people who cannot count on others for support, and hence must depend on the state. In other words, social capital theory replaces an ignorance of nature with an ignorance of people. The problem, of course, is that there may be people whom no one needs to know (and hence trust) to ensure their own welfare. At that point, the role of public goods in fostering universalism (see **UNIVERSALISM VERSUS RELATIVISM**) becomes apparent.

FURTHER READING

R. Aron, *Main Currents in Sociological Thought* (1965).

P. Bourdieu, "The Specificity of the Scientific Field and the Social Conditions of the Progress of Reason" (1975).

S. Fleischacker, *A Short History of Distributive Justice* (2004).

F. Hirsch, *Social Limits to Growth* (1976).

B. Latour, *The Pasteurization of France* (1988).

R. K. Merton, *The Sociology of Science* (1977).

J. Ravetz, *Scientific Knowledge and its Social Problems* (1971).

J. Rawls, *A Theory of Justice* (1971).

SOCIAL CONSTRUCTIVISM

The leading research orientation in contemporary SCIENCE AND TECHNOLOGY STUDIES, social constructivism has been controversial since its inception in the 1970s. It is primarily a set of methodological imperatives for the study of science and technology that focus on the means by which people, ideas, interests and things are organized in specific places and times to produce knowledge that carries authority throughout society, especially among those not originally involved in the knowledge-production process. Thus, social constructivists tend to stress the diversity of interpretations and applications of knowledge across social contexts. However, where philosophers and scientists might regard this variety as different representations or instantiations of an already completed form of knowledge, social constructivists treat the variety as part of the ongoing core knowledge-production process.

It follows that social constructivists do not recognize a sharp distinction between the production and consumption of knowledge. Thus, social constructivism has a "democratizing" effect on epistemology by levelling traditional differences in the authority granted to differently placed knowers. To a social constructivist, a technologist using a scientific formula is "constructing" the formula as knowledge in exactly the same sense as the scientist who originated the formula. Each depends on the other to strengthen their common "cycle of credibility" or "actor-network", in the words of Bruno Latour, perhaps the leading social constructivist today. In contrast, most philosophers and scientists would raise the epistemic status of the original scientist to a "discoverer", while lowering the status of the technologist to an "applier". Fuller's version of social epistemology accepts these basic tenets of social constructivism.

In philosophical terms, social constructivism is a form of anti-realism. This means that social constructivists do not presuppose the existence of a reality independent of the procedures available to the agents under study for deciding the truth-value of their assertions. In this respect, social constructivism has affinities with German idealism, pragmatism, phenomenology and even logical positivism. All of these movements agree that aspects of the world that have traditionally been cited as evidence for "external reality" are in fact the intended and unintended products of human practices. However, this common insight has led to rather different philosophical responses. For example, positivists and phenomenologists strived to design criteria that could command universal assent, while idealists and pragmatists regarded the resolution of conflict in the application of such procedures as the basis of future epistemic developments.

Social constructivists differ from these earlier anti-realists by challenging their common fundamental assumption of a centralized decision-making environment, be it a unified self or a unified society. In contrast, they presuppose that the social world where construction occurs is highly dispersed. It implies that rather different decisions are taken across many places and times. This is often considered a postmodern (see **POSTMODERNISM**) feature of social constructivism. Fuller's version of social epistemology shares this feature of social constructivism only as an empirical starting-point, not a normative conclusion. The construction of science as common public thing, or *res publica*, is a major project of social epistemology (see **FREE ENQUIRY** and **EPISTEMIC JUSTICE**), whereas most social constructivists are happy to see scientific activity remain in its normally dispersed condition. Despite paying lip-service to fashionable French poststructuralist thinkers such as Michel Foucault and Gilles Deleuze, social constructivists have derived their decentralized view of science from the social phenomenologists Peter Berger and Thomas Luckmann's classic *The Social Construction of Reality*.

Berger and Luckmann descend from a Viennese heritage of Alfred Schutz, Friedrich Hayek and Ludwig von Mises, all of whom were dedicated to turning Adam Smith's "invisible hand" into the meta-narrative of social life. Just as Hayek had argued in the 1930s (against the socialists) that no central planner could determine fair prices more efficiently than the spontaneous self-organization of buyers and sellers, social constructivists deny that a single philosophical method can determine the course of science more efficiently than the spontaneous self-organization of scientific practitioners. It is worth noting that Hayek had grounded his own argument on the unique *knowledge* possessed by people differently placed in the market. Thus, the social construction of scientific knowledge can be seen historically as an extension of a market mentality into an aspect of social life, science, which for much of the twentieth century had tied its legitimacy to the control mechanisms of the state. (See **KNOWLEDGE SOCIETY**.)

Despite often being portrayed as antiscientific, social constructivism's anti-realism has precedents in the history of science, specifically doctrines of *indeterminism*. These start with Aristotle's view of matter as an indeterminate potential that is given form through human intervention. In the nineteenth and early-twentieth centuries, the constructivist position was most clearly represented by chemists who contested the idea of an ultimate form to physical reality, as defined by, say, "atoms". Instead, chemists appealed to "energy" as an updated version of the Aristotelian potential. Current versions of constructivism further "socialize" this perspective by invoking concepts such as "work" and "practice" as the medium through which scientific objects are brought in and out of existence. (There is a precedent for this usage: in the late-nineteenth and early-twentieth centuries, the

Marxist concept of labour-power and the physical concept of power as potential energy were frequently fused in the German word *Kraft*.) According to its proponents, social constructivism is the spontaneous philosophy of the working scientist, who is concerned more with making things happen in the laboratory (and society at large) than completing some philosophically inspired picture about ultimate reality. Not surprisingly, Latour and other leading social constructivists have flourished in engineering schools rather than pure science faculties.

Social constructivism is normally defined in terms of its opposition to two familiar, albeit extreme, views that might be called "philosophical rationalism" and "sociological determinism". Philosophical rationalism implies that science is ultimately driven (in that sense, determined) by a concern for the truth, perhaps even a desire to provide a comprehensive and unified picture of reality. From that standpoint, the social dimension of science functions as either a facilitator or inhibitor of this quest. Sociological determinism implies that the science of a time and place is an ideological reflection of the social conditions that sustain it. In that case, the development of science is dependent on its larger societal functions. Social constructivism differs from these two perspectives by denying any strong ontological distinction between the cognitive (or natural) and social (or cultural) dimensions of science. Both dimensions are co-produced in any episode of scientific activity. As a result, social constructivists see science as much more subject to agency and contingency than either philosophical rationalism or sociological determinism allowed.

David Bloor's *Knowledge and Social Imagery* was the first book to put forward the social constructivist case against both philosophers and sociologists. Bloor, himself a trained mathematician and psychologist, had been influenced by Wittgenstein's later writings on rule-following. These implied that there is no correct way to continue a number series (e.g. 2, 4, 6, 8, ...) other than to abide by the judgement of the community of counters, since arithmetic itself is open to infinitely many continuations, depending on what is taken to be the rule underlying the number series. Bloor generalized this insight in the name of a thoroughly naturalistic (see **NATURALISM**) approach to the study of knowledge, which he called the "strong programme in the sociology of scientific knowledge". The approach involved suspending all external normative judgements about the validity or rationality of knowledge claims. Bloor would have us look only to the standards of reasoning and evidence available to those who must live with the consequences of what they do. This approach encouraged what Bloor called a "symmetrical" attitude towards the various competing beliefs or courses of action in a given situation. In other words, the enquirer is to treat them as seriously as the situated agents treat them, suspending any knowledge the enquirer might have about their likely or (in the case of historical cases) actual consequences. The import of this approach was to neutralize specifically philosophical appraisals of knowledge claims, which typically appeal to standards of rationality and validity that transcend the interests or even competence of the agents.

Whereas Bloor – along with his Edinburgh colleague Barry Barnes – mapped out the conceptual terrain defined by social constructivism, the 1980s and 1990s brought about a plethora of historical and sociological case studies inspired by the position. Constructivist historical studies characteristically reinterpret landmark scientific debates, so that what had traditionally been seen as an instance of truth clearly triumphing over falsehood now appears as a more equally balanced contest, in which victory was secured at considerable cost and by means quite specific to the contest. Attached to these reinterpretations is a view, traceable to Thomas Kuhn (see **KUHN, POPPER AND LOGICAL POSITIVISM**), whereby every scientific success entails a rewriting of history so as to make it appear inevitable. In this respect, social constructivist history of science aims to "deconstruct" the narratives of scientific progress typically found in science textbooks and science popularization.

Steven Shapin and Simon Schaffer's *Leviathan and the Air-Pump* is perhaps the most influential work of this sort. It deals with Robert Boyle's successful blocking of Thomas Hobbes's candidacy for membership in the Royal Society. This episode is normally told in terms of Hobbes's persistent metaphysical objections to the existence of a vacuum long after it was scientifically reasonable. However, it turns out that Hobbes was defending the general principle that experimental demonstrations are always open to philosophical criticism, even if the philosopher could not have designed such an experiment. Hobbes's failure on this score set a precedent for the competence required for judging experiments that began to insulate science from public scrutiny.

Constructivist case studies typically draw on the sociological method of "grounded theory", according to which the enquirer introduces a theoretical concept or perspective only if the agents under study do so. Grounded theory was originally used to oppose structural-functionalism, the leading school of US sociology, associated with Talcott Parsons and Robert Merton. It postulated that deviance is a well-defined role that performs specific functions in the social system. In contrast, for grounded theorists, the deviant role – say, in the context of asylums and hospitals – had to be constructed from moment to moment, since, generally speaking, there was no clear observable difference between the behaviour of so-called normals and deviants.

The perverse genius of Latour and Woolgar's *Laboratory Life*, Knorr-Cetina's *The Manufacture of Knowledge*, and the other early constructivist sociologists was to imagine that "deviance" may apply to people on the positive as well as the negative extreme of a normal distribution curve. Thus, in their daily laboratory tasks, scientists do not sound or look especially different from people working in an industrial environment subject to an intensive division of labour. Nevertheless, they are socially constructed as exceptionally rational, producing knowledge that commands authority throughout society. How is that possible? For the constructivist sociologist, the answer lies in the "made for export" language that scientists use to describe their activities and the specific distribution channels in which this language – as expressed in journal articles, preprints and press releases – circulates. This produces a forwards momentum, involving many other people, laboratories, interests and so forth, that eventually turns a unique set of events into a universally recognizable fact.

There is little doubt that social constructivism has provided an important challenge to standard historical, philosophical, and sociological accounts of science. The open question is its implications for science itself. Constructivism's steadfast adherence to the symmetry principle has been both a great strength and weakness. Its strengths extend beyond intellectual insight to the ease with which constructivism can be used in science policy research, especially in a time when constrained budgets and sceptical publics demand that science be evaluated by its actual consequences rather than its professed norms. In this respect, social constructivism has been a success of the marketplace, proving especially attractive to the increasing proportion of academic researchers who depend on external contracts for their livelihood. But beneath this success lies constructivism's weakness: it lacks a clear normative perspective of its own. This largely reflects its decentralized vision of social life. While constructivists excel in revealing the multiple directions in which science policy may go, it refuses to pass judgement over any of them or even the means by which their differences might be resolved. In this respect, social constructivism is indifferent to the future of science and its role as the vanguard of rationality and progress in society at large. The project of "social epistemology" has attempted to redress this imbalance, explicitly arguing that social constructivism can foster an approach to science policy that is both genuinely democratic and experimental.

FURTHER READING
P. Berger & T. Luckmann, *The Social Construction of Reality* (1967).
D. Bloor, *Knowledge and Social Imagery* (1976).
G. Deleuze, *Difference and Repetition* (1994).
M. Foucault, *The Order of Things* (1970).
N. Gilbert & M. Mulkay, *Opening Pandora's Box* (1984).
B. Glaser & A. Strauss, *The Discovery of Grounded Theory* (1967).
F. Hayek, "The Use of Knowledge in Society" (1945).

K. Knorr-Cetina, *The Manufacture of Knowledge* (1981).
I. Lakatos, *Proofs and Refutations* (1976).
B. Latour & S. Woolgar, *Laboratory Life* (1986).
A. Pickering (ed.), *Science as Practice and Culture* (1992).
A. Schutz, "The Well-Informed Citizen" (1964).
S. Shapin & S. Schaffer, *Leviathan and the Air Pump* (1985).

SOCIAL EPISTEMOLOGY

Social epistemology is a naturalistic (see **NATURALISM**) approach to the normative (see **NORMATIVITY**) questions surrounding the organization of knowledge processes and products. It seeks to provide guidance on how and what we should know on the basis of how and what we actually know. The subject matter corresponds to what the pragmatists used to call "the conduct of enquiry" and what may appear to today's readers as an abstract form of science policy. (See **KNOWLEDGE POLICY**.) Social epistemology advances beyond other theories of knowledge by taking seriously that knowledge is produced by agents who are not merely individually embodied but also collectively embedded in certain specifiable relationships that extend over large chunks of space and time.

The need for social epistemology is captured by an interdisciplinary (see **DISCIPLINARITY VERSUS INTERDISCIPLINARITY**) gap between **PHILOSOPHY AND SOCIOLOGY**: philosophical theories of knowledge tend to stress normative approaches without considering their empirical realizability or political consequences. Sociological theories suffer the reverse problem of capturing the empirical and ideological character of knowledge, but typically without offering guidance on how knowledge policy should be conducted. Social epistemology aims to consolidate the strengths and eliminate the weaknesses of these two approaches. Even the traditionally conservative analytic school of philosophy has been increasingly forced to treat social epistemological themes as they come to accept the findings of historical, sociological, psychological and economic studies of science as constraints on the advice they issue about the pursuit of knowledge.

Social epistemologies may be compared along three dimensions: (i) whether "the problem of knowledge" is envisaged in terms of acts of knowing or access to knowledge; (ii) their specification of the relationship between the normative and empirical dimensions of enquiry; and (iii) the presumptive answers to their research questions. I shall consider each in turn.

First of all, it makes a big difference whether one regards "the problem of knowledge" as pertaining primarily to the verb "to know" or the noun "knowledge". In the former case, the problem becomes a matter of getting outside one's head (i.e. to engage in an act of knowing); in the latter, a matter of managing certain products and processes (i.e. to gain access to knowledge). **ANALYTIC SOCIAL EPISTEMOLOGY** has been fixated on the former, but Fuller's social epistemology is mainly concerned with the latter. This contrast may be expressed more formally in terms of two strategies (*A* and *B*) for generating philosophically interesting problems of knowledge:

Strategy A

1. The thing I know best is the thing with which I have had the most direct acquaintance, namely my own mind. After all, without it, I could not have made this very observation. But my mind is possibly not all that exists.
2. How, then, do I determine whether other possible things exist, and, if they exist, how can I know them, given that they seem quite different from my own mind?

Strategy B

1. We ordinarily experience everyone (and everything) as living in the same world. Yet, as people articulate their experience, it becomes clear that there are significant differences in the aspects of the world to which we have direct access.
2. What, then, accounts for these differences in access to our common reality, and what enables us to ignore them in everyday life, as we suppose that our own access is the one shared by all right-minded people?

Thus, Strategy A poses the problem of knowledge *inside-out*: how do we get out of our individual heads and into some common reality? It captures the tradition of enquiry that unites Descartes and Bertrand Russell, as well as W. V. Quine's progeny in analytic philosophy, especially once translation and communication are treated as versions of the problem of access to other minds. Strategy B poses the problem of knowledge *outside-in*: how do we get beyond our common reality and into the mindsets that separate people? It extends from Augustinian theodicy through Leibniz, Hegel and Marx, as well as the SOCIOLOGY OF KNOWLEDGE, SCIENCE AND TECHNOLOGY STUDIES and Fuller's social epistemology.

Whereas Strategy A sets the task of epistemology as generalizing from the individual case, Strategy B sets the task as fully realizing the universal. The former task involves adding something that is missing, such as insight into other times, places and people that cannot be inferred through either deductive or inductive inference. The latter task involves redistributing something that is already present, be it called knowledge or power. (See EPISTEMIC JUSTICE.) Strategy A regards knowledge as a problem for each individual to solve by approximating a standard to which the cognitive agent may or may not have conscious access. There is no sense that epistemic access may be a scarce good, with one agent's access to knowledge perhaps impeding, competing with or making demands on the epistemic access of some other agent. This would be more in accord with Strategy B. Here the cognitive agent is portrayed as choosing between one of two or more alternative research trajectories, fully realizing that resources are limited and that other agents will be making similar decisions at roughly the same time. Advocates of Strategy B are moved by the different fates that befall people, even though everyone is supposed to be equal members of humanity.

Strategies A and B both operate with epistemological premises that are taken to be liabilities in advancing the search for knowledge. Historically speaking, they are epitomized by, on the one hand, the Cartesian evil demon and, on the other, the Hegelian master–servant dialectic. For Strategy A, a self-centred RELATIVISM is the initial liability that needs to be overcome: I am in my own head, but I suspect that there are other things out there different from me. How do I find out? Not surprisingly, this strategy stresses methods that are biased towards realism, such as looking for (primary) qualities that remain invariant under a variety of observations and transformations and hence escape the tricks that an evil demon might play on our naive minds. For Strategy B, on the other hand, a totalizing realism is the initial liability: we all live in the same world, therefore everyone must think like me, at least when they are thinking right. But why does this not seem to be the case? (Are they crazy?) The relevant corrective here is methodological relativism: precisely *because* our reality is common, it cannot explain our palpable differences. We are thus better off regarding claims to a common reality as disguised partial perspectives, ideologies or standpoints that may gain certain local material advantage by capitalizing on our weakness for thinking in terms of totalizing forms of realism. In this context, relativism invites CRITICISM to ensure that subordinate (or subaltern) social groups do not adopt perspectives (a.k.a. false universals or hegemonies) that simply serve the interests of the superior groups. (See FEMINISM and MULTICULTURALISM.)

Secondly, social epistemologies may be contrasted in terms of how they specify the relationship between the normative and empirical dimensions of enquiry. The two major historical models of this relationship are the *geometrical* and the *dialectical*, so named after their roots in ancient Greek practices: land surveying and public defence (or, in modern academic terms, natural science and SOCIAL SCIENCE). The origins vividly contrast the difference between a sense of knowledge that presumes stability and one that presumes volatility. According to the geometrical model, the normative dimension is cast as "basic" or "pure" enquiry, in which the enquirer's value orientation is inscribed in a set of objects or concepts (sometimes called "intuitions") upon which the empirical dimension is then constructed. This latter dimension is defined as "deductions" or "applications", depending on whether the enquiry is science or technology. As in geometry, the first principles circumscribe the range of permissible inferences. In contrast, the dialectical model shifts the terms of the relationship between the normative and empirical dimensions from a hierarchical to a conflictual one. Specifically, the normative dimension appears as an ideal or goal that is then realized within constraints and in spite of resistance, which together define the empirical dimension. As in dialectics, what results from this tension is a synthesis that *realizes* the ideal in a sense more akin to completion than instantiation. Whereas geometrical enquiry proceeds *ab initio*, dialectical enquiry proceeds *in medias res*.

Philosophers have usually opted for either the geometrical or the dialectical model of enquiry, with a few attempting to integrate the two into one system: for example, Kant's system, which specifies the terms in which objects of cognition are, respectively, constituted and regulated. Outside of philosophy, the difference between the two models is typically exemplified by the distinction between *science* (geometrical) and *politics* (dialectical). (See RHETORIC.) However, the natural descendants of these models are better seen in purely sociological terms: the geometrical model is exemplified by the Kuhnian paradigm (see KUHN, POPPER AND LOGICAL POSITIVISM) and the dialectical model by SCIENCE AS A SOCIAL MOVEMENT. Both science and politics can adopt either form, such that science may be movement-like (as it arguably was during the eighteenth-century Enlightenment) and politics may be paradigm-like (as it arguably was in Marxist ideology). Nevertheless, for analytic purposes it is useful to keep the geometrical–dialectical distinction sharp in order to track the fortunes of the normative and empirical dimensions of enquiry. Whereas the geometrical model treats the empirical as already normatively infused, the dialectical model treats the empirical as a challenge for the normative to overcome. In short, the geometrical model will tend to characterize the world in ways it can accept, whereas the dialectical model will tend to characterize it in ways it would correct. (See RATIONALITY.) This captures the difference in philosophical style between analytic social epistemology and Fuller's version.

Finally, social epistemologies may also be compared in terms of the presumptive answers they provide to the following research questions:

- Are the norms of enquiry autonomous from the norms governing the rest of society?
- Is there anything more to a "form of enquiry" than the manner in which enquirers are arranged?
- Do truth and the other normative aims of science remain unchanged as particular forms of enquiry come and go?
- Is there anything more to "the problem of knowledge" than a matter of *whose* actions are licensed on the basis of *which* claims made under *what* circumstances?
- Is the social character of knowledge reducible to the aggregated beliefs of some group of individuals?

- Is social epistemology's purview limited to the identification of mechanisms and institutions that meet conceptually satisfying definitions of knowledge?

Social epistemologists inclined towards positive answers to these questions remain close to the Cartesian starting-point of classical epistemology, which focuses on the individual's orientation to the truth. This is the standpoint of analytic social epistemology, which does not turn to the social (or even psychological) factors relevant to knowledge production until the relevant definitions of knowledge and related concepts have been established by such folk epistemological methods (see **FOLK EPISTEMOLOGY**) as conceptual analysis and pre-analytic intuitions. In contrast, Fuller's interdisciplinary but philosophically grounded approach offers a programme of empirical research and social policy based on negative answers to the above questions. However, this is not to deny the desirability of some of the classical ideals of epistemology, especially autonomous enquiry. Nevertheless, these ideals remain empty words without some clear strategy for overcoming the obstacles that block their successful institutionalization (See **UNIVERSITY**). In this respect, Fuller's version of social epistemology upholds positivist strictures about the need to operationalize, proceduralize and standardize key concepts that might otherwise have no clear meaning whatsoever. (See **TRUTH, RELIABILITY AND THE ENDS OF KNOWLEDGE**.)

FURTHER READING

S. Fuller, *Social Epistemology* (1988).
S. Fuller & J. Collier, *Philosophy, Rhetoric and the End of Knowledge* (2004).
A. Goldman, *Knowledge in a Social World* (1999).
F. Remedios, *Legitimizing Scientific Knowledge* (2003).
P. Roth, *Meaning and Method in the Social Sciences* (1987).
J. Rouse, *Knowledge and Power* (1987).
F. Schmitt (ed.), *Socializing Epistemology* (1994).

SOCIAL SCIENCE

The social sciences were inspired by the eighteenth-century European Enlightenment, when political theorists began to argue for a more integral connection between a state and its inhabitants than had been previously urged – by, say, Plato, Machiavelli and Hobbes. In particular, a ruler should not simply keep the peace but also provide for their welfare. Statecraft thus had to go beyond the usual threats and deceptions. Rulers were now expected, as Adam Smith would say, to increase the wealth of their nations. This historic change of attitude had three important consequences. First, it led to a managerial conception of the state, in which economic matters acquired a public significance that had been previously left in the hands of private households and corporations. Secondly, it fostered a more discriminating sense of citizenship as "contribution to society", especially for purposes of raising and distributing revenue. Finally, it led to the systematic collection of data about people's lives, culminating in a hardening of social categories (into classes and even races), which were then projected backwards as having been implicit throughout history. In this respect, social science and socialism were born joined at the hip, specifically in France in the 1820s, courtesy of Henri de Saint-Simon and especially his understudy, Auguste Comte, who coined both "positivism" and "sociology". Fuller's version of **SOCIAL EPISTEMOLOGY** is alive to this heritage. (See **PHILOSOPHY VERSUS SOCIOLOGY**.)

Given the multiple definitions that are often attached to positivism, it is worth observing two senses in which the natural sciences might be seen as the basis for the social sciences. One, due to Francis Bacon, simply involves the application of natural science theories and methods to social phenomena: a fairly straightforward case of what might be called reductionism or scientism. However, Comte's own view – shared by Fuller – presupposes a more reflexive attitude towards the history of science. In other words, as the natural sciences have expanded their sphere of applicability, they have also learned more about how scientific enquiry itself works. Thus, a second-order discipline, called "methodology" and later "philosophy of science", is a by-product of scientific progress, which then feeds back to steer the subsequent course of science. In that respect, sociology – as the historically final science – is also the one with the capacity to comprehend all that has gone before it as a coherent point of view that can then be used to govern society. Broadly speaking, it was this Comtean image of social science that enabled its development to be aligned with the growth of the nation state in the nineteenth and twentieth centuries.

Generally speaking, social scientists have provided a layer of mediation between the governors and the governed in complex democracies, especially with respect to those governed whose opinions the governors do not trust. Of course, the governors need to know what their various constituencies think, but it is not clear that putting government policies to a direct test, such as an election, will result in an outcome that is either favourable to the governors or faithful to the beliefs of the governed. Thus, social scientists armed with surveys, focus groups and participant-observation techniques have given voice to the people without directly inserting them into the policy-making process. A government that wishes to keep its options open will find frequent and decisive elections inconvenient, not least because it then must accept the legitimacy of the outcome, even if it goes against what the government would want or expect. However, once social scientists deliver public opinion as data to policy-makers who are allergic to direct accountability, the data function as a vaccine, that is, inoculation against further charges of accountability. Thus, policy-makers say that the people have been heard and their views are taken "under advisement".

The capture of public opinion as data defers the need for an immediate government response: analysis and interpretation must come first! This conclusion unites the most earnest social scientist and the most cynical policy-maker. For social scientists, the drive to empirical work has often been motivated by the perception that there are norms already in place in society that escape what the government wants to impose. For policy-makers, however, once these norms are revealed, they enable greater control of the potentially recalcitrant subjects. Moreover, at a reflexive level, the social scientist is herself subject to a similar sort of capture. The policy-maker refuses to interfere with the social scientist in her work, just as the social scientist refuses to interfere with her subjects in their day-to-day business. In both cases, autonomy enables greater instrumentality because just as the subjects do not interfere with the social scientific account of their activities, social scientists (as value-free enquirers) do not interfere with the political use of their research. (See **KNOWLEDGE POLICY**.)

Seen in the broader sweep of Western cultural history, the rise of the social sciences also marks an important stage in the secularization of the monotheistic religious (see **RELIGION**) perspective represented by Judaism, Christianity and Islam. (Indeed, the fourteenth-century Muslim scholar Ibn Khaldun had produced the earliest attempt at laws of historical change that displayed the modern social scientific aspiration of systematically interrelating political, cultural, economic and even ecological factors.) Of special relevance is the unique position of human beings in relation to the divine creator, in whose "image and likeness" *Homo sapiens* is said to have been created. The two implied theological traits – the separateness of human beings from other animals and the equality of all human beings in the eyes of God – have anchored subsequent discussion about the distinctiveness of the social sciences from the other two great bodies of academic knowledge, the natural sciences and the humanities. On the one hand, the natural sciences traditionally have presupposed that everything can be studied in terms of their external relations with other things, without considering their inner life (or soul). On the other hand, the humanities traditionally have presupposed a strong hierarchy of merit among individual members of *Homo sapiens*, with categories such as "genius" and "classic" playing significant evaluative and even explanatory roles.

Put more prosaically, the two great academic cultures prefer to study humanity without having to mingle with flesh-and-blood human beings. Thus, evolutionary psychologists infer what makes us who we are from the remains of our Stone Age ancestors (including their DNA), whereas humanists focus on artefacts of a more recent and literate age. In contrast, the social sciences adhere to the maxim that the best way to study human beings is to interact with them, typically by getting them to do and say things that they might not otherwise. This profoundly simple idea, common to experiments and ethnographies, has inspired the triumphs and disasters that punctuate the history of modern politics. It has required an increasingly controversial assumption: all human beings – whatever their achievements, competences, status or health – are equally significant members of society, whose strength ultimately lies in what they can do together.

Thus, the distinctiveness of the social sciences may be summed up in two words used to characterize the objects of their enquiry: meaning and welfare. The former captures what marks the social sciences from the natural sciences, the latter what marks the social sciences from the humanities. Both words have been invoked to call into question the status of a species-based "human nature". The uniqueness of individual consciousness associated with meaningfulness points to irreducible differences in personal histories, whereas the concept of welfare presupposes that humanity can collectively transcend the fatalism implied in our mortality as individuals. On the one hand, the appeal to meaning has served to remind would-be reformers that effective social change requires recognizing that individuals already have standpoints that inform their actions and out of which they need to be persuaded to do otherwise. On the other, the appeal to welfare has inspired the creation of political units, nation states, designed to instil a sense of social solidarity among biologically unrelated individuals (a.k.a. citizens) by providing them with health, education and even minimal subsistence in return for participation, most notably at elections and in war. Thus, the first professor of sociology, Émile Durkheim, used his discipline as a vehicle for importing into France the welfare state from Germany, where it had been a Bismarckian innovation.

From their inception, the social sciences have been subject to a pincer attack from the humanities and the natural sciences. On the one hand, the natural sciences have tried to reduce consciousness to a complex form of animal sensation;

on the other, the humanities have tried to reduce welfare to an artifice designed to cheat fate. The attack began to intensify in the late-nineteenth century, as the Darwinian focus on differential reproductive success as the key to **EVOLUTION** provided a natural scientific interpretation of fate – as "survival" – that humanists had previously lacked. The standard social science response to this pincer attack has been to convert what natural scientists and humanists see as brute facts into social problems, which are the proper subject matter of the social sciences. In short, what might be otherwise regarded as irreversible features of the human condition, with which we can do no better than cope, are treated as challenges to be overcome on the path to **PROGRESS**.

Indeed, Darwin's staunchest defender in his own day, Thomas Henry Huxley, held precisely this view: that an "evolutionary ethics" is a non-starter because humanity is distinguished by its *organized resistance* to natural selection. Huxley meant the various ways in which human beings have transformed the natural environment to enable the flourishing of those who, from a strictly biological standpoint, are by no means the fittest. Huxley's own field of medicine comes most readily to mind, especially its modern concern with prolonging life rather than simply letting nature take its course. But also included here are legal arrangements, in which succession to a corporate post or institutionalized role is prescribed on the basis of examination or election, that is, *not* family lineage. It is significant that the historically leading institutions in Western society – from the church and the **UNIVERSITY** to the state and the firm – have progressed by *discarding* whatever links their membership may have initially had to kinship, the point at which biological factors normally gain a foothold in explaining the human realm. In that respect, the history of humanity can be traced by following the development of the Western legal category of the corporation, or *universitas*, its name in Roman law.

However, the social sciences have been in steady decline since the late 1970s. Several concurrent tendencies point in this general direction. The political projects historically associated with the social sciences – socialism, the welfare state and international development policy – fell far short of expectations. All of these projects shared the ambition of redistributing effort and income to enable humanity to become a whole greater than the sum of its parts. To be sure, the gap between the rich and the poor had begun to close, when compared to the previous century of European imperial expansion. Nevertheless, progress was painfully slow and costly. Thus ensued what Marxists call "the fiscal crisis of the state", which led to the curtailment of welfarist initiatives and the toppling of socialist regimes worldwide. Also cut were the social science research programmes devoted to identifying and overcoming systemic social problems. As the nation state devolved its powers to the private sector, eighteenth-century arguments concerning the unnaturalness of large social units (e.g. nation states) and limitless human expansion have been revived, resulting in a revalorization of families and markets as natural forms of social life. However, this traditionally right-wing message is now aligned with recent research in sociobiology, evolutionary psychology and behavioural genetics.

The normative side of this shift is most evident in the conversion of "red" to "green" in the politics of self-avowed progressive thinkers and politicians. Thus, the older focus on the alleviation of specifically human misery has shifted to care for the environment at large. At a superficial level, this shift marks an increase in ambition. However, at a deeper level, it marks an admission of defeat, as policy goals are now defined primarily in terms of human self-restraint, such as birth control and pollution reduction. The ultimate goal appears to be not welfare maximization, but suffering minimization. Moreover, the criteria for success are more abstractly specified and hence potentially less controversial: politics is made easier if one needs to achieve a certain carbon emissions standard – which can be accomplished by whatever means – than a certain level of minimum income, which clearly would require some form of economic redistribution. Not surprisingly, recent years have witnessed the rise of corporate environmentalism, whereby labour exploitation is rendered compatible with clean environments.

Lurking behind this greening of the political left is the most fundamental challenge facing the future of the social sciences: *are human beings always the privileged members of society?* The question arises once we consider that the neo-Darwinian synthesis of Mendelian genetics and evolutionary biology does not privilege *Homo sapiens* above other animals. Because animals share possibly 95 per cent of their genes, species turn out to be convenient taxonomic schemes, not natural kinds. From a strictly neo-Darwinian perspective, even commonsensical appeals to a "human nature" that sharply distinguishes us from the "brutes" is little more than a myth. Of course, the myth lives on in the normative use still made by Noam Chomsky and Jürgen Habermas of our allegedly species-unique linguistic capacities. Nevertheless, species egalitarianism has expanded beyond Peter Singer's animal liberation movement, as greater comparative research into human beings and other animals tends to minimize the traditional differences between them. The more we study animals, it seems, the smarter they become, on the basis of which they then acquire greater normative significance.

At the same time, there has been a return to fatalism in the humanities. It is not quite a return to the original Graeco-Roman paganism, but it does share the same element of what Heidegger calls our "thrownness" into a world not of our own making. This newfound fatalism has been especially influential in French poststructuralist thought, especially following the work of Roland Barthes, Michel Foucault and Jacques Derrida on the "death of the subject". It is a sensibility born of the perceived failure of humanism, as the final moment in the Christian worldview, to prevent the atrocities of the twentieth century. It has even affected conceptions of language, which, following Heidegger, is now often said to "speak us", rather than the other way round. Indeed, the cognitive scientist Steven Pinker – not normally known for his poststructuralist sympathies – has argued that there may be a natural scientific basis for this sense of "fate". The configuration of our brains and genes may be ultimately out of our control, however deeply we come to understand them. Pinker's message will appeal to those eager to avoid political reforms that would compel a greater sense of collective responsibility. The social sciences historically offered empirical support and spiritual hope for just such reforms, which are increasingly dismissed by both natural scientists and humanists as utopian.

Moreover, we are beginning to see a generation of scientifically literate postmodernists (see **POSTMODERNISM**), followers of Bruno Latour and Gilles Deleuze, who under the rubric of "political ecology" extol the virtues of selectively including (and hence excluding) a variety of human beings, animals and even machines in the name of some advanced hybrid collective order: what ecologists call a "maximally inclusive fitness landscape". Such "cyborg worlds", as these heterogeneous regimes are now popularly known, have some disturbing precedents in the history of totalitarian politics. These include the origins of California-style clean environments in the racial hygiene of Nazi Germany. Consequently, we live in a time when an unprecedented openness to the inclusion of non-human members in the social order is combined with a heightened sensitivity to the difference between normal and pathological members. Of course, with the devolution of state authority, the drive to eradicate pathology nowadays often takes less direct and centralized forms than in the heyday of eugenics: for example, the decisions are individually taken and may be prenatally or subconsciously applied. This state of affairs has been called "bioliberalism".

The normative and empirical options for social science in the twenty-first century are summarized in the four "visions" depicted in Figure 1. The visions are defined in terms of two dimensions: whether or not society consists exclusively of human beings, and whether or not the human population will increase. For each vision,

	"we" = human bodies	**"we" ≠ human bodies**
Increase population	Enlightenment progress (welfarism or totalitarianism?)	Cyborg utopia (hybridization or purification?)
Decrease population	Darwinian survival (liberalism or indifference?)	Karmic balance (cosmic benevolence or inhumanity?)

Figure 1. Visions for social science in the twenty-first century.

the utopian and dystopian versions are presented. "Enlightenment progress" and "Darwinian survival" are options carried over from the nineteenth century, with the latter coming to dominate over the former. "Cyborg utopia" and "Karmic balance" are visions added only in the last generation. Clearly, they complicate matters by presenting the prospect of a largely dehumanized (or posthuman) social science.

- *Enlightenment progress* (= Marquis de Condorcet): Population increase provides an incentive to innovation, which will enable the earth to be remade into a human paradise, via state intervention.
- *Darwinian survival* (= Thomas Malthus): Population is naturally selected according to fitness to an environment that human artifice (including the state) cannot substantially change.
- *Cyborg utopia* (= Donna Haraway): Genetic engineering, prosthetic technologies and computer simulations create new entities, which become "our" new identities, replacing earlier human forms.
- *Karmic balance* (= Peter Singer): Evolutionary psychology creates new affiliations between human beings and non-human beings, which equalize cross-species sentiment and thereby diminish the value of individual human lives.

FURTHER READING

R. Aron, *Main Currents in Sociological Thought* (1965).
D. T. Campbell, *Methodology and Epistemology for the Social Sciences* (1988).
G. Deleuze, *Difference and Repetition* (1994).
P. Dickens, *Social Darwinism* (2000).
S. Fleischacker, *A Short History of Distributive Justice* (2004).
M. Foucault, *The Order of Things* (1970).
S. Fuller, *The New Sociological Imagination* (2006).
D. Haraway, *Simians, Cyborgs, Women* (1991).
B. Latour, *Politics of Nature* (2004).
W. Lepenies, *Between Literature and Science* (1988).
R. Macksey & E. Donato (eds), *The Structuralist Controversy* (1970).
J. Milbank, *Theology and Social Theory* (1990).
P. Mirowski, *Machine Dreams* (2002).
J. S. Nelson, A. Megill & D. McCloskey (eds), *The Rhetoric of the Human Sciences* (1986).
D. Noble, *The Religion of Technology* (1997).
S. Pinker, *The Blank Slate* (2002).
R. Proctor, *Value-Free Science?* (1991).
H. Simon, *The Sciences of the Artificial* (1977).
P. Singer, *A Darwinian Left* (1999).
T. Sorell, *Scientism* (1991).
C. Taylor, "Interpretation and the Sciences of Man" (1971).
I. Wallerstein, *Open the Social Sciences* (1996).
E. O. Wilson, *Consilience* (1998).

SOCIOLOGY OF KNOWLEDGE

The empirical side of social epistemology is rooted in the sociology of knowledge, whose history is a tale of two traditions, French and German, both coming to fruition in the period 1890–1930. They are based on the proximity of knowers in *space* and *time*, respectively. Thus, the French tradition focused on how people of different origins who are concentrated in one space over time acquire a common mindset, whereas the German tradition focused on how people dispersed over a wide space retain a common mindset by virtue of having been born at roughly the same time. (See UNIVERSALISM VERSUS RELATIVISM and MULTICULTURALISM.) The first strategy is exemplified by Lucien Levy-Bruhl and Émile Durkheim, the second by Wilhelm Dilthey and Karl Mannheim. An assumption common to both traditions is that collective patterns of thought are constituted as collective acts of resistance to the environment. The exact nature of the resistance is explainable by the spatiotemporal arrangement of the people concerned. Religious movements and political parties are thus obvious targets for the sociologist of knowledge. A Durkheimian might show how religious rituals enable the faithful to escape the limitations of their material conditions and stand up to potential oppressors, while a Mannheimian might show how a persistent ideology enables the experience of a particular generation to define the parameters of policy for the entire society. In both cases, the sociology of knowledge is meant to complement, not replace, the psychology of normal thought processes through which individuals adapt to a world that is largely not of their own making. (See COMMON SENSE VERSUS COLLECTIVE MEMORY)

The sociology of knowledge finds itself in a peculiar normative (see NORMATIVITY) position. Is its object of enquiry, organized resistance to reality, to be valorized or pathologized? Are RELIGIONs and ideologies instances of thought operating at a standard, as it were, above or below that of everyday reasoning? Are they vocations or manias? The two sociology of knowledge traditions are themselves ambivalent on this point, and the addition of science as a potential object of enquiry has only complicated the matter. (See EXPLAINING THE COGNITIVE CONTENT OF SCIENCE.) To be sure, some classical sociologists, notably Vilfredo Pareto, were very clear about the "non-logical" status of the forms of knowledge eligible for sociological scrutiny. Unsurprisingly, philosophers of science from Hans Reichenbach to Larry Laudan have followed Pareto's lead by dividing the labour between the epistemology and the sociology of knowledge along the border of the rational and the irrational. (See PHILOSOPHY VERSUS SOCIOLOGY.) Interestingly, with the onset of the Second World War, Mannheim himself shifted from this view to one closer to American pragmatism, which would have judgements about the rationality of science – as of any belief system – turn on the consequences of actions taken in its name. This shift seeded C. Wright Mills's political CRITICISM of science as a military–industrial complex during the Cold War.

However, science cannot be easily assimilated to the pragmatist model because science has not always had rational consequences outside the controlled mental and physical spaces – say, seminars and laboratories – in which its distinctive forms of knowledge have been produced. If judgements about the rationality of religion and politics were analogously confined to, say, theological disputation and parliamentary debate, would judgements of their rationality suffer significantly by comparison with science? Probably not. Consider the extended legacy of the Vienna Circle (see KUHN, POPPER, AND LOGICAL POSITIVISM). In most general terms, the Vienna Circle regarded conceptual frameworks in a generally Kantian fashion. Thus, the external question of which framework should be selected was treated as practical, whereas the internal question of what follows from a selected framework was treated as theoretical. This led to what social constructivists (see SOCIAL CONSTRUCTIVISM) would call an "asymmetrical" treatment of framework origins and consequences. The former represented an existential choice; the latter was determined by logic.

Mannheim departed from this asymmetrist legacy by interpreting the consequences of such a framework in existential, not logical, terms. In other words, before 1940 Mannheim excluded the natural sciences and mathematics from the purview of the sociology of knowledge, but after 1940 he began to include these disciplines, which implied that their RATIONALITY became an empirically open question. After all, the traditional "purest" of the sciences – mathematics and physics – were integral to some of the most oppressive and destructive episodes in human history during the Second World War, which were then normalized in the Cold War. Thus, the original turn to "symmetry" in the sociology of knowledge, nowadays associated with the studied neutrality of SCIENCE AND TECHNOLOGY STUDIES research, came less from an open-mindedness to alternative research trajectories than an openly critical attitude towards the dominant trajectory that had valorized science without taking its negative consequences into account. (See EXPLAINING THE NORMATIVE STRUCTURE OF SCIENCE.)

However, the overall history of science and technology studies has gradually removed the normative sting of Mannheim's later sociology of knowledge, largely by attenuating science's status as a form of organized enquiry that offers collective resistance to the world in which it finds itself. In the end, science comes to blend into other socio-technical practices with no special normative status of its own. Science and technology studies has facilitated this blending through three successive solutions to the problem of scientific rationality, each of which breaks down the distinction between science and the rest of society more fundamentally: (i) relativize scientific rationality; (ii) bracket scientific rationality; and (iii) eliminate scientific rationality:

(i) Science must be seen as organized resistance, much like a religious (see RELI-GION) or political movement, and hence its rationality seen exclusively in terms of its internal workings. Ludwig Fleck's pioneering application of the French sociology of knowledge tradition to biomedical "thought collectives" and Kuhn's generalized model of scientific change are cases in point.

(ii) The entire question of scientific rationality needs to be bracketed, specifically by presuming that apparent differences in the rationality of, say, science and religion or politics – or even what passes for true or false – is an artefact of whether one has chosen an evaluative framework internal or external to the practice in question. Otherwise, there is no empirical reason for treating one set of practices as more rational than another set. This is the once infamous but now widely accepted symmetry principle of the "strong programme" of the Edinburgh School of science and technology studies.

(iii) Most recently Bruno Latour's Paris School has challenged the idea that science can be clearly separated from the rest of society, especially once one examines *all* (not just the theoretically prescribed) consequences of a scientific practice. In that case, epistemic rationality collapses into a special case of political rationality in an undifferentiated world of "technoscience". Those maintaining the longest networks for the longest time simply come to be defined as both the most knowledgeable *and* most powerful, with the former predicate used to explain the latter by obscuring the local struggles faced along the way.

By the time we reach stage (iii), it is legitimate to ask whether what is described is any longer a sociology of *knowledge*. After all, stage (iii) does not recognize knowledge as having a distinct normative character that could channel the development of scientific institutions. To appreciate what the sociology of science looks like once it has lost its moorings in the sociology of knowledge's traditional preoccupation with institutionalized rationality, one need only turn to the practice of KNOWLEDGE MANAGEMENT and its Orwellian correlate, the so-called KNOWLEDGE SOCIETY.

FURTHER READING
R. Aron, *Main Currents in Sociological Thought* (1965).
D. Bloor, *Knowledge and Social Imagery* (1976).

G. Delanty, *Challenging Knowledge* (2001).
L. Fleck, *The Genesis and Development of a Scientific Fact* (1979).
D. Frisby, *The Alienated Mind* (1992).
L. Laudan, *Progress and its Problems* (1977).
K. Mannheim, *Ideology and Utopia* (1936).
K. Mannheim, *Man and Society in an Age of Reconstruction* (1940).
R. Proctor, *Value-Free Science?* (1991).

TRANSLATION

Social epistemology's interest in translation comes from Kuhn's (see **KUHN, POPPER AND LOGICAL POSITIVISM**) *incommensurability* thesis, which implies that scientists cannot normally translate between conceptual schemes, or "paradigms". Thus, most scientists fail to see beyond the paradigm in which they are trained. It is left to more recent initiates, relatively inexperienced in the old paradigm, to appreciate fully a scientific revolution as converts to the new paradigm. However, according to Kuhn, true scientific revolutionaries such as Galileo and Einstein can switch back and forth between the old and new paradigm in their understanding of the world, a capacity he likened to bilingualism. While **SCIENCE AND TECHNOLOGY STUDIES** tends to stress the relativist (see **RELATIVISM VERSUS CONSTRUCTIVISM**) implications of Kuhn's thesis – to change one's paradigm is effectively to change one's world – professional translators normally possess the scientific revolutionary's capacity to live in two worlds at once. Their translations, however, are epistemic hybrids, attempts to render alien lines of thought in a native medium. These are largely exercises in intellectual diplomacy that scientists themselves do not normally face. After all, physicists are not concerned with capturing the full sense of Aristotelian physics in Newtonian mechanics. Rather, they happily relinquish all interest in Aristotle on the assumption that most of what is worthwhile in Aristotle can be better expressed in Newtonian terms and what cannot be so expressed is not worth expressing.

This distinction between the translator and the scientist reappears in the counterfactuals implicitly presupposed by, respectively, historians and philosophers of science. In this sense, Kuhn thought like a historian. He was led to the incommensurability thesis when he tried to imagine how Aristotle could have thought as he did. He thus counterfactualized from the present to the past by positioning himself as an observer or re-enactor of past events who, like a guest in a foreign land, tries to learn the natives' customs. In contrast, philosophers regularly counterfactualize from the past to the present. In this case, it would mean that Aristotle is reincarnated as the ultimate adult student, someone sufficiently rational and obliging to learn how to get from his physics to ours through a combination of logical inferences and empirical observations that he himself would have made, under the right conditions. By appealing to these complementary counterfactuals, historians and philosophers of science maintain an *entente cordiale*. Thus, Kuhn's incommensurability thesis may cause us to question our understanding of Aristotle but not our own self-understanding, since both counterfactual excursions assume the legitimacy of the norms governing their respective destinations.

Nevertheless, this *entente cordiale* stretches credulity as a strategy for how alien visitors should approach native norms. It simply reflects the artificial separation of history and philosophy of science that is characteristic of Prig HISTORIOGRAPHY. Since virtually all societies manifest internal conflicts, any uniform NORMATIVE display is bound to be an official story (perhaps even one "made for export") that represents an expedient resolution of those conflicts. The exigencies of imperial rule in the early-twentieth century help to explain the status of such stories as interpretive benchmarks. But there is no reason to suppose that the alien visitor could not criticize (see CRITICISM) or even change native norms by appealing to these internal conflicts. In other words, why must counterfactual time travel be asymmetrical, with historians always transporting themselves to the past and philosophers always importing the ancients into the present? Why not portray the ancients as our historians or ourselves as philosophical missionaries in their worlds? In both cases, we would be forced to persuade the ancients that we could bring (or have brought) out the best of their scientific projects, and defend ourselves against the charge of taking (or having taken) them in wayward directions. Recovering this pre-Kuhnian appeal to counterfactuals would be a valuable first step in the normative integration of history and philosophy of science. Here RHETORIC would play a central role.

Generally speaking, what is typically worth recovering from past figures is less the *content* of their ideas than the *contexts* that brought them forth. Professional translators follow the biblical scholar Eugene Nida, an influence on both W. V. Quine and Kuhn, who drew a distinction between providing the *formal* and *dynamic* equivalent of an original utterance. The former aims at reproducing the content of the original in a new context, the latter the context of the original, even if that means providing substantially new content. This distinction is sometimes drawn in terms of the translator focusing, respectively, on the semantic and pragmatic dimension of the text. Thus, a text of Shakespeare's *Romeo and Juliet* that includes notes explaining its archaic expressions provides a formal equivalent of the original, whereas the text of *West Side Story*, a mid-twentieth-century adaptation of Shakespeare's play, provides a dynamic equivalent.

The difference between a stilted but literally rendered *Romeo and Juliet* and an accessible but loosely rendered *West Side Story* casts the trade-off in translation strategies in very bold relief. But how does it appear in works more relevant to social epistemology? Take Plato, for example. (See PHILOSOPHY VERSUS SOCIOLOGY.) There are two basic ways of rendering Plato for contemporary philosophical audiences. Formal equivalence is normally given precedence. Thus, the interpreter focuses on the ontology of Pure Forms that figures so prominently in Plato's writings. Plato's arguments are presented, explicated, supplemented and/or refuted.

As much as possible, the interpreter draws on Plato's actual utterances to make sense of his arguments. When this strategy fails, Plato is presumed to be saying something unusually subtle, which then calls forth alternative interpretations. The overall effect of this hermeneutical activity is to suggest that Plato's text ought to be read with a care that is normally not extended to texts written in the reader's own time. Thus, Plato is, so to speak, "performed" as a classic. By restricting the role of Plato's original context in his thought, Plato is simultaneously made *both* more and less accessible to today's interpreter. He is more accessible because relatively little knowledge of Plato's sociohistorical background is needed to make sense of what he says. (Indeed, texts written by Plato's contemporaries and precursors are more likely to be used in "intertextualizing" Plato.) But, ultimately, Plato is rendered less accessible, since his text appears *prima facie* quite alien, and hence in need of extended interpretation.

In contrast, the social epistemologist would argue that Plato's greatness lies less in his specific utterances than in the exigencies that gave rise to his utterances, specifically the fall of Athens to Sparta in the Peloponnesian War, which Plato witnessed during his youth. This context was perhaps most clearly articulated in his day in the chronicles of the failed Athenian general Thucydides. Basically, the Athenians deployed the dialectic indiscriminately in the public sphere, which enabled virtually anyone with a quick wit to steer the city state in what invariably turned out to be disastrous directions. (See **FREE ENQUIRY** and **RHETORIC**.) Recognition of this Athenian trait motivated Plato's hatred of those who taught the dialectic, the Sophists, his fixation on the fate of Socrates as an object lesson in the dark side of the "open society" and his formation of a school that developed the arts of reasoning in a setting more akin to a monastery than a courtroom.

Bearing Plato's context in mind, then, we can understand his ideal realm as a form of indirect speech that, in other times and places, would have been expressed rather differently. Corresponding to the Pure Forms that played such a central role in Plato's own ontology might be God or even a sense of society whose existence transcends that of social facts and social relations. In that sense, those who want to follow the spirit of Plato should not follow him literally (or repeat him mindlessly, which amounts to the same thing), but try to translate his sociohistorical context into our own, so that we may learn from it. Friedrich Nietzsche, Leo Strauss and Alvin Gouldner are examples of interpreters of Plato who adhered precisely to these strictures, albeit drawing predictably different ideological lessons for their own times.

FURTHER READING

S. Fuller, *Social Epistemology* (1988).
W. Fusfield, "To Want to Prove it ... is ... Really Superfluous" (1997).

A. Gouldner, *Enter Plato* (1965).

T. S. Kuhn, *The Structure of Scientific Revolutions* (1970).

T. S. Kuhn, *The Essential Tension* (1977).

W. V. O. Quine, *Word and Object* (1960).

J. Rawls, *A Theory of Justice* (1971).

L. Strauss, *Persecution and the Art of Writing* (1952).

S. P. Turner, *Sociological Explanation as Translation* (1980).

TRUTH, RELIABILITY AND THE ENDS OF KNOWLEDGE

The traditional strategy for instilling a common sense of collective enquiry has been to engage in a transcendental **RHETORIC** of truth, whereby enquirers are led to believe (usually with the help of a philosophical theory) that they are all *already* heading in a common direction, fixated on a common end (a.k.a. truth), and that all subsequent discussion should be devoted to finding the most efficient means towards that end. **RATIONALITY** and **PROGRESS** are often invoked in this context. Most versions of **ANALYTIC SOCIAL EPISTEMOLOGY** are truth-oriented in this broad sense. Some advocates, such as Alvin Goldman, even believe that there is an interesting – and superior – sense of enquiry common to all those who seek the truth of whatever domain that interests them.

Fuller's version of social epistemology denies this doctrine, which Goldman calls "veritism", for two main reasons. The first is that, in practice, veritism is not quite as it seems. Indeed, the doctrine is applied selectively, as Plato and Machiavelli might: knowledge is fashioned as an instrument of power for stabilizing the social order. (See **CONSENSUS VERSUS DISSENT**.) In Goldman's own formulation, truth is necessary but not sufficient for knowledge worth having. Some truths may not be worth "knowing" – in the sense of publicly disseminated – not simply because their content is trivial but because the knower is incapable of drawing valid inferences from those truths. Moreover, in order to maximize the number of truths that are known, it may be necessary to plant some strategic falsehoods in the public consciousness. In short, the end justifies the means, when the end is truth. The profoundly anti-Enlightenment sensibility informing this policy is revealed in Goldman's own name for it, "epistemic paternalism", which implies that some – if not most – people need to be treated as children who cannot be trusted to draw their own conclusions and make their own mistakes. (For contrast, see **FREE ENQUIRY**.)

The second reason Fuller opposes veritism is that it pre-empts the articulation of significant disagreements over the ends of enquiry and the standards used to evaluate progress towards them. Sometimes truth is invoked to argue that social interests are not always relevant for evaluating knowledge claims. After all, the round-earth theory is an improvement on the flat-earth theory, regardless of our interests in wanting to know about the shape of the earth. This is presumably because the former is true, the latter false. Again, the European scientific community came to be convinced of the truth of Newtonian mechanics because the planets really do move as Newton predicted. Nevertheless, we are justified in believing that the round-earth theory is an improvement on the flat-earth theory because our theory turns out to be better by standards *that have themselves changed* so as to render the flat-earth theory a non-starter. "Standards" here mean the **NORMATIVE** contexts in which we are most likely to want to know the shape of the earth. In this sense, interest is integral to the nature of knowledge claims. The people who found the flat-earth theory persuasive were generally not interested in the earth's shape for the same reasons that now persuade us that the round-earth theory is true. In particular, they did not wish to embed the earth's shape in a unified theory of physical reality, *à la* Newtonian mechanics.

One need not be a sceptic or even a **RELATIVIST** to insist that the standards for evaluating knowledge claims be made explicit at the outset in order to argue sensibly about which claims are better than others. For example, this point has been repeatedly urged by all kinds of positivists against all transcendental forms of philosophy. Moreover, if these standards are not to appear arbitrary, they must make reference to the reasons *why* one wishes to acquire knowledge, so that the knowledge so acquired turns out to be of the appropriate kind. "Justified true beliefs" – the classical definition of knowledge – are all too easy to accumulate, as long as we are not too fussy about the relevance of what is accumulated to what we care about. Indeed, the classical definition of knowledge seems to have been designed more for conservers than stakeholders or even funders of knowledge.

Admittedly, the reasons for wanting knowledge are not normally made explicit in the conduct of science. (See **KNOWLEDGE POLICY**.) Unless that time-honored epistemic device – the budgetary constraint – intervenes, we do not normally worry much about the relative value of pursuing physics *vis-à-vis* biology. Both disciplines are simply taken to be worth pursuing as well as possible. That is because it is presumed that, at a certain level, we all have the *same* reasons for wanting to engage in scientific enquiry. Thus, logical positivist (see **KUHN, POPPER AND LOGICAL POSITIVISM**) appeals to the "unity of science" presume a unified conception of both reality and the community of enquirers. And to be sure, in many contexts, the standards for adequate knowledge are common to most of those who would want such knowledge, regardless of their other personal and social differences. However, this convergence on epistemic standards does not, strictly speaking, reflect a convergence of independently reasoned judgements. As Kuhn realized, that members of a well-defined scientific community can usually agree on which theories to accept or reject is largely explainable by their common training and their desire to follow wherever the pack seems likely to go.

Only an Orwellian sense of history would have us believe that the scientists behind the acceptance of Newtonianism in the eighteenth century constituted a relatively unified, consensus-seeking community. Indeed, before disciplinary boundaries hardened in the second half of the twentieth century, a scientist would normally pursue multiple research agendas with varying degrees of enthusiasm, resources and results. A formal vote would never be taken to ratify a paradigm. Rather, something closer to a statistical drift in scientific allegiances occurred over time, the phenomenon that Kuhn dramatized as the "invisibility of scientific revolutions". In such a diffuse field of play, in which many different parties pursue a variety of theories for only partially overlapping reasons, it is unclear *a priori* what might count as epistemic success. Each theory has its own way of prioritizing evidence and arguments, suited to its own particular strengths, which appeal to constituencies who may or may not determine the course of science in the long run. Consequently, a successful scientific research programme has typically had to score on two fronts at once: it has not only had to overcome rivals, but has had to do so according to rules that are biased to its strengths. These rules then become the basis for evaluating new players and are retrospectively used to explain the failure of old rivals. In short, *any major success in science is simultaneously a meta-success.* Indeed, the part of Newton's success that is usually explained by appealing to "nature" or "reality" is nothing more than this meta-success.

Thus, once Newtonian mechanics had been widely accepted, textbooks gave the impression that everyone accepted it for the same set of "good reasons" that now allow the theory to be integrated into the larger body of scientific knowledge, on which the next generation of enquirers may build. Somewhat more credible cases of independent individuals converging on the same scientific judgements may be found in the widespread lay acceptance of the professional standards of engineers and medical doctors. But these cases usually presuppose that it is rational for individuals to defer to those who have been certified by the relevant disciplinary community, who in turn typically consist of those who have been subject to common training, which brings us back to the textbooks and what amounts to a blind trust in their Orwellian view of history. (See **HISTORIOGRAPHY**.) This last point is related to two features of our epistemic predicament that philosophers often seem to regard as desirable but should be treated as problematic.

The first concerns what Aant Elzinga, the first Scandinavian social epistemologist, calls "epistemic drift", that is, the tendency for epistemic criteria to drift from ones that are likely to push back the frontiers of knowledge to ones that are likely to serve some socially desirable ends. Elzinga introduced epistemic drift to highlight potential perversions of the research agenda that result from the existence of a state monopoly on research funding. However, the legacy of epistemic drift is far subtler, namely, the tendency for measures of *reliability* to become proxy measures of *validity* in the evaluation of knowledge claims. In other words, while scientists are officially concerned with whether their theories get closer to their target realities, they nevertheless measure success in terms of the regularity with which they can achieve more limited goals that are said to "model" those realities. This epistemic bait-and-switch is most familiar from biomedical research, in which laboratory experiments on rats provide the basis for claims about how to treat disease in human beings. But the same also applies to particle accelerator experiments that are made to settle questions about the origins of the universe, to aptitude tests whose efficient sorting of schoolchildren is said to tap into native intelligence, and to public opinion surveys that supposedly capture the mood of a nation. In both cases, the instrument's reliability in producing similar results is made to stand for its ability to represent a reality beyond the research environment.

Moreover, currently popular versions of analytic social epistemology are based precisely on this overestimation of reliability. The overestimation lies in supposing that doing something well can trump whether it is what we want to do. In other words, validity can drift into reliability by shifting the goalpost for adequate knowledge over time. Such drifts and shifts are very much the stuff of politics and perhaps even essential for maintaining a stable social order. Social psychologists speak of *adaptive preference formation* to capture this pervasive phenomenon, which enables people to minimize cognitive dissonance by coming over time to want what they are most likely to get. This applies to scientists no less than politicians. Moreover, a demonstrably reliable process has precisely the sorts of virtues that policy-makers like. Thus, the hypodermic injection that alleviates the laboratory rat of an experimentally induced illness in most cases suggests the presence of a closed system that can be inserted – as one might a machine – to increase the efficiency of a larger healthcare system. Of course, complications can be added to this example but it is important in such matters to return periodically to the core intuitions that anchor the epistemological discussions.

The second problematic feature of our epistemic predicament is a generalization of the first. The drift from validity to reliability is part of a more global tendency towards what economists call "screening" and "signalling" criteria, whereby a readily accessed indicator is made to stand for the thing we really care about. The relevant euphemisms are "bounded rationality" and "heuristics", popularized by the late Herbert Simon. The classic example is letting academic credentials determine judgements of job suitability. In these cases, we imagine that credentials stand for some unknown track record: for example, Harvard graduates who have performed well at their jobs. Yet, this is no more than an endless cycle of hearsay, anecdote and folklore. Despite all the talk of reliability in contemporary epistemology and philosophy of science, there really is nowhere to turn to learn the actual track records of the competing research programmes. In this respect, we continue to live in a "Baconian fantasy".

To see the Baconian fantasy in action, consider Goldman's version of analytic social epistemology. His conception of reliability – the proportion of true beliefs to the sum of true and false beliefs generated by a knowledge system – is operationalized as "epistemic power", what is normally called EXPERTISE, although the exact bearer of this power (human, machine, network, etc.) remains unspecified. Unlike Goldman, however, Francis Bacon – England's Lord Chancellor in the early-seventeenth century and the guiding spirit behind the Royal Society – realized that demonstrating reliability requires work. Specifically, Bacon envisaged that the state would need to get into the business of counting, recording and publicizing the relevant beliefs, thereby producing, so to speak, a consumer report of knowledge. SCIENCE AND TECHNOLOGY STUDIES acquires much of its rhetorical sting from taking reliability seriously and then looking for the evidence, and finding that it is either lacking or ambiguous, not least because we lack authoritative accounts of epistemic track records.

That philosophers have developed some sophisticated, probability-based definitions of reliability only shows that we now probably have a much better understanding of what reliability means. Unfortunately, these wonderful definitions have yet to be systematically implemented in the record-keeping practices of scientific disciplines and liberal professions, let alone the state. Thus, scepticism about reliabilist social epistemologies ultimately rests on the reliabilists' own failure to develop – or even suggest – the appropriate institutions for assessing the reliability of knowledge claims. Matters are not helped by reliability's multiple ordinary meanings. It not only refers to the capacity of the same process to produce the same result, but also our propensity to trust someone's judgement – presumably because we have been satisfied by that person's judgement in the past, a criterion rather different from whether the judgement has displayed consistency across similar cases. In this latter, looser sense, reliability is simply equated with blind trust in EXPERTISE and, especially in educational contexts, reliabilists appear happy to capitalize on the association.

In general terms, matters of efficiency too easily override larger concerns about how, why and for whom knowledge is produced. A failure to check the work of others because of a lack of resources to do so has metamorphosed into a transcendental justification of "trust" as the ultimate social bond. Never before has the "two wrongs make a right" principle insinuated itself so insidiously in social life. Perhaps the public is risk-averse not because it places such a high value on reliable knowledge (so as to want to avoid anything that smacks of unreliability), but because it is currently peripheral to the knowledge-policy process. Public caution, then, is more an expression of political disaffection than brute ignorance. Were the public more directly involved, and hence forced to find out more about what is going on, they would probably be willing to take more risks, thereby dispelling the Baconian fantasy.

FURTHER READING

D. T. Campbell, *Methodology and Epistemology for the Social Sciences* (1988).

J. Elster, *Sour Grapes* (1984).

S. Fuller, *Kuhn vs Popper* (2003).

S. Fuller & J. Collier, *Philosophy, Rhetoric and the End of Knowledge* (2004).

R. Giere (ed.), *Cognitive Models of Science* (1992).

A. Goldman, *Epistemology and Cognition* (1986).

A. Goldman, *Knowledge in a Social World* (1999).

J. Hecht, *Doubt* (2003).

S. Shapin & S. Schaffer, *Leviathan and the Air Pump* (1985).

H. Simon, *The Sciences of the Artificial* (1977).

UNIVERSALISM VERSUS RELATIVISM

Many philosophically inspired approaches to knowledge attempt to show that certain claims to knowledge are true regardless of time and place. They are true or false everywhere and always. This position is *universalism*. In contrast, there are broadly sociological approaches, which argue that the validity of a knowledge claim is specific to time and place. What passes as knowledge in one culture may not pass in another. This position is *relativism*. The import of relativism is best understood if one thinks of cultures as well-defined spatiotemporal units that are the subjects of national histories or tribal lore. Without these clear boundaries, it is difficult to specify the extent of a knowledge claim's validity. In that sense, relativism loses its meaning if one cannot specify relative to *what* exactly. But do claims to knowledge naturally carry such clearly marked jurisdictions (a.k.a. validity conditions), or must these be actively constructed and maintained? If these jurisdictions are indeed constructed, can they not also be constructed to constitute a universe, a single polity that at least potentially includes everyone? This is the *constructivist universalism* common to the idea of the UNIVERSITY, LOGICAL POSITIVISM and Fuller's social epistemology. (See RELATIVISM VERSUS CONSTRUCTIVISM.)

A well-defined sense of culture – and the epistemological relativism it breeds – is itself relative to a certain period in the history of Western culture, one that roughly began in the late-eighteenth century, and is unravelling today in the midst of postmodern (see POSTMODERNISM) patterns of communication and migration (a.k.a. globalization). The historically specific character of relativism – "metarelativism", if you will – is lost in introductory philosophy courses that portray the debates between the Sophists and Socrates in Plato's *Dialogues* as the prototype of the zero-sum dialectical game nowadays defined by universalism and relativism. Thus, philosophers ask, is man (or woman) the measure of all things, or are there ideal forms in terms of which all knowledge must measure up? This forced choice misleads because the ancient statements of relativism were not usually formulated as negations of universalism. Take Bishop Ambrose's seasoned advice to the young Augustine: "When in Rome, do as the Romans do". He did not mean that what Romans do applies *only* in the city of Rome. After all, in Ambrose's day (fourth century CE), Roman customs were prevalent in many precincts throughout Europe, Asia and Africa. All that the slogan prohibits is a disregard for the customs already in place, but it leaves open just how extensive the "place" happens to be and, more importantly, the extent to which different customs may coexist in the same place. For example, after a relatively brief period of persecution, Christians coexisted with pagans in Rome and its foreign spheres of influence.

Before the aggressive campaigns to spread Christianity and Islam as "world RELIGIONS", there were few, if any, instances of culture clash that could be reasonably cast in terms of "universalism versus relativism". Most such clashes were more or less tolerated in an eclectic environment of *cosmopolitanism*. This applied even in cases of imperial domination, where one would most suspect universalist tendencies at work. Because it was in an imperial power's own interest to economize on the use of force, local customs were usually left in place as long as the locals regularly paid their taxes. Thus, the Romans would have been hard-pressed to disavow Jesus's original instruction to his disciples to "Give Caesar what is Caesar's, but give God what is God's". In this respect, the tribute-based character of imperial rule in the ancient world contrasts sharply with the culturally disruptive, capital-driven forms of imperialism in the modern world, as epitomized by the need to reorganize the local workforce in order to render it an efficient source of surplus value.

That the recognition of local customs might come into conflict with forms of life that aspired to universality first arose in international law, under the rubric of *the standard of civilization*, during the sixteenth-century European colonial expansion into the Americas. Much of the early discussion was concerned with reconciling the avowed universality of Christian ethics with the fact that Christian colonists often slaughtered vast portions of native populations before establishing permanent settlements. The legal solution was to define a "civilized" country as one that allowed Europeans to do business peacefully. Moreover, this definition was reintroduced to Europeans in the eighteenth century as the concept of "civility". By that time, Enlightenment intellectuals had come to believe that another form of life had to replace the role that Christendom had traditionally played in disciplining the passions, as sectarian struggles among Christians were seen as the source of two centuries of almost uninterrupted warfare within Europe itself. That new form of life was *commercialism*, or the pursuit of wealth.

The equation of civility with commerce – and the associated image of the humble merchant seeking recognition from others by catering to their needs – seemed to epitomize the essence of tolerance. But in fact it opened a Pandora's box of problems, especially outside Europe. Expatriate European merchants, keen to set up as many exchanges as possible, effectively rendered native goods commensurable with – and hence potentially replaceable by – European ones. Taken to the limit, everything would eventually have its price. To open the door to Europeans *de jure* was *de facto* to Europeanize one's own culture. It seemed, then, that the only salient differences between the aggressive campaigns mounted by Christian and Islamic proselytizers and such open-door trade policies were that the latter enabled the natives to lose their cultural identity in a less violent, more piecemeal fashion. Moreover, it did not require historical hindsight to appreciate this point.

The decline of India after the influx of European trade in the sixteenth century discouraged China and Japan from opening their doors until they were effectively forced open in the mid-nineteenth century. The worldwide diffusion of the commercial ethic revealed that the historical longevity of a set of social practices did not prevent people from exchanging them for other practices that they perceived to be better, be it by force or by choice. This turned out to be universalism in action. It continues to animate debates surrounding the cultivation of *indigenous* versus *relevant* knowledge in the developing world.

When Kant's student Johann Gottfried von Herder first introduced *Kultur* in academic German in the 1780s, it referred to the handicrafts cultivated by rural folk. It played on the etymological kinship of *culture* and *agriculture*, which associated intellectual depth with geographical rootedness during a period when it was widely thought that traits acquired through experience could be transmitted to one's offspring not only legally – in terms of land ownership – but also biologically. In this respect, *Kultur* was born with racialist overtones. English turned out to be the last major European language in which "culture" appeared in ordinary usage, mainly because the word had originated in opposition to the perceived British tendency to encourage (or force) nations to exchange their native products for more efficiently produced foreign ones in a universal regime of free trade. It was only once the British thought that their own native traditions were under threat that Matthew Arnold – especially in his 1869 essay "Culture and Anarchy" – popularized in English the idea that culture was something worth preserving and nurturing in the face of what Arnold called "philistines".

Much of what passes for relativism today is really a pluralism that refuses to take a clear stand on whether multiple perspectives can coexist. This means that relativism is most persuasive when there are no resource constraints on realizing alternative worlds. If everything can be realized without interfering with anything, then relativism is vindicated. However, whenever and wherever there are conflicts, and we are forced to make trade-offs, then relativism turns out to be obscurantist. This situation does not necessarily vindicate some absolute conception of truth or reality, but it may vindicate a constructivist universalism. In any case, it means that we must ascend to the second order and construct a decision procedure that could reach judgements binding on all the conflicting parties, even – or perhaps especially – if subject to appeal. This is the topic of EPISTEMIC JUSTICE.

Of course, universalists can easily mystify their own position by overinterpreting the fact that the range of acceptable opinion on any topic in any society is always much narrower – and subject to much more cross-cultural overlap – than is logically possible. An antidote to such overinterpretation is what Paul Ricoeur called the "hermeneutics of suspicion" (see PHILOSOPHY VERSUS SOCIOLOGY). Here, two strategies prove helpful. First, the appearance of universalism may simply be the product of a *post facto* harmonization of rather different events that, in the hands of the adept author of a scientific textbook, provide independent support for the reality of a research finding. (See **EXPLAINING THE COGNITIVE CONTENT OF SCIENCE**.) Secondly, universalism may be more prosaically the result of a subtly intertwined common history that has escaped naive observers. For example, Westerners often interpret the relatively easy acceptance of Darwinism in the Far East as evidence for the universal truth of evolution. But this is to look at matters the wrong way round. More likely is that the monotheistic privileging of human beings over other life forms has impeded the acceptance of Darwinism at home, since religions upholding the unity of nature and the fundamental equality of life forms should find – and have found – Darwinism metaphysically quite congenial.

There is a general lesson here: claims to epistemic universalism are often little more than a superstitious response to a tortuous tale of legitimization. "Independent corroboration" may be an intellectual mirage that emerges from multiple interpretations of the same work that never come into contact with each other, because in each case they are judged by local standards, but the overall effect is to suppress intellectual differences and perhaps even disagreements, resulting in what is called "incommensurability" in Fuller's social epistemology. (See **TRANSLATION**.)

In short, the relativist–universalist distinction is itself not universal but part of Western **FOLK EPISTEMOLOGY**. On the contrary, the universalist–relativist distinction has appeared vivid only for a limited period: from Britain's aggressive pursuit of a free-trade policy in the 1780s to the end of colonialism in the 1960s. The idea of culture as something attached to a particular people who are, in turn, attached to a particular place – the typical image of relativist knowledge production – emerged in reaction to the palpable disintegration of traditional forms of life by the spread of commercial values. During this period, utilitarianism was often demonized for reducing qualitative distinctions to a universal calculus of commensurable quantities, which later came to be seen as a general tendency towards "scientization". The reaction took the form of consolidating a unique cultural identity around the nation state, mainly through uniform schooling and military service, two processes that did much to restrict people's spontaneous cognitive plasticity and physical mobility. By the end of this period, less than fifty years ago, the second major round of nation-state building – this time in Africa and Asia – had occurred, during which similar arguments for cultural identity were made, this time in the face of the post-Second World War Euro-American hegemony. Much of what cultural studies today discusses as "identity politics" descends from this form of relativism.

FURTHER READING

A. Ahmad, *In Theory: Classes, Nations, Literatures* (1992).

A. G. Frank, *Re-Orient* (1998).

S. Fuller, *Social Epistemology* (1988).

S. Fuller, *Science* (1997).

S. Harding, *Whose Science? Whose Knowledge?* (1991).

M. Hollis & S. Lukes (eds), *Rationality and Relativism* (1982).

T. Masuzawa, *The Invention of World Religions* (2005).

Z. Sardar, *Postmodernism and the Other* (1997).

C. Taylor, *The Politics of Recognition* (1992).

S. P. Turner, *Sociological Explanation as Translation* (1980).

I. Wallerstein, *Open the Social Sciences* (1996).

B. Wilson (ed.), *Rationality* (1970).

UNIVERSITY

Universities are social technologies for the production of universal knowledge. (See **UNIVERSALISM VERSUS RELATIVISM**.) Historically they have been distinguished from other advanced training centres by their institutional autonomy. That alone has placed universities periodically at odds with the surrounding society. It represents a dynamism most clearly expressed in the university's dual role as producers and distributors of knowledge, via its joint research and teaching functions. This ideal was updated in 1810 by Wilhelm von Humboldt, the first rector of the University of Berlin. Anticipating by a century Joseph Schumpeter's definition of the entrepreneur as the "creative destroyer" of markets, Humboldt conceived of universities as engaged in an endless cycle of creating and destroying social capital (see **SOCIAL CAPITAL VERSUS PUBLIC GOOD**), that is, the comparative advantage that a group or network enjoys by virtue of its collective capacity to act on a form of knowledge. Thus, as researchers, academics create social capital because intellectual innovation necessarily begins as an elite product available only to those on the cutting edge. However, as teachers, academics destroy social capital by making the innovation publicly available, thereby diminishing whatever advantage was originally afforded to those on the cutting edge. In this respect, the university is naturally a dispenser of **EPISTEMIC JUSTICE** and the enemy of intellectual property.

However, if the university's research and teaching functions are not integrated, the results can be perverse, as credentials depreciate as more people seek them. That a bachelor's, or even a master's, degree does not offer the same labour-market advantage as in the past is sometimes blamed on low-quality academic instruction or the irrelevance of academic to vocational training. More likely, though, the loss of advantage is simply a straightforward result of more job seekers now possessing the relevant degrees, and hence cannot be so easily discriminated on that basis. In this case, knowledge has lost its former social power. A natural academic response is to call for more research, so as either to discriminate more effectively among current degree-holders or to establish yet still higher degrees for satisfying the Sisyphean search for credentials.

The closeness – ideally the identity – of researchers and teachers in the university context has tended to overturn the initial advantage enjoyed by the creators and funders of new knowledge. This process mimics the welfare state's dual economic function of subsidizing capitalist production (research) and redistributing its surplus (teaching). Not surprisingly, universities magnified in size and significance with the expansion of the welfare state, and have now been thrown into financial and wider institutional uncertainty with the welfare state's devolution. From this standpoint, the recent drive to have universities mimic business firms as generators of intellectual property amounts to no less than a campaign of institutional dismemberment, in which the university's research function is severed from the teaching function. Thus, we have seen the emergence of quasi-private science parks at the edge of campuses, home to an increasing number of entrepreneurial academics. The profitable ventures associated with these facilities threaten to arrest the normal flow of knowledge, perhaps enabling the emergence of a knowledge-based class structure. (See KNOWLEDGE MANAGEMENT.)

In its pursuit of universal knowledge, the university has always regarded the status quo as no more than a stage towards something greater. (See SCIENCE AS A SOCIAL MOVEMENT.) Thus, its involvements with current regimes have always been expedient and uneasy. The first great modern philosophy professors, the German idealists (Kant, Fichte, Schelling and Hegel) both explained and exemplified how universities could be progressive institutions. The Hegelian dialectic, originally a pedagogical device, makes the case most clearly. The first moment of the dialectic – the *abstract universal* – reflects the university's mission prior to its realization. There is much talk about universal knowledge but much is also left out of that talk. The second moment of the dialectic – the *concrete particular* – redresses this imbalance by incorporating people and perspectives whose absence had made the university's claim to universality a mere idea. However, the result of this incorporation is a form of knowledge – the *concrete universal* – that is rather different from what both the original ideologues and the newly included others had envisaged. Hopefully, but not always, it combines the best of both aspirations. The controversies surrounding *affirmative action* as a vehicle of epistemic justice fall under this rubric. (See FEMINISM.)

The ideal of universal knowledge is defined by the problem of making elite knowledge (i.e. knowledge as social capital) available to everyone, so that (objectively) universal applicability is matched by (subjectively) universal accountability. *Everything* is thus rendered knowable to *everyone*. This situation raises a fundamental normative question about how the university is supposed to instantiate universal knowledge and, in that sense, render the universal concrete. For example, one might hold the *liberal* view that universal knowledge is simply what individuals should know to satisfy their respective interests. Or, one might hold a more *communitarian* view that universal knowledge consists of knowing how particular beliefs acquire the status of knowledge by the relevant experts. Already here is encapsulated the difference between a purely instrumental (or "vocation-based") and a purely disciplinary (or "major-based") approach to the curriculum. However, there is a third way, which Fuller has called *republic* or *movement*, depending on whether the opposition is, respectively, a "liberal" or a "communitarian" view of universal knowledge. (See FREE ENQUIRY.) Universal knowledge requires more institutional safeguards than liberalism (hence "republic") without demanding the consensus (see CONSENSUS VERSUS DISSENT) orientation of the communitarian standpoint (hence "movement"). The republican and movement approaches share the view that universal knowledge is an emergent feature of the interaction of all those who would use that knowledge for quite different ends and evaluate it by quite different standards.

To be sure, not all historical visions of universal knowledge have counted on the university as their vehicle of realization. Typical have been the difficulties faced by Hegel's contemporaries Auguste Comte and William Whewell in trying to institutionalize their respective quests for universal knowledge in the universities of France and Britain. In these countries, a different ideal predominated, one that dissociated the validity of knowledge from claims to what was earlier called "subjective universality". Here it was simply assumed that cutting-edge knowledge would be of direct use only to an elite, who would then be able to govern the masses more benevolently. The model was Plato's Academy, which Leibniz and later the French *philosophes* tried to recreate throughout Europe in the seventeenth and eighteenth centuries as state-protected associations for the promotion of scientific research, such as the Royal Society of London and the Parisian Académie des Sciences. The educational system, then, could be left to reproduce the traditional social order by providing different training to different classes.

An important reason why Germany was less susceptible to this easy conversion of scientific knowledge to elite power is that it was historically a consumer, not a producer, of intellectual innovation. It enjoyed what economic historians call the "relative advantage of backwardness" (see MULTICULTURALISM). Like the medieval scholastics who originated the university as the crucible for synthesizing Christian and non-Christian knowledge, the German idealists excelled at giving shape and direction to disparate alien bodies of superior knowledge. They viewed the university from the standpoint of the curriculum committee, where teachability counts as a validity condition for research. But teachable to whom? With the gradual eclipse of the classical liberal arts model of the university as preparing students for citizenship, Germany's distinctiveness lay in its institutional imperative to convert (often British) eccentric geniuses into employment schemes for ordinary trainee academics: that routinization of charisma that Kuhn (see KUHN, POPPER AND LOGICAL POSITIVISM) called a "disciplinary matrix, the backbone of modern graduate education. In this way, say, Newton's *Principia Mathematica* would be regarded not as an imperfectly realized masterwork but as the blueprint for a collectively realizable project. In this way, Hegel's concrete universal acquired a scientific face.

Like both social movements and classical republics, the idea of the university is also predicated on the presence of an external enemy that threatens all their members equally. Regardless of their other differences, academics and citizens, respectively, can always focus their political energies on how to deal with this foe. In the history of republics, the foe has tended to be a larger empire or political entity that threatens to obliterate the republic's autonomy and hence the liberties enjoyed by its citizens. The common foreign foe that has confronted the university has been alternatively called "error", "falsehood", "prejudice" or "ignorance". The university has traditionally tackled this common foe through the curriculum, especially in the task of *canon formation*, which functions much like a written constitution (including the provision for revision and amendments) in republics. In both cases, it provides the backbone of governance, underwriting both the autonomy and dynamism of republics and universities. Deft curriculum design has prepared the conditions for the wider reception of the innovative and often controversial research. Even during the scientific and industrial revolutions, when the universities were rarely the source of new discoveries or inventions, they nevertheless helped to normalize those developments as part of the public knowledge of the day, if only by immunizing the next generation of elites against a knee-jerk negative reaction to innovation and controversy.

Thus, rather than being a burden on the free spirit of research, teaching has conferred legitimacy and relevance on ideas and techniques that would otherwise fall victim to either benign neglect or charges of blasphemy. Towards this end, curriculum design has compelled the maintenance of a lingua franca for a single academic subject and sometimes even the entire university. This has enabled the expression of intellectual disagreements that arise in the academy to have larger societal import. For example, one should not underestimate the long-term role that the scholastic artifice of reducing complex differences of opinion to binary oppositions has played in fuelling the political imagination. The intellectual basis of virtually every modern social movement is an us-versus-them dichotomy, such as nature versus nurture, rulers versus ruled or simply traditional versus modern.

A subtler effect of the academic fixation on a lingua franca has been a search for second-order categories to organize the curriculum that neither simply reproduce traditional prejudices nor cater to specific professional training needs. Such categories need to be specified at a level of abstraction that does not presuppose the content of any of the particular disciplines to which they are meant to apply. The result is that the university generates what Fichte called a "science of knowledge" out of what was originally a practical device for providing a structure to the courses given at the university. The main legacy has been the medieval scholastic three-part formal classification of all knowledge into grammar, dialectic and rhetoric, which reappeared in the work of Charles Sanders Peirce and especially the logical positivists as syntax, semantics and pragmatics. These categories have enabled non-specialists to evaluate the epistemic merit of specialist knowledge claims and disciplines, as in criteria of verifiability and falsifiability to demarcate science from non-science.

Moreover, just as civic republicans would have it, universities have traditionally been run according to a system of checks and balances in which faculty and students exercised mutually countervailing powers. Faculty determined the curriculum, but students could voice their objections by refusing to pay for lectures, which would ultimately, albeit indirectly, affect course content. In the medieval period, the university's corporate character was modelled on the trade guilds that positioned students as apprentices in their field of study. However, the British settlers in seventeenth- and eighteenth-century America innovated the idea of the university as an *independent church* that, lacking either a state monopoly or a natural clientele, had to actively solicit its student base as a constituency that would support the institution even after graduation. This "evangelical" attitude has anchored higher-education policy in the US more generally, even in the public sector, most notably through the philanthropic mission of university alumni associations. While the best American private universities officially charge the world's highest tuition fees, few students actually pay them because their education is subsidized by generous alumni who want others to have the same formative experiences they had.

The anchoring effect of the origins of US higher education on attitudes towards tuition raises the important issue of the political economy under which universities have been able to retain their autonomy. To be sure, both the original guild and the later independent church models have provided an initial basis for autonomy. In addition, there have been two long-term autonomizing strategies that have involved academics in, respectively, a *priestly* and a *monastic* mission. In the priestly mode, universities *expand* to become sovereign states in their own right, or at least to acquire many of the powers typically held by states. During the politically disorganized Middle Ages, this was a common path for universities to take, given that they were in the business of training the next generation of civil and religious officials. In the nineteenth century, this strategy was updated for a modern secular society in the land-grant mission of American universities. In the monastic mode, universities *contract* so as to be free of benefactors who might try to pervert the path of enquiry with their donations. In *The Governance of Science*, Fuller presented an updated version of this ascetic orientation, namely, that universities would refuse big corporate grants in favour of functioning as critics, quality control checks and "reverse engineers" (i.e. those who lend their EXPERTISE to opening up knowledge markets by providing the same utilities by more efficient means) – all in the name of an Enlightenment conception of **RATIONALITY** that aims to remove barriers to the free flow of knowledge. In this respect, the innovative function of universities would be limited to opening up channels for the distribution of already existing knowledge.

In fact, the historic tendency of universities has been to drift from a monastic to a priestly mode, much as republics have tended to become empires. Perhaps the clearest epistemic marker of this drift is the benchmark for original research. In the monastic mode, the enquirer's empirical resources are typically confined to the university's grounds. This implies a reliance on the campus library or oneself (or sometimes students) as primary databases. Under the circumstances, historical and philosophical studies provided the *via regia* to knowledge of the particular and universal, respectively. As the university extended its political ambitions into the priestly mode, these two disciplines were replaced by field- and laboratory-based work, respectively. This shift has required that the university undertake a substantial commitment to transform and govern its own environment. It has included not only enabling researchers to roam far away from their teaching sites but also turning the university itself into a participant in a power structure about which many of its staff had serious reservations. Moreover, faced with a more attractive work environment, staff members trained in the research orientation associated with the priestly mode are more inclined to leave, rather than change, their home university.

FURTHER READING

W. Clark, *Academic Charisma and the Origins of the Research University* (2006).
R. Collins, *The Sociology of Philosophies* (1998).
G. Delanty, *Challenging Knowledge* (2001).
E. Eyerman & A. Jamison, *Social Movements* (1991).
S. Fuchs, *The Professional Quest for Truth* (1992).
S. Fuller, *The Governance of Science* (2000).
S. Fuller & J. Collier, *Philosophy, Rhetoric and the End of Knowledge* (2004).
R. Hofstadter & A. Metzger, *The Development of Academic Freedom in the United States* (1955).
E. Krause, *The Death of the Guilds* (1996).
J. Schumpeter, *Capitalism, Socialism and Democracy* (1950).
M. Weber, *The Sociology of Religion* (1965).

BIBLIOGRAPHY

Adorno, T. (ed.) 1976. *The Positivist Dispute in German Sociology*. London: Heinemann.

Ahmad, A. 1992. *In Theory: Classes, Nations, Literatures*. London: Verso.

Ainslie, G. 1992. *Picoeconomics*. Cambridge: Cambridge University Press.

Aron, R. 1965. *Main Currents in Sociological Thought*, 2 vols. Garden City, NY: Doubleday.

Ayer, A. J. 1936. *Language, Truth and Logic*. London: Gollancz.

Bazerman, C. 1987. *Shaping Written Knowledge*. Madison, WI: University of Wisconsin Press.

Bell, D. 1973. *The Coming of Post-Industrial Society*. New York: Basic Books.

Berger, P. 1967. *The Sacred Canopy*. New York: Free Press.

Berger, P. & T. Luckmann 1967. *The Social Construction of Reality*. Garden City, NY: Doubleday.

Bergson, H. 1935. *The Two Sources of Morality and Religion*. London: Macmillan.

Bernal, J. D. 1939. *The Social Function of Science*. London: Macmillan.

Bhaskar, R. 1987. *Scientific Realism and Human Emancipation*. London: Verso.

Bloor, D. 1976. *Knowledge and Social Imagery*. London: Routledge & Kegan Paul.

Bourdieu, P. 1975. "The Specificity of the Scientific Field and the Social Conditions of the Progress of Reason". *Social Science Information* **14**(6): 19–47.

Burke, K. [1945] 1969. *A Grammar of Motives*. Berkeley, CA: University of California Press.

Bury, J. B. [1920] 1956. *The Idea of Progress*. New York: Dover.

Butler, J. 1990. *Gender Trouble*. London: Routledge.

Butler, J. 1997. *Excitable Speech*. London: Routledge.

Campbell, D. T. 1988. *Methodology and Epistemology for the Social Sciences*. Chicago, IL: University of Chicago Press.

Campbell, J. A. & S. Meyer (eds) 2003. *Darwin, Design and Public Education*. East Lansing, MI: Michigan State University Press.

Cassirer, E. 1950. *The Problem of Knowledge: Philosophy, Science, and History since Hegel*. New Haven, CT: Yale University Press.

Castells, M. 1996–8. *The Information Age*, 3 vols. Oxford: Blackwell.

Ceccarelli, L. 2001. *Shaping Science with Rhetoric: The Cases of Dobzhansky, Schrödinger, and Wilson*. Chicago, IL: University of Chicago Press.

Clark, W. 2006. *Academic Charisma and the Origins of the Research University*. Chicago, IL: University of Chicago Press.

Cohen, L. J. 1986. *The Dialogue of Reason*. Oxford: Oxford University Press.

Collins, H. M. 1990. *Artificial Experts*. Cambridge, MA: MIT Press.

Collins, H. M. & M. Kusch 1999. *The Shape of Actions*. Cambridge, MA: MIT Press.

Collins, H. M. & T. J. Pinch 1993. *The Golem: What Everyone Needs to Know about Science*. Cambridge: Cambridge University Press.

Collins, R. 1998. *The Sociology of Philosophies: A Global Theory of Intellectual Change*. Cambridge, MA: Harvard University Press.

Degler, C. 1991. *In Search of Human Nature*. Oxford: Oxford University Press.

Delanty, G. 2001. *Challenging Knowledge: The University in the Knowledge Society*. Milton Keynes: Open University Press.

Deleuze, G. [1968] 1994. *Difference and Repetition*. New York: Columbia University Press.

De Mey, M. 1982. *The Cognitive Paradigm*. Dordrecht: Kluwer.

Derrida, J. 1976. *Of Grammatology*. Baltimore, MD: Johns Hopkins University Press.

Dickens, P. 2000. *Social Darwinism: Linking Evolutionary Thought to Social Theory*. Milton Keynes: Open University Press.

Dollimore, J. 1996. "Bisexuality, Heterosexuality, and Wishful Theory". *Textual Practice* **10**: 523–39.

Drucker, P. 1993. *Post-Capitalist Society*. New York: HarperCollins.

Elster, J. 1980. *The Logic of Society*. Chichester: John Wiley.

Elster, J. 1984. *Sour Grapes*. Cambridge: Cambridge University Press.

Elster, J. 1999. *Alchemies of the Mind*. Cambridge: Cambridge University Press.

Evans, G. 2003. *A Brief History of Heresy*. Oxford: Blackwell.

Eyerman, E. & A. Jamison 1991. *Social Movements: A Cognitive Approach*. Cambridge: Polity Press.

Feyerabend, P. 1975. *Against Method*. London: Verso.

Feyerabend, P. 1979. *Science in a Free Society*. London: Verso.

Fleck, L. [1935] 1979. *The Genesis and Development of a Scientific Fact*. Chicago, IL: University of Chicago Press.

Fleischacker, S. 2004. *A Short History of Distributive Justice*. Cambridge, MA: Harvard University Press.

Forman, P. 1971. "Weimar Culture, Causality, and Quantum Theory: 1918–1927". *Historical Studies in the Physical Sciences* **3**: 1–115.

Foucault, M. 1970. *The Order of Things: An Archaeology of the Human Sciences*. New York: Random House.

Frank, A. G. 1998. *Re-Orient: Global Economy in the Asian Age*. Berkeley, CA: University of California Press.

Frank, P. 1949. *Modern Science and its Philosophy*. New York: Collier Books.

Franklin, J. 2001. *The Science of Conjecture*. Baltimore, MD: Johns Hopkins University Press.

Frisby, D. 1992. *The Alienated Mind: The Sociology of Knowledge in Germany*. London: Routledge.

Fuchs, S. 1992. *The Professional Quest for Truth*. Albany, NY: SUNY Press.

Fuller, S. 1988. *Social Epistemology*. Bloomington, IN: Indiana University Press.

Fuller, S. [1989] 1993. *Philosophy of Science and Its Discontents*, 2nd edn. New York: Guilford Press.

Fuller, S. 1997. *Science*. Milton Keynes: Open University Press.

Fuller, S. 2000a. *The Governance of Science*. Milton Keynes: Open University Press.

Fuller, S. 2000b. *Thomas Kuhn: A Philosophical History for Our Times*. Chicago, IL: University of Chicago Press.

Fuller, S. 2002. *Knowledge Management Foundations*. Woburn, MA: Butterworth-Heinemann.

Fuller, S. 2003. *Kuhn vs Popper: The Struggle for the Soul of Science*. Cambridge: Icon.

Fuller, S. 2005. *The Intellectual*. Cambridge: Icon.

Fuller, S. 2006a. *The Philosophy of Science and Technology Studies*. London: Routledge.

Fuller, S. 2006b. *The New Sociological Imagination*. London: Sage.

Fuller, S. & J. Collier [Fuller 1993] 2004. *Philosophy, Rhetoric and the End of Knowledge: A New Beginning for Science and Technology Studies*, 2nd edn. Mahwah, NJ: Lawrence Erlbaum.

Fusfield, W. 1997. "To Want to Prove it … is … Really Superfluous". *Quarterly Journal of Speech* **83**: 133–51.

Galison, P. & D. Stump 1996. *The Disunity of Science*. Palo Alto, CA: Stanford University Press.

Gibbons, M., C. Limoges, H. Nowotny *et al.* 1994. *The New Production of Knowledge*. London: Sage.

Giere, R. (ed.) 1992. *Cognitive Models of Science*. Minneapolis, MN: University of Minnesota Press.

Gilbert, N. & M. Mulkay 1984. *Opening Pandora's Box*. Cambridge: Cambridge University Press.

Glaser, B. & A. Strauss 1967. *The Discovery of Grounded Theory: Strategies for Qualitative Research Practice*. Chicago, IL: Aldine.

Goldman, A. 1986. *Epistemology and Cognition*. Cambridge, MA: Harvard University Press.

Goldman, A. 1999. *Knowledge in a Social World*. Oxford: Oxford University Press.

Gouldner, A. 1965. *Enter Plato*. London: Routledge & Kegan Paul.

Gouldner, A. 1970. *The Coming Crisis in Western Sociology*. New York: Basic Books.

Gouldner, A. 1979. *The Future of Intellectuals and the Rise of the New Class*. London: Macmillan.

Gross, P. & N. Levitt 1994. *Higher Superstition: The Academic Left and Its Quarrels with Science*. Baltimore, MD: Johns Hopkins University Press.

Habermas, J. 1983–7. *Theory of Communicative Action*, 2 vols. Boston, MA: Beacon Press.

Habermas, J. [1962] 1989. *The Structural Transformation of the Public Sphere*. Cambridge, MA: MIT Press.

Hacking, I. (ed.) 1981. *Scientific Revolutions*. Oxford: Oxford University Press.

Hacking, I. 1998. *The Social Construction of What?* Cambridge, MA: Harvard University Press.

Hacohen, M. 2000. *Karl Popper: Politics and Philosophy in Interwar Vienna*. Cambridge: Cambridge University Press.

Haraway, D. 1989. *Primate Visions*. London: Routledge.

Haraway, D. 1991. *Simians, Cyborgs, Women*. London: Free Association Books.

Harding, S. 1986. *The Science Question in Feminism*. Ithaca, NY: Cornell University Press.

Harding, S. 1991. *Whose Science? Whose Knowledge?* Ithaca, NY: Cornell University Press.

Hardwig, J. 1985. "Epistemic Dependence". *Journal of Philosophy* **82**: 335–49.

Hayek, F. 1945. "The Use of Knowledge in Society". *American Economic Review* **35**: 519–30.

Hecht, J. 2003. *Doubt*. London: HarperCollins.

Hirsch, F. 1976. *Social Limits to Growth*. London: Routledge & Kegan Paul.

Hofstadter, R. & A. Metzger 1955. *The Development of Academic Freedom in the United States*. New York: Random House.

Hollis, M. & S. Lukes (eds) 1982. *Rationality and Relativism*. Cambridge, MA: MIT Press.

Irwin, A. 1995. *Citizen Science*. London: Routledge

Jansen, S. C. 1991. *Censorship: The Knot that Binds Power and Knowledge*. Oxford: Oxford University Press.

Jarvie, I. C. 2001. *The Republic of Science: The Emergence of Popper's Social View of Science*. Amsterdam: Rodopi.

Kadvany, J. 2001. *Imre Lakatos and the Guises of Reason*. Durham, NC: Duke University Press.

Keith, W. 2007. *Democracy as Discussion*. Lanham, MD: Lexington Books.

Kitcher, P. 1993. *The Advancement of Science*. Oxford: Oxford University Press.

Kitcher, P. 2001. *Science, Truth and Democracy*. Oxford: Oxford University Press.

Knorr-Cetina, K. 1981. *The Manufacture of Knowledge*. Oxford: Pergamon.

Knorr-Cetina, K. 1999. *Epistemic Cultures*. Cambridge, MA: Harvard University Press.

Krause, E. 1996. *The Death of the Guilds: Professions, States, and the Advance of Capitalism*. New Haven, CT: Yale University Press.

Kuhn, T. S. [1962] 1970. *The Structure of Scientific Revolutions*, 2nd edn. Chicago, IL: University of Chicago Press.

Kuhn, T. S. 1977. *The Essential Tension*. Chicago, IL: University of Chicago Press.

Kusch, M. & P. Lipton (eds) 2002. *Studies in History and Philosophy of Science* **33**, special issue on testimony: 209–423.

Lakatos, I. 1976. *Proofs and Refutations*. Cambridge: Cambridge University Press.

Lakatos, I. & A. Musgrave (eds) 1970. *Criticism and the Growth of Knowledge*. Cambridge: Cambridge University Press.

Latour, B. 1987. *Science in Action*. Milton Keynes: Open University Press.

Latour, B. 1988. *The Pasteurization of France*. Cambridge, MA: Harvard University Press.

Latour, B. 1993. *We Have Never Been Modern*. Cambridge, MA: Harvard University Press.

Latour, B. 1999. *Pandora's Hope*. Cambridge, MA: Harvard University Press.

Latour, B. 2004. *Politics of Nature: How to Bring the Sciences into Democracy*. Cambridge, MA: Harvard University Press.

Latour, B. & S. Woolgar [1979] 1986. *Laboratory Life: The Construction of Scientific Facts*, 2nd edn. Princeton, NJ: Princeton University Press.

Laudan, L. 1977. *Progress and its Problems*. Berkeley, CA: University of California Press.

Lepenies, W. 1988. *Between Literature and Science: The Rise of Sociology*. Cambridge: Cambridge University Press.

Lippmann, W. 1922. *Public Opinion*. New York: Macmillan.

Longino, H. 1990. *Science and Social Values*. Princeton, NJ: Princeton University Press.

Lyotard, J.-F. [1979] 1983. *The Postmodern Condition*. Minneapolis, MN: University of Minnesota Press.

Machlup, F. 1962–80. *The Production and Distribution of Knowledge*, 4 vols. Princeton, NJ: Princeton University Press.

Machlup, F. & U. Mansfield (eds) 1983. *The Study of Information: Interdisciplinary Messages*. New York: John Wiley.

Macksey, R. & E. Donato (eds) 1970. *The Structuralist Controversy: The Languages of Criticism and the Sciences of Man*. Baltimore, MD: Johns Hopkins University Press.

Mandelbaum, M. 1971. *History, Man and Reason*. Baltimore, MD: Johns Hopkins University Press.

Mannheim, K. [1929] 1936. *Ideology and Utopia*. New York: Harcourt, Brace.

Mannheim, K. 1940. *Man and Society in an Age of Reconstruction*. London: Routledge & Kegan Paul.

Masuzawa, T. 2005. *The Invention of World Religions*. Chicago, IL: University of Chicago Press.

Merton, R. K. 1977. *The Sociology of Science*. Chicago, IL: University of Chicago Press.

Merz, J. T. [1861–1914] 1964. *A History of European Thought in the Nineteenth Century*, 4 vols. New York: Dover

Milbank, J. 1990. *Theology and Social Theory*. Oxford: Blackwell.

Mirowski, P. 2002. *Machine Dreams: Economics Becomes a Cyborg Science*. Cambridge: Cambridge University Press

Mirowski, P. 2004. *The Effortless Economy of Science?* Durham, NC: Duke University Press.

Mirowski, P. & E.-M. Sent (eds) 2002. *Science Bought and Sold*. Chicago, IL: University of Chicago Press.

Nelson, J. S., A. Megill & D. McCloskey (eds) 1986. *The Rhetoric of the Human Sciences*. Madison, WI: University of Wisconsin Press.

Nichols, S., S. Stich & J. Weinberg 2003. "Meta-Skepticism: Meditations on Ethno-Epistemology". In *The Skeptics: Contemporary Essays*, S. Luper (ed.), 227–48. Aldershot: Ashgate.

Nisbett, R. 2003. *The Geography of Thought: How Asians and Westerners Think Differently – and Why*. London: Nicholas Brealey.

Noble, D. 1997. *The Religion of Technology*. Harmondsworth: Penguin.

Noelle-Neumann, E. 1982. *The Spiral of Silence*. Chicago, IL: University of Chicago Press.

Norman, D. 1993. *Things that Make us Smart*. Reading, MA: Addison-Wesley.

Pettit, P. 1993. *The Common Mind*. Oxford: Oxford University Press.

Pettit, P. 1997. *Republicanism*. Oxford: Oxford University Press.

Pickering, A. (ed.) 1992. *Science as Practice and Culture*. Chicago, IL: University of Chicago Press.

Pinker, S. 2002. *The Blank Slate*. New York: Random House.

Polanyi, M. 1957. *Personal Knowledge*. Chicago, IL: University of Chicago Press.

Popper, K. 1945. *The Open Society and its Enemies*, 2 vols. New York: Harper & Row.

Popper, K. 1957. *The Poverty of Historicism*. New York: Harper & Row.

Popper, K. 1963. *Conjectures and Refutations*. New York: Harper & Row.

Popper, K. 1972. *Objective Knowledge*. Oxford: Oxford University Press.

Price, C. 1993. *Time, Discounting and Value*. Oxford: Blackwell.

Price, D. de S. [1963] 1986. *Big Science, Little Science, ... and Beyond*, 2nd edn. New York: Columbia University Press.

Proctor, R. 1991. *Value-Free Science? Purity and Power in Modern Knowledge*. Cambridge, MA: Harvard University Press.

Quine, W. V. O. 1960. *Word and Object*. Cambridge, MA: MIT Press.

Quine, W. V. O. 1969. *Ontological Relativity and Other Essays*. New York: Columbia University Press.

Ravetz, J. 1971. *Scientific Knowledge and Its Social Problems*. Oxford: Oxford University Press.

Rawls, J. 1971. *A Theory of Justice*. Cambridge, MA: Harvard University Press.

Reisch, G. 2005. *How the Cold War Transformed the Philosophy of Science*. Cambridge: Cambridge University Press.

Remedios, F. 2003. *Legitimizing Scientific Knowledge: An Introduction to Steve Fuller's Social Epistemology*. Lanham, MD: Lexington Books.

Richards, R. 1987. *Darwin and the Emergence of Evolutionary Theories of Mind and Behavior*. Chicago, IL: University of Chicago Press.

Ricoeur, P. 1972. *Freud and Philosophy*. New Haven, CT: Yale University Press.

Robertson, J. M. 1929. *A History of Free-Thought in the Nineteenth Century*. London: Watts & Watts.

Rorty, R. 1979. *Philosophy and the Mirror of Nature*. Princeton, NJ: Princeton University Press.

Ross, A. (ed.) 1996. *Science Wars*. Durham, NC: Duke University Press.

Roth, P. 1987. *Meaning and Method in the Social Sciences*. Ithaca, NY: Cornell University Press.

Roth, P. 1991. "The Bureaucratic Turn: Weber contra Hempel in Fuller's Social Epistemology". *Inquiry* **34**: 365–76.

Rouse, J. 1987. *Knowledge and Power*. Ithaca, NY: Cornell University Press.

Sardar, Z. 1997. *Postmodernism and the Other*. London: Pluto.

Sassower, R. 1993. *Knowledge without Expertise: On the Status of Scientists*. Albany NY: SUNY Press.

Sassower, R. 2006. *Popper's Legacy*. Chesham: Acumen.

Schaefer, W. (ed.) 1984. *Finalization in Science*. Dordrecht: Kluwer.

Schmitt, F. (ed.) 1994. *Socializing Epistemology*. Lanham, MD: Rowman & Littlefield.

Schumpeter, J. 1950. *Capitalism, Socialism and Democracy*. New York: Harper & Row.

Schutz, A. [1932] 1964. "The Well-Informed Citizen: An Essay in the Distribution of Knowledge in Society". In *Collected Papers*, volume II, 120–34. The Hague: Martinus Nijhoff.

Segerstråle, U. 2000. *Defenders of the Truth.* Oxford: Oxford University Press

Shadish, W. & S. Fuller (eds) 1994. *The Social Psychology of Science.* New York: Guilford.

Shapin, S. & S. Schaffer 1985. *Leviathan and the Air Pump.* Princeton, NJ: Princeton University Press.

Simon, H. 1977. *The Sciences of the Artificial,* 2nd edn. Cambridge, MA: MIT Press.

Singer, P. 1999. *A Darwinian Left.* London: Weidenfeld & Nicolson.

Sokal. A. & J. Bricmont 1998. *Fashionable Nonsense: Postmodern Philosophers' Abuse of Science.* London: Profile. Originally published in French in 1997.

Sorell, T. 1991. *Scientism.* London: Routledge.

Sperber, D. 1996. *Explaining Culture: A Naturalistic Approach.* Oxford: Blackwell.

Stehr, N. 1994. *Knowledge Societies.* London: Sage

Stich, S. & R. Nisbett 1984. "Expertise, Justification, and the Psychology of Inductive Inference". In *The Authority of Experts,* T. Haskell (ed.), 226–41. Bloomington, IN: Indiana University Press.

Strauss, L. 1952. *Persecution and the Art of Writing.* Chicago, IL: University of Chicago Press.

Swanson, D. 1986. "Undiscovered Public Knowledge". *Library Quarterly* **56**(2): 103–18.

Taylor, C. 1971. "Interpretation and the Sciences of Man". *Review of Metaphysics* **25**: 3–51.

Taylor, C. 1992. *The Politics of Recognition.* Princeton, NJ: Princeton University Press.

Toulmin, S. 1972. *Human Understanding.* Princeton, NJ: Princeton University Press.

Toulmin, S. 2003. *Return to Reason.* Cambridge, MA: Harvard University Press.

Turner, S. P. 1980. *Sociological Explanation as Translation.* Cambridge: Cambridge University Press.

Turner, S. P. 1994. *The Social Theory of Practices.* Chicago, IL: University of Chicago Press.

Turner, S. P. 2002. *Brains/Practices/Relativism: Social Theory after Cognitive Science.* London: Sage.

Turner, S. P. 2003. *Liberal Democracy 3.0: Civil Society in an Age of Experts.* London: Sage.

Wallerstein, I. 1996. *Open the Social Sciences.* Cambridge: Cambridge University Press.

Weber, M. 1965. *The Sociology of Religion.* Boston: Beacon.

Weinberg, S. 1992. *Dreams of a Final Theory.* New York: Pantheon.

Willard, C. A. 1983. *Argumentation and the Social Grounds of Knowledge.* Tuscaloosa, AL: University of Alabama Press.

Willard, C. A. 1996. *Liberalism and the Problem of Knowledge.* Chicago, IL: University of Chicago Press.

Wilson, B. (ed.) 1970. *Rationality.* Oxford: Blackwell.

Wilson, E. O. 1998 *Consilience: The Unity of Knowledge.* New York: Knopf.

Winch, P. 1959. *The Idea of a Social Science.* London: Routledge & Kegan Paul.

Wolpert, L. 1992. *The Unnatural Nature of Science.* London: Faber.

Wuthnow, R. 1989. *Discourse Communities.* Cambridge, MA: Harvard University Press.

INDEX

Russell, Bertrand   5, 55, 57, 178